# Heads or Tails

*To my wife and my son.*

# Heads or Tails

Financial Disaster, Risk Management and Survival Strategy in the World of Extreme Risk

EVGUENI IVANTSOV

Routledge
Taylor & Francis Group

LONDON AND NEW YORK

First published 2013 by Gower Publishing

2 Park Square, Milton Park, Abingdon, Oxon OX14 4RN
711 Third Avenue, New York, NY 10017, USA

*Routledge is an imprint of the Taylor & Francis Group, an informa business*

First issued in paperback 2016

**British Library Cataloguing in Publication Data**
A catalogue record for this book is available from the British Library.

**The Library of Congress has cataloged the printed edition as follows:**
Ivantsov, Evgueni.
    Heads or tails : financial disaster, risk management and survival strategy in the world of extreme risk / By Evgueni Ivantsov.
       pages cm
    Includes bibliographical references and index.
    ISBN 978-1-4094-6073-2 (hardback : alk. paper)
  1. Risk management. 2. Financial institutions. I. Title.

    HD61.I93 2013
    332.1068'1–dc23

                                       2013016868

ISBN 978-1-4094-6073-2 (hbk)
ISBN 978-1-138-27264-4 (pbk)

# Contents

# List of Figures and Tables

## Figures

## Tables

# Reviews of *Heads or Tails*

*Risk managers that want to survive the next ice age in the financial system must read this book. Ivantsov lucidly explains what went wrong in the Great Recession and why financial institutions and their regulators remain ill-prepared for the next extreme event. They need to change, and this book tells them how.*

**Mark Zandi, Chief Economist of Moody's Analytics, co-founder of Economy.com and advisor to US policymakers**

Heads or Tails *is an indispensable rethinking of extreme risks for the rebuilding of the financial services industry.*

**Lee Howell, Managing Director and Member of the Managing Board, World Economic Forum, Editor in Chief, Global Risks 2013**

Head or Tails *is a thorough and readable account of the extreme dangers ... Dr Ivantsov offers many suggestions as to how current risk management practices, regulation and culture should be changed to ensure that extreme risks are managed properly, to ensure the safety of the organisation and the stability of the financial system as a whole.*

**Michael Imeson, Associate Editor, Financial Times Live, Contributing Editor, *The Banker* Magazine**

*This book is an excellent read for anyone that has been involved with, or wants to learn about, the recent financial crisis. The author provides thought provoking analysis and presents a very engaging section that challenges the regulatory response to the crisis. The book is a joy to read. It is written in a forthright style using irrefutable empirical evidence and effective demonstrative analogies to great effect. As a risk practitioner I thoroughly enjoyed this book however I believe the author has approached the subject in such an engaging manner that its appeal will span a much wider audience.*

**Kevin O'Rourke, Chief Risk Officer & General Manager,
Mizuho Bank (Europe)**

*Evgueni's book, which is studded with interestingly relevant examples, reminds us that there is more to ensuring banks do not fail than the regulator's more capital, more liquidity mantra. He encourages us to step outside the risk management comfort zone and think about managing tail risk by devising scenarios that push managers to consider extreme 'what-ifs', which can act as a flight simulator, so that they are better able to cope with tail risks when they crystallise. His is an important and very readable book for all those searching for a more creative approach to risk management.*

**Simon Hills, Executive Director, the British Bankers Association**

*A brilliant review of the financial crash and the problems associated with calculating actual risk exposure in the financial markets. Dr Ivantsov applies supreme logic and intellectual acumen when dissecting the topics of bank capital and risk management, and the result is incisive. Everyone with an interest in the events of 2007–2009, from students to CEOs to regulators, should read this clear, accessible and coherent account of the causes of the crash and its accompanying critique of the legislators' response that was Basel III. Unlike most authors on this subject, Dr Ivantsov also presents his recommended policy response, which is excellent. An absolute classic, and an exceptional and worthy addition to the finance literature.*

**Moorad Choudhry, Group Treasury, Royal Bank of Scotland
and Visiting Professor, Department of Mathematical Sciences,
Brunel University**

*In this book Evgueni explains in ways that are accessible to a broad range of persons, who may have no great command of financial mathematics, the role reliance on models played in the financial crisis. In particular he analyses the problems of the ballooning of risk in a crisis and the enormous problems associated with trying to model risk in extreme outcomes. He illustrates the limitations of risk models with clear and interesting examples and gives us some powerful insight aimed at improving our current regulator reaction to the crisis. Above all his message is 'Tail risk is different', I could not agree more.*

**Brandon Davies, Chairman, Premier European Capital and former Non-Executive Board Director and Chairman, Audit and Risk Committee, Gatehouse Bank**

*Dr Ivantsov is one of the leading strategic thinkers in the risk industry today. Often firms establish conventional risk frameworks that capture transaction driven high-frequency low-impact events, and evaluate capital adequacy accordingly. Dr Ivantsov highlights the need to redirect our focus to the catastrophic events, the low-frequency high-impact incidents that really cause companies to fail, the compounding of sequences of extreme risk, and proposes approaches needed to tackle such extreme risks. This is a must read for risk managers across all disciplines and industries.*

**Harry Rogers, Head of Risk Management, Bank of China (UK)**

*This book provides fresh and valuable insights into the extent of our continued ignorance of the changing nature of risk and the inadequacy of current responses.*

**Professor Ian Goldin, Director, Oxford Martin School, University of Oxford**

# About the Author

Dr Evgueni Ivantsov is a financial practitioner and an internationally recognised specialist in risk management with a successful career of more than 20 years in some of the global financial services industry's top banks. Dr Ivantsov is also the Chairman of the European Risk Management Council (since 2011), a think tank of risk executives and risk 'gurus' from the leading financial institutions and global corporates operating in Europe. He has been a member of the Advisory Board for European Capital Markets of *The Economist* magazine and the author of numerous publications in the area of risk management. He is also a member of the Advisory Group on Global Risks of the World Economic Forum.

Dr Ivantsov spent most of his career in risk and portfolio management. He has recently joined Lloyds Banking Group as the Head of Portfolio Management and Strategy, responsible for improving the risk/return profile of LBG Retail and Wealth portfolios. Before that, Dr Ivantsov was the Head of Portfolio Risk and Strategy at HSBC Bank plc, where he implemented the strategic enterprise-wide risk management framework and solutions for risk mitigation for major European portfolios. Prior to this role, he led the Basel II model development and implementation at HSBC Group, being the Head of Global Analytics. Before his move to HSBC, he worked in Brussels at ING Group as the Senior Manager of Credit Portfolio Group and the Senior Financial Analyst of Large Corporate Rating Agency at BBL (Banque Bruxelles Lambert).

Dr Ivantsov has ample academic experience. He was an adjunct Professor of International Economics at Boston University (MBA course), and the Professor of Money, Banking and Credit at the United Business Institutes in Brussels (MBA programme).

Dr Ivantsov lives in West London with his wife and his son.

# Preface

While this book focuses on the modern financial services industry and describes how to successfully manage extreme risk and mitigate its devastating impacts, the theme of the book is much wider. The connotation of the book includes an eternal subject: a human being and extreme risks. This multi-thousand-year-old theme has been at the centre of the human survival and people have always searched for an answer to the question of how to live and survive in a world where extreme risks are always close by.

At the time of publication, the British Museum had opened a new exhibition called 'Life and Death in Pompeii and Herculaneum'. When I visited the exhibition, the main discovery for me was that Pompeii's citizens made the same mistakes that modern bankers made during the years preceding the global financial crisis of 2007–9. The main difference between these two cases was the price that people paid for their negligence regarding extreme risk threats. In 79 AD, a catastrophic eruption of Mount Vesuvius destroyed the city of Pompeii. This large centre of the Roman region with a population of circa 15,000 was wiped out. The financial 'eruption' in the twenty-first century destroyed some financial institutions, yet most bankers walked out relatively unharmed.

The mistakes that the Pompeii citizens made almost 2,000 years ago were similar to those made by modern bankers in the 2000s. For example, why did people decide to settle so close to Mount Vesuvius? They were attracted by the extremely rich fertility of the soil with volcanic ash and the trading hub of the Bay of Naples. Translating into modern language, we can say that those who ran their businesses close to the volcano enjoyed a higher return on equity than the people in other areas of this Roman region.

Did they understand the risk? Well, they understood to some extent the 'normal' risks of living near a volcano – frequent earthquakes and periodic eruptions – but considered this risk tolerable and justifiable. What they underestimated was what we today call 'tail risk'. Like modern bankers,

Pompeii's citizens chased short-term economic benefits and ignored long-term extreme risks. But this strategy appeared to be unviable, taking into account what price Pompeii's citizens eventually paid.

Did people expect the major eruption of Vesuvius in AD 79? Unfortunately, the catastrophic eruption was absolutely unexpected for them in spite of various signs of an upcoming major eruption such as numerous earth tremors. The problem was that Pompeii citizens did not understand the link between seismic activity and volcanic activity. They ignored the 'early warning signals' like the severe earthquake which happened 16 years prior to this major eruption.

Pompeii citizens also ignored recurrent activity of Vesuvius or what we would call 'cyclicality'. Mount Vesuvius' activity changes: a period of active eruptions followed by a period of inactivity. The length of inactivity correlates positively with the magnitude of the forthcoming eruption. The eruption which wiped out Pompeii followed a long calm period. The Pompeii citizens made the same mistake as modern bankers made in years of financial bonanza which preceeded the catastrophic year 2008: the law of recurring activity suggests that each calm year implies a greater eruption in the future, but Pompeii's citizens treated the long period of volcanic inactivity as a sign of security.

A look at Pompeii's tragedy from an extreme risk management perspective creates a bridge from modern days to the Roman Empire era. Of course, modern society has made a huge step since then: we can predict volcanic eruptions with a high level of accuracy. But I am not sure that our progress in dealing with extreme financial risks is as impressive as that in dealing with natural disasters. I have a feeling that like the Pompeii citizens, we are struggling to understand the cause of a major disaster in the financial world. We have serious difficulties in comprehending and interpreting signs and signals of the forthcoming crisis. Time and time again, we ignore extreme risks for the sake of short-term financial benefits. I am afraid that in our financial and risk thinking, we are stuck in the Roman ages. If in the first decade of the twenty-first century, modern bankers made broadly the same mistakes and exhibited similar reckless behaviour towards extreme risks as Pompeii's citizens did 2,000 years ago, then the problem is worth scrutinising closely. Now should be the time to learn these painful lessons.

Interestingly, by coincidence the exhibition 'Life and Death in Pompeii and Herculaneum' at the British Museum was sponsored by Goldman Sachs, one of the victims of the global financial crisis.

This book would not have been possible without the help and contribution of many people who generously shared their ideas with me and provided feedback on my work. I have been very fortunate to meet many people in my life who gave me invaluable advice and immense support. I am grateful to all of them and would like to mention some specifically.

I would like to express my gratitude to Jonathan Norman, Publisher at Gower Publishing, who dedicated a lot of his time to making this book better. He read each and every page of my drafts and provided many helpful suggestions on the book's structure and content and enthusiastically supported me during my work thereon. He went the extra mile and expressed this personal interest in my work above and beyond what was required by his role as a publisher. Thank you to all the great people at Gower who helped me with this book.

I owe a special thanks to Kevin O'Rourke, Chief Risk Officer & General Manager of Mizuho Bank (Europe) for his collaboration. He was one of the first people who I showed the 'blueprint' of the extreme risk management framework to and who enthusiastically supported these ideas and provided practical suggestions.

There were two men who actively encouraged me to write a book. When I shared my dream to write a book about extreme risk with Dr Oliver Backhouse, he convinced me to start doing this sooner rather than later in spite of all the obstacles I faced at that time. Nick Obolensky, CEO of Complex Adaptive Leadership, who was my teacher of the leadership course at university many years ago, not only encouraged me to write the book but shared with me his personal experience of publishing and put me in contact with Gower. I really appreciate the support that both Oliver and Nick provided to me.

I am greatly indebted to Brandon Davies, Non-Executive Director of the Board and Chairman of Risk and Audit of Gatehouse Bank. His view on uncertainty in the financial world and measurability of tail risk that he shared with me helped me narrow down my approach in dealing with extreme risk challenges. I am also grateful to Charles Stewart, Senior Director of Moody's Analytics and Bill Rickard, Head of Regulatory Development at RBS for the long friendship and collaboration. Our intellectual, thought-stimulating discussions greatly influenced my view of modern risk management and regulation.

I should also mention Michael Roseman, the former Global Chief Risk Officer and EVP at MF Global, who shared with me his invaluable experience in practical risk management and explained how the underestimation of risk factors and aggressive business strategy could quickly ruin a firm. Thank you, Michael, for your time and support.

I am greatly indebted to two people from Bank of New York Mellon – Michael Cole-Fontayn, Chairman of Europe, Middle East and Africa and John Johnston, Chief Risk Officer EMEA. Michael Cole-Fontayn is a rare example of a business leader in the financial sector who has a genuine interest in the deep understanding of all aspects of risk and incorporating modern risk solutions in the business practice far beyond what the regulators ask for. I really appreciate the fact that Michael and John supported me when I shared my draft of the extreme risk framework with them. In addition, our intellectual discussions on risk management stimulated me to think about the paramount role of risk culture and include the risk culture aspect in this book.

I would like to say my big thanks to Eugen Buck, Managing Director of Rabobank (London Branch). He provided me with an insightful view on what risk culture and firms' governance should look like to ensure that all strategic decisions undergo thorough risk control.

Finally, my special thanks to Simon Hills, Executive Director of British Bankers' Association. Simon was one of the people who enthusiastically supported my initial ideas on extreme risk management and who became my co-author in a later publication. Our discussions on risk and regulation and his view on the lessons of the global financial crisis greatly influenced my thinking on how extreme risk challenges should be addressed.

Last, but not least, I am grateful to all the people who invited me to speak at various professional conferences, summits and gatherings in Europe, the USA and Asia, where I had a lucky opportunity to present my ideas covered in this book to hundreds of business and risk professionals. Their feedback helped me to improve the content of this manuscript immensely.

# Introduction

*All truths are easy to understand once they are discovered: the point is
to discover them.*

(Galileo Galilei)

The times were great and the investor conference on 5 August 2007 went even
smoother than before. 'It is hard for us, without being flippant, to even see a
scenario within any kind of realm of reason that would see us losing $1,' said
Joseph Cassano, AIG Financial Products Executive. AIG's President and CEO
Martin Sullivan added: 'That's why I am sleeping a little bit easier at night.' He
never suspected that the time remaining for his peaceful sleep was running low.
Only a few months were left before the AIG disaster happened, which brought
the largest US insurance company to its knees and cost the US taxpayers over
$180 billion.

How come one of world's largest and strongest financial institutions,
which owned more than $1 trillion of assets and generated annual revenues
of above $100 billion, failed so quickly and miserably? Just a few months
before the collapse, AIG's top managers were convinced that the company
was overcapitalised and the state-of-the-art economic capital model confirmed
AIG's exceptionally strong capital position. On 16 March 2007, AIG's CEO
Martin Sullivan wrote to the shareholders:

> *The Economic Capital modeling analysis has reinforced our view that
> AIG's capital position is strong with an estimated $15 billion to $20
> billion in excess capital at the end of 2006. This analysis supported the
> decision by the Board of Directors to announce a new dividend policy
> with a plan of increasing the common stock dividend by approximately
> 20 percent annually, under ordinary circumstances. The new policy
> will be effective with the dividend to be declared in May of 2007.
> Additionally, the Board expanded AIG's existing share repurchase*

*program by authorizing the repurchase of up to $8 billion in common
stock.*

*(AIG 2007: 7)*

It can sound almost unbelievable but the insurance giant had been brought to
its knees by the business of a very small London-based unit – AIG Financial
Products – with just 377 employees, which represented about 0.3 per cent of
AIG's total workforce!

The *New York Times* wrote: 'It is beyond shocking that this small operation
could blow up the holding company' (Morgenson 2008).

While the collapse of AIG looks surrealistic, this story is a very typical
example of how a firm suddenly finds itself dancing in the financial "minefields"
and how an extreme risk event can unfold and smash it to pieces.

One of the main questions that keeps bank executives up at night nowadays
can be formulated as follows: 'Are we dancing in the 'minefields' and are we
exposed to potential large or even catastrophic losses?' The fear is reasonable.
Since the global financial crisis hit the industry, we have witnessed a number of
spectacular failures among those financial institutions which were previously
regarded as solid and successful.

Even the best are not immune. The surprising larger complex derivatives
trading loss of JP Morgan revealed in April 2012 not only crashed the bank's
share price and immediately ignited investigations from Senate, SEC, OCC
and even FBI, it led to very severe reputational damage. This case of a huge
trading loss attributable to the so-called 'London Whale' complex derivatives
deals (amounting to $5.8 billion by July 2012) is a reminder to all financial
institutions: regardless of how big you are and how smart you are, if you keep
on dancing in the minefields you need to be equipped with the robust purpose-
built framework preventing large and catastrophic losses.

The lesson that we ought to learn from recent experience is that every
organisation urgently needs to develop and implement solutions addressing
extreme risk events, which are often called 'black swans'. The recent macroeconomic trends in Europe and the US give no hope of 'black swans'
disappearing from the economic landscape any time soon.

I would like to shape your expectations about this book. It will help you to
answer several questions:

- Why do financial firms so often become victims of extreme risk events?

- Why don't modern 'sophisticated' risk management frameworks, strong capitalisation and liquidity prevent banks from failure in the 'perfect storm' of the systemic crisis?

- What does it mean to build an effective defence against large systemic and catastrophic losses?

- How do the modern risk management practices, regulation and culture need to change in order to ensure the sustainability of the financial sector?

In this sense, the following aspects, presented in the book, could be of interest:

- The analysis of extreme risk events provided in this book allows one to understand the special nature of extreme risks and how these risks differ from day-to-day risks. Numerous cases of a devastating nature of idiosyncratic and systemic extreme risk events are discussed throughout the book (including some cases from the recent global financial crisis). Through these case studies, typical scenarios of how extreme risk events unfold are revealed.

- The book provides a view on risk management in financial institutions from, to a large extent, an unfamiliar angle: from the angle of assessing, managing and mitigating extreme risk events. Many known things look different from this angle, which allows us to challenge a generally accepted truth about risk management practice and regulation.

- Extreme risk is the most complex and the most difficult threat to deal with. If somebody tells you that you can solve tail risk problems with a magic formula or a magic model or a magic trading strategy, think twice. The most complex task about risk management is unlikely to be solved by any 'Mickey Mouse' solution. There is no 'silver bullet' against tail risk.

- Efficient risk management of extreme risk events is about the enhancement of most elements of contemporary risk management practice by adding new anti-tail risk methods, tools and processes.

- In order to build robust protection against large systemic and catastrophic losses, an organisation is required to make changes in 'hard' (e.g. models, data, systems) and 'soft' (e.g. governance, decision-making processes, the business strategy and risk culture) components of the traditional risk management framework.

One of the purposes of writing this book was to analyse how contemporary risk management practices and regulations address the challenges of extreme risks. Therefore, I dedicate special attention to the analysis of the effectiveness of the measurement and prediction of extreme risk events. In addition, the analysis of the evolution of the financial regulation is provided to show where regulators lead (and mislead) us and why. The special focus is for the new banking regulatory agenda widely known as Basel III and its 'silver bullets'.

The second part of the book, from, Chapter 5 onwards, focuses on the solutions that financial firms need to implement in order to build an effective extreme risk management framework. I will describe the 'heads or tails' dilemma. The proposed approach to focus on 'tails' is purely additive and extends the risk framework to effectively cover the entire risk spectrum: from recurring regular daily risks to extreme and very rare ones. I will discuss how to examine a firm's business and risk strategy and to 'diagnose' the areas of extreme risk exposure by applying a concept of 'comfort zones' and 'risk zones'. A further approach is given on how to build the map of a firm's business 'genome' and how to connect the concept of 'comfort zones' with a firm's risk appetite and to transform the risk appetite concept into a powerful extreme risk management tool.

Stress testing is another important area of the analysis. The book describes the stress-testing approach for extreme scenarios that allows us to maximise value for the firm and to avoid typical pitfalls and conflicts of interest.

The effective risk management of extreme risk events includes not only the solutions that help to escape the crisis (pre-emptive solutions), but also solutions that allow us to successfully mitigate the impact of the crisis in case the 'perfect storm' hits the organisation. I will provide a detailed description of how a firm can build a robust crisis management framework to ensure its resilience to extreme risk shocks. When an extreme risk event occurs and all hell breaks loose, the last line of defence will be the factor which determines whether the firm survives or disappears.

Like in a marathon run, where the last mile is crucial, in this book the last chapter provides the crucial ingredient for understanding how the financial industry as a whole can develop the robustness with regard to extreme risks. In the last chapter, I will analyse why regulators, as well as part of the financial elite, were and still remain blind to the threats of extreme risk. I believe that this is a question of culture, values and people.

While the last several years have been rather grim for the financial industry in Europe and the USA, I remain optimistic. The global financial crisis has been a cold 'sober up' shower which helps us to understand why dancing in the financial minefields is not a smart business strategy. The crisis also indicated that the financial sector has entered a 'little ice age'. Those who will be able to build a robust framework for extreme risk management and adopt the culture of survival in the adversely changing environment will thrive. Those who will stay blind to the tail risk will disappear. I believe that the majority will choose to survive. That hope motivated me to write this book.

.

PART I

# *Dancing in the Minefields*

# 1

# Beware of the Tail:
# The Dark Nature of Extreme Risk

*The greatest happiness is to know the source of unhappiness.*
*(Fyodor Dostoyevsky)*

After the global financial crisis hit the economy, risk management in the financial sector became an important area for investors, regulators, politicians and the general public. The crisis started suddenly and spoiled the party of the financial bonanza. It rolled out like a tsunami, first hitting the US financial sector as the US sub-prime mortgage crisis developed in 2007. Then the wave covered Europe, the Middle East and some Asian countries, achieving a global scale in 2008–9. The next wave hit the Eurozone sovereign debt, pushing the entire Governments of some European countries to the brink of default. We have been witnesses to a huge detrimental power of extreme risk events.

The crisis raised many questions regarding the resilience of financial business and efficiency of its risk management and regulation. In the last 10–15 years preceding the crisis, risk management and banking regulation have made significant progress; they were supposed to be able to successfully sustain systemic shocks. Huge losses and write-downs of financial institutions in 2007–9 and spectacular failures of global and large banks and financial firms came as a surprise. Clearly something went terribly wrong.

Before we start analysing why risk management failed to address properly such extreme risk events and what has to be done, let's discuss some fundamentals of risk in general.

## How the Risk Factory Works

We live in a world of risk: risk is always around, and we are not the first generation of human beings who live immersed in risk. All human history has been co-living with risk every day, hour and minute. Each of us has a life-long job contract with the risk factory, where we constantly produce risks and manage them. After thousands and thousands of years of evolution in the world of risk, we human beings should be the masters of risk. Yet we are not …

### RISK AND KNOWLEDGE

If you ask 100 random people on the street if they are good at understanding and managing risks in their lives, most of the respondents would give you a positive answer. If you also ask them the simple question: is it very risky to jump from an aeroplane which is flying at 20,000 feet without a parachute? You can expect that the vast majority of your respondents would say 'Oh, it is huge risk' – and this answer would be wrong. It would just demonstrate how the risk concept is difficult to understand and embrace. It sounds very strange as we deal with different risks every day throughout our entire lives. But, to us, risk remains an enigma to some extent: a strange creature, often invisible, intangible, immeasurable and unpredictable.

The risk of jumping from the aeroplane without a parachute is literally zero. It can sound bizarre at first glance, but it appears quite logical. Many people confuse 'risk' and 'danger'. While danger is a hazard or troublesome situation, a risk is uncertainty of future outcomes. In the case of jumping from an aeroplane, it is indeed extremely dangerous but clearly has no uncertainty of the outcome: the chance of survival is zero, while the probability of being killed is 100 per cent. There is no room for ambiguity and there is no risk.

Risk not only depends on the degree of uncertainty of the future outcomes, but also on exposure to that uncertainty. We can reduce or increase risk by reducing or increasing our exposure to that uncertainty. Let me demonstrate the risk concept by telling my personal story.

I was born and brought up in Siberia near Lake Baikal, the deepest lake in the world. In the middle of the lake there is an island called Olkhon. The island is about 70 km long and 15 km wide and is larger than the Mediterranean islands of Corfu or Ibiza. There are several villages on the island. A deep strait separates the island from the mainland. You can get to the island by ferry or boat when the lake is not frozen or by car when the strait is frozen into a thick layer of ice during the winter period. However, during the spring, over a period of several weeks, all communication with the island stops when the ice becomes too thin for car crossing. The local administration warns people when the ice crossing becomes dangerous yet many motorists ignore the warnings and take the risk of crossing the strait on thin ice. As a result, each year several cars end up at the bottom of world's deepest lake and several people lose their lives.

Several times in my life, I have been a witness of how some motorists were crossing the strait during this dangerous period. Was it any risk for me? No, because I was on the coast watching somebody else's reckless driving on ice. I had no personal exposure to the uncertainty of the thin ice crossing adventure. At the same time, people in the car were experiencing the huge risk that their lives were exposed to. The situation, however, would be different for me if somebody was crossing the strait in my car. Although my life would still not be in any form of danger, my risk would not be zero any more as my exposure to the uncertainty would be my car.

The conclusion is very simple – there are three ways to reduce risk:

1.     reduce uncertainty of the outcome, keeping the exposure constant;

2.     reduce exposure to the uncertainty;

3.     reduce simultaneously both uncertainty and exposure.

When some business people say that they like risk because the risk is an opportunity, it is important to remember that the risk is a subjective category and reflects one's knowledge about this subject. The same situation or business opportunity can represent a substantial different degree of risk to different people.

Consider an example: a person is going to open a restaurant in New York. This person has never been involved in the restaurant business before and has recently migrated to the USA from Romania. At the same time, another person is also starting a restaurant business next door. The second person has 20 years of successful career experience in the restaurant business in New York. All other things being equal, it is obvious that the first person is exposed to a higher risk than the second one although both are exposed to identical projects. Risk is about personal knowledge and may come from not knowing what you're doing.

Therefore, the pursuit of reducing risk (in other words, of decreasing an uncertainty by building knowledge and skills to understand and control the situation, business or processes) should always be the prevailing desire of a business person or an organisation, even if this person likes to take more risk or the organisation chooses a risky business strategy.

## TURNING BLACK SWANS TO WHITE SWANS

Since the global financial crisis happened and we all witnessed some spectacular failures in the financial sector, discussions around extreme events in the economy have become very central. I would like to bring my contribution to this topic. To ensure that we really talk about the same events, a clarification is needed about what we mean when we mention an extreme risk event or a so-called black swan – a popular cliché for an extreme risk event.

Often when we talk about a black swan we mean an event which is highly improbable, unpredictable from knowledge and past experience of an observer, and has a massive impact (Taleb 2007). I would prefer a wider definition of black swan events as extreme risk events which are either totally unpredictable or events that *could be foreseen* but have not been considered by an observer as plausible.

The wider definition has a more practical application. A human being with a good imagination could envisage numerous outcomes from very trivial to absolutely fantastic. The main point is that the observer discards most of these potential outcomes as unrealistic and does not take any actions to be ready for the situation if one of these 'unrealistic' scenarios suddenly unfolds. And when it happens, it comes as a surprise for the observer. Consider the 9/11 terrorist attack as an example of a black swan event. The scenario of the aeroplane hijacks and using jets as bombs was to some extent predicted by US anti-terrorism forces but was not considered as a realistic threat.

The whole history of human civilisation is a journey from the world of black swans to the world of white swans. Many events that today we categorise without any doubt as white swans were black swans at some point in the past. The most notorious examples of how a black swan turned into a white swan event are from the areas of the natural sciences and medicine.

A solar eclipse is a good example: a few hundred years ago a solar eclipse was an unexplainable and entirely unpredictable event, considered by people as an act of God, and it often had a massive impact on the ancient society.

Each time it happened, it ruined the picture of the normal order of things that people had at those times: suddenly a bright day turns to a dark night. The fact that it happened extremely rarely (on average, once every 370 years in the the same area) and without any easily observable regularity made this natural phenomenon a great mystery in the people's eyes. The psychological effect of a solar eclipse on people in ancient times was always deeply shocking. The ancient literature contained descriptions of people's reactions to a solar eclipse. For example, an eclipse which happened during the war between the Medians and the Lydians (presumably about 585 BC in the middle of modern Turkey) was so shocking for soldiers that both fighting sides put down their weapons and declared peace.

A solar eclipse is no longer a black swan. Nowadays, a solar eclipse, thanks to achievements in modern astronomy, is an ordinary white swan event which can be predicted for hundreds of years ahead with pinpoint accuracy.

By considering the way in which we turn black swans to white swans, we uncover the nature of the phenomenon and the mechanism (cause–effect relationships), which leads to a sudden change in the properties of the object. As soon as the nature of the phenomenon is clear, its prediction and the subsequent prevention (mitigation) of a potentially negative impact (or the exploitation of its positive effect) become an achievable task. Our level of understanding of the nature and cause–effect relationships of the phenomenon is exactly what separates black and white swan types of events. If the nature of a phenomenon is unknown, we are exposed to 'highly improbable' and 'unpredictable' events. I use quotation marks here because improbability and unpredictability are not properties of this phenomenon. They reflect our subjective knowledge and as soon as we uncover the driving forces of the phenomenon, the event becomes plausible and predictable and ceases to belong to the category of extreme risk events (Figure 1.1).

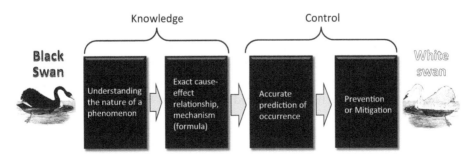

Figure 1.1    Eliminating extreme risk: turning black swans into white swans

Lots of natural phenomena have been getting removed from the black swan territory during the last few centuries thanks to the development of science and the accumulation of empirical knowledge. Physical processes, weather forecasting, agriculture, medicine, modern industry – all these areas benefited from the removal of black swan events. The risk of many extreme events that have shaken the world in the past (e.g. plague or smallpox outbreaks) has been eliminated completely. Many other diseases, which for ages have been black swans – unpredictable and fatal – became predictable, avoidable and curable. Hurricanes, thunderstorms and many other black swan types of weather phenomena have become entirely predictable and as a result of pre-emptive mitigating actions, the severity of the impact of these 'acts of God' is reduced substantially. All this becomes a brilliant demonstration that black swans exist until the moment when human beings uncover their fundamental nature and learn how to prevent them or mitigate their impact. The restless human activity on discovering the nature of extreme risk events around us has brought and keeps on bringing tangible results in 'killing' black swans and eliminating extreme risks.

## UNDERSTANDING THE EXTREME RISKS OF SOCIO-ECONOMIC SYSTEMS

The success in turning black swans to white swans, however, has been uneven. In some areas of human activity, such as meteorology, agriculture and medicine, the progress is much more noticeable than, for example, economics and sociology, where economic crises or social shocks (e.g. political regime overthrown, riots, civil wars) remain in black swan territory. Why has the progress in extreme risk elimination been so uneven?

Herbert Spencer, an English philosopher and sociologist, who is best known for his expression 'survival of the fittest' with respect to Darwin's concept, developed an all-embracing concept of evolution as the progressive movement of the physical world, biological organisms and human culture and societies. In his book *Principles of Biology*, published in 1864, he conceptualised that all structures in the universe develop from simple, undifferentiated homogeneity to a complex, differentiated heterogeneity, while being accompanied by the process of greater integration of the differentiated parts. Spencer distinguished three main systems when he formulated an evolution of complexity:

- non-organic nature;

- organic nature (biological systems);

- social systems.

If we adopt Spencer's classification for our analysis of extreme risks, the non-organic system is clearly the simplest one, which can be described by relatively simple terms. All changes in this system (its evolution) are slow and many relationships can be measured and quantified by applying simple maths. The simplicity of the non-organic world allows us to use scientific experiments to uncover relationships in the system and, in some cases, even to use linear equations to describe processes.

Biological systems include elements and relationships of the non-organic world but the level of complexity increases dramatically. Even very simple forms of life are much more dynamic compared to non-organic nature. An advanced biological system such as a human body represents something of an extremely complex nature. An interaction among different organic forms and between the organic and non-organic world is not easy to quantify. It is the world where there is almost no space left for linear relationships. The number of factors that should be taken into account when we formalise the relationship is normally very high. There is some room left for scientific experiments with biological systems; however, the process and interpretation of results often become cumbersome.

Finally, social systems are at the top of the pyramid of complexity (Figure 1.2). They inherit all the complexity of both non-organic and organic systems but also produce the new complexity of a human mind, social behaviour and economic life.

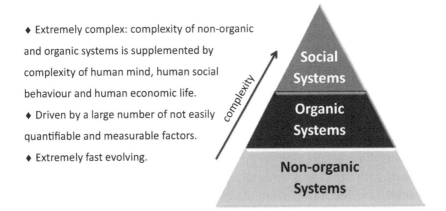

♦ Extremely complex: complexity of non-organic and organic systems is supplemented by complexity of human mind, human social behaviour and human economic life.

♦ Driven by a large number of not easily quantifiable and measurable factors.

♦ Extremely fast evolving.

**Figure 1.2    Characteristics of socio-economic systems from the risk perspective**

The complexity of the system, with its mosaic of a large number of factors affecting the state of the system and its fast evolution, results in a very high level of uncertainty of the future state of the system. So many moving parts and high dynamism create uncertainty. More uncertainty means more risk. This explains why the modern economic system becomes an area where a lot of black swans still comfortably live.

We, as the human race, have spent thousands of years studying and empirically exploring the natural world around us and succeeded in understanding many enigmas of this world. It was necessary for the successful survival of human beings. Yet much less time has been spent on understanding how socio-economic systems work. Human society is a very complex and messy system. I have no doubt that key developments and trends of the socio-economic systems are not random and follow a particular logic and rules. However, these rules are often much more complex than that of the physical world. Moreover, the physical world around us looks almost unchanged (at least in comparison to a human life). The key principles and laws of the physical world stayed the same for millions of years (even the evolution of a human body is slow enough to reasonably assume that it is unchanged). Knowledge about particular phenomena comes from the past and is accumulated by observers. At a certain point, the breakthrough idea connects all the jigsaw pieces of knowledge together in the right order and the nature of the phenomenon becomes clear.

In contrast, socio-economic systems are evolving quickly, and this makes it more difficult to understand their underlying principles and driving forces. While we are struggling to understand one socio-economic black swan, the system moves to its new state and much of the past knowledge becomes obsolete or inapplicable. Thus, the world economic system in the seventeenth century bears little resemblance to the modern economy, and knowledge of the seventeenth century economy does not look very valuable for explaining economic processes of the global economy.

Moreover, socio-economic systems are ones in which the processes have large numbers of drivers (much larger than in the physical world) and these drivers are not easily quantifiable and measurable. Even when the key drivers are known, the relationships are normally very complex. They are always non-linear, with rapid and unexpected changes in the power of the drivers (a linear relationship is the dream of any researcher but hardly exists in reality outside a few areas of precise science). All these difficulties in understanding and predicting black swan events in socio-economic systems can explain the limited progress in turning black swans into white swans in this area, but this should not be used for stopping researchers and practitioners trying to make the complex systems more transparent, predictable and black swan free.

I can recognise that our achievements are very modest so far, but without the efforts of scientists, economists, statisticians, philosophers, business and risk practitioners our knowledge of socio-economic systems would be even smaller than they are now. Efforts that we make today are necessary to pave the way for future discoveries and making social and economic phenomena more predictable and better manageable. The notion of 'Don't try to explain the black swan because it is impossible' sounds odd to me. I do hope that my efforts to understand extreme risks and ways to mitigate them described in this book become my two cents of contribution to the process of turning black swans into white ones.

## RISK AND VOLATILITY

Often, people associate financial risk with volatility and use volatility as a measure of risk. However, it is important to understand how these two notions differ.

Risk represents uncertainty regarding future outcomes. The more uncertain future outcomes are (in the financial world, it can be asset prices, return on investments, losses of the credit portfolio, operating profit, etc.), the more risk we deal with. Risk depends on our knowledge, skills and ability to keep the situation under control. If a person (or organisation) has the necessary knowledge and skills, the risk is low because this increases certainty about future outcome (e.g. return on investment). Therefore, the more knowledge and control over a situation we have, the less risk we are exposed to.

On the other hand, volatility is a statistical measurement of fluctuations of a particular factor (for example, an asset's price) over time. There are clearly some important differences:

- Risk always characterises a future situation. There is no risk in the past as all outcomes are known with 100 per cent certainty. While risk is always about the future, volatility is a backward-looking statistical characteristic which reflects the past events. Future volatility, by definition, is unknown and can only be predicted with a particular level of certainty.

- Risk is always subjective and the same situation means different risks for different parties. A party that has better knowledge and insight of the situation and stronger ability to control the processes has less risk (remember my example above, when the risk of starting a new restaurant business is different for an amateur entrepreneur and for an experienced and successful restaurant expert). In contrast, volatility is an objective characteristic (e.g. volatility of asset prices) and does not depend on any subjective factors.

These two differences between risk and volatility can explain why volatility cannot be used as a reliable measure of risk. Consider the following situation: there are ten investors who are going to invest an equal amount of money into their real estate portfolios by buying property in the London area. From a risk perspective, in spite of investing the same amount of money to the same market, each one has a different investment risk which depends on individual knowledge of the London property market and ability to exercise effective control over investments (e.g. ability to obtain up-to-date and accurate information, ability to have the right business connections, ability to strike the best possible deal). However, volatility of the London property index reflects the general market behaviour. If volatility of the London property index is used as a measure of risk, it can be misleading as it would suggest that all property investors are exposed to the same risk, which is not the case.

Volatility of the market value of different asset classes can reflect the perception of market participants towards risk associated with different asset classes. But it should not be mistaken for the actual risk. This market volatility is driven by expectations of market participants and reflects their collective behaviour. If market participants start to believe (rightly or wrongly) that risk of a particular class of asset is growing, it usually leads to higher volatility of the market value. In this sense, market volatility can be a proxy of awareness of market participants regarding asset class risk. But quite often, our perceptions towards risk are wrong and do not correctly reflect the real state of things. It is especially true when we deal with extreme risks.

Extreme risks characterise events having a very low likelihood of occurance but when they occur, they create a massive impact. We also call such risk tail risk. Although the impact of tail risk can be negative as well as positive, from a risk management perspective, in this book we will focus on negative impact events. As extreme risk drivers are often unknown in advance and tail risk events have a very low perceived likelihood of occurrence, the market often stays unaware of extreme risks and these events often come 'out of the blue'.

That is why these events are called black swans: to reflect that they look improbable and almost entirely unpredictable.

It means that the market volatility of a particular asset price can stay low just because market participants collectively overlook, or are not aware of, important risk factors. And then suddenly, when at a particular point in time these risk factors are finally spotted, the market panics and volatility rockets. It does not mean that risk grows overnight. In fact, risk stays largely the same as it was during the low volatility period or grows marginally. The only thing that changed was the market recognition of the existing risk.

Consider the oil price before the oil crisis of 1973. After the Second World War, in 1946–7, the oil price experienced a high volatility and doubled just in three years (Figure 1.3).

If you had used price volatility as a proxy of risk in 1948, you would be completely fooled because after 1948, the oil market entered the era of full certainty – from 1948 until 1953 the price remained unchanged. Overall between 1948 and 1973, the oil price demonstrated an amazingly low volatility. For these 25 years it increased only by 39 per cent, or less than 1.5 per cent per annum,

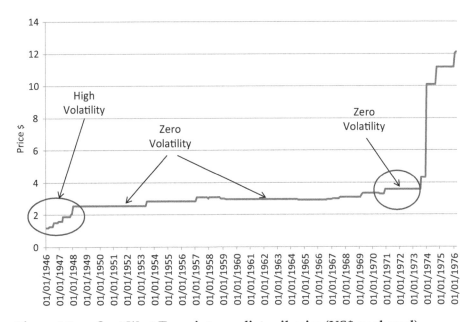

**Figure 1.3    Spot West Texas intermediate oil price (US$ per barrel)**

*Source*: Author's own figure using data from Financial Forecast Center, LLC.

without any substantial jumps. From 1948 to 1973, in 292 out of 307 months (95 per cent) the prices remained unchanged!

In the period preceding the oil crisis, from 1971 to the middle of 1973, the price was at US$3.56 per barrel with zero volatility for 2.5 years! If volatility was a good proxy of future risk, then the obvious conclusion would be: the risk of the future price change was close to zero. But suddenly, the oil price skyrocketed and almost tripled in six months by the end of 1973. The oil price shock had a dramatic impact far beyond the energy market. It led to the stock market crash in G7 countries and global stagflation (the low or negative economic growth combined with a very high inflation).

Did the risk of an oil price shock exist for example in 1972 during the period of zero oil price volatility? Yes, key factors of risk were already there:

- OPEC was created in 1968 and in early 1972 OPEC expanded by adding Algeria, Iraq, Syria and Egypt.

- The confrontation between Israel and Arab countries existed and after the Six-Day War in 1967 the chance of the new 'hot' conflict remained very high.

- USA supported Israel in the Six-Day War and continued to be Israel's key ally.

- The shortage of US oil production was recognised in 1970 with zero spare capacity and increasing dependency on oil export.

The risk of the oil price shock was viewed by the markets as unrealistic until the crisis started. As usual, there were some people who correctly put all of the pieces of the puzzle together regarding this risk and warned the market in advance. In 1972, James Akins, Director of fuels and energy at the US State Department, correctly predicted a risk of an oil embargo and its dramatic consequences. But the markets rejected this scenario as implausible.

Therefore, in many cases and almost always in the case of extreme risks, volatility is a lagging risk indicator and not a reliable proxy of tail risk. If it were known in advance, future volatility could be used as a proxy, but only historical volatility is observable. As volatility remains the widely used measure of risk, this often misleads market participants. Mark Carney, the governor of the Bank of England, formulated the problem very clearly: 'Risk appears to be at its greatest when measures of it are at their lowest' (Carney 2010: 5).

## Every Troubled Firm is Troubled in its Own Way ...

> *Happy families are all alike; every unhappy family is unhappy in its own way ...*
>
> *(Leo Tolstoy,* Anna Karenina*)*

Leo Tolstoy knew maybe more than anybody else how difficult and unpredictable family life could be. His novel, *Anna Karenina* provides a deep psychological analysis of why and how a family life can go off the cliff and end with a tragedy. It was not coincidental that in the first sentence of the novel Tolstoy tells us that 'every unhappy family is unhappy in its own way'. When I started to study numerous cases of firms collapsing due to the force of extreme risk events, I found this thought applicable to troubled companies. Each story of corporate failure has been pretty unique. At the beginning, I saw little commonalities of how all these 'fallen angels' have run into big problems. However, as I study more and more cases, the picture of a 'typical' scenario has emerged and crystallised.

In this book, I will analyse many firms' failures, but I would like to start here with two very different stories of a bank's failure – Halifax Bank of Scotland (HBOS) and Royal Bank of Scotland (RBS). While these stories have two obvious similarities – both banks were British and both failed in the midst of the financial crisis in 2008 – these two parallels are not really important for the context of their collapse stories. What's important is that both banks became victims of extreme risk, which their bosses readily took and which resulted in catastrophic losses and, eventually, the collapse of the firms. In this case, the similarities can be clearly seen.

### THE PROFIT ENGINE AND THE BLINDFOLDED DRIVER

HBOS was formed as a result of the merger of Halifax, British largest building society, and the Bank of Scotland in 2001. The new merged entity became the largest mortgage lender in the UK and retail business remained the core business of the banking group. The retail division was almost four times larger by assets than its corporate division. However, the strategy of HBOS included the ambitious growth target for its corporate portfolio. In the period of 2001–7, loans and advances of the corporate division experienced an astonishing compound annual growth rate of 45 per cent (Figure 1.4)! As a result of the aggressive penetration into the UK corporate loan market, the gap between HBOS' retail and corporate portfolios reduced substantially. While the retail portfolio remained more than twice as big as the corporate one by assets, in 2007 the latter overtook the former in terms of profit generation (Figure 1.5).

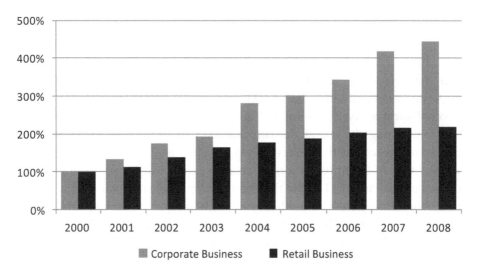

**Figure 1.4    HBOS loans and advances growth (2000=100%)**

*Source*: Author's own figure using data from HBOS annual reports.

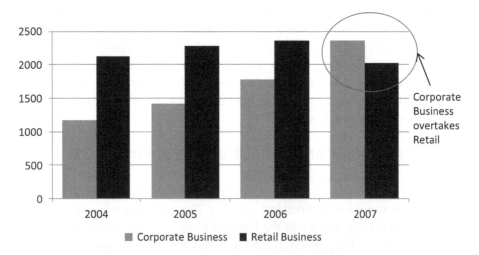

**Figure 1.5    HBOS divisional profit before tax (£ million)**

*Source*: Author's own figure using data from HBOS annual reports.

The year 2007 was the most successful in HBOS's history. The bank's net profit managed to break the £4 billion mark and the £600 billion one of total assets. HBOS reached the lowest ever cost/income ratio, the best ever earnings per share and paid record high dividends. The bank reported a strong capitalisation with the Tier 1 ratio of 7.7 per cent and the total capital ratio of 11 per cent (much higher than minimum Basel requirements). The corporate division became a 'profit engine', delivering the highest profit margin, the fastest asset growth and contributing the largest portion of HBOS's profit.

However, the macroeconomic situation in the UK began its deterioration in the second half of 2007. The sub-prime mortgage crisis started to bite. Did the HBOS management expect the financial disaster? Well, in the 2007 annual report, which was published in the first quarter of 2008 – just a few months before the collapse – its CEO, Andy Hornby, wrote:

> We expect financial markets to be difficult in 2008 but our combination of balance sheet strength, diversified business mix and stringent cost control, together with relative margin stability, leaves us well positioned to take opportunities presented in these markets and deliver good growth in shareholder value over the next few years.
>
> (HBOS 2007: 3)

For the 'profit engine', the strategy remained largely unchanged. The corporate division intended to keep on dancing until the music stopped. The annual report shed light on the corporate business strategy: 'The recent market dislocation has not changed our long held strategy of lending through the cycle. As competition has lessened over the last few months, we have seen more opportunity to use our underwriting and pricing skills to capture additional market share' (HBOS 2007: 30).

The music suddenly stopped. In the first half of 2008, the bank faced growing loan impairments and announced a £4 billion rights issue. After the Lehman Brothers default, HBOS share price started its freefall and the bank experienced massive deposit withdrawals (£35 billion in the last three months of 2008). HBOS's rival bank, Lloyds TSB, stepped in and acquired HBOS, preventing it from financial disaster. Simultaneously, the British government partly nationalised Lloyds Banking Group by injecting £11.5 billion of capital as a bail-out deal.

What exactly went wrong for HBOS? It might sound strange but the HBOS retail portfolio, in spite of its large size and heavy exposure to the problem mortgage market, performed satisfactorily. Its impairment losses rose substantially (Figure 1.6), but overall, in 2008, the division reported a profit before tax of £1.4 billion. But HBOS's 'profit engine' – the corporate portfolio – became the real trouble-maker.

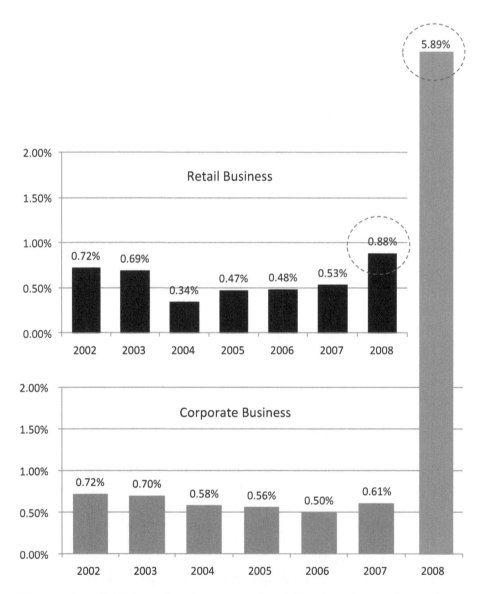

**Figure 1.6      HBOS retail and corporate portfolios: impairment losses as a percentage of average advances**

*Source*: Author's own figure using data from HBOS annual reports.

I paid special attention to how the management assessed future risks for its corporate portfolio at the beginning of 2008. HBOS bosses believed that they ran a sound business:

> Our market understanding, asset quality, sound customer and partner base, proven track record and sector intelligence ... are all designed to manage the balance between risk and return ... In mitigation, we have a well diversified Corporate business which we believe will continue to generate sound returns ... The tough economic climate is likely to see a rising trend in impairments, but we expect this to lead to only a modest increase in impairment losses in 2008.
>
> (HBOS 2007: 32)

So they expected a modest increase in impairments. In reality, the impairments as a percentage of average advances grew from 0.61 per cent to 5.89 per cent! (see Figure 1.6). This 'modest' increase of 961 per cent became the factor that brought HBOS to its knees.

In 2008, HBOS reported a loss of £8.5 billion, of which £6.8 billion was the contribution of the former 'profit engine' – the corporate division. That was not the end of the story. Later, Lloyds Banking Group wrote off almost £20 billion of HBOS's corporate division portfolio of £116 billion or 17 per cent (Aldrick 2012).

But what about the high asset quality and well diversified corporate portfolio that HBOS bosses proudly highlighted in the annual report? All these were no more than illusions. In reality, the portfolio was badly diversified. By March 2008, £34 billion (or one quarter of the total portfolio) was exposed to just 30 clients – over half of whom were in commercial property (Aldrick 2012). As for the real credit quality of assets, it can be comprehensively described by the fact that 17 per cent of HBOS's corporate portfolio was later written off!

At a parliamentary hearing in November 2012, Peter Cummings, former Chief Executive of HBOS Corporate Banking, said about the HBOS collapse: 'I watched a train crash for nine months and could not do anything about it ... I was a spectator of world events that I could not control' (Treanor 2012). No, Cummings was not a spectator. He was the blindfolded driver of this train. Before the train crashed, he created a 'culture of optimism', ignored all red lights and accelerated the train to excessive speeds before completely losing control.

Interestingly, HBOS used the Leadership Index as their key performance indicator. Derived from the annual Colleague Opinion Survey, the Index reflected the percentage of colleagues who agreed with 12 statements about good leadership in HBOS (HBOS 2007: 10). In 2006 and 2007, HBOS was proud that the Index stood as high as 76 per cent. In 2008, HBOS did not report the Leadership Index any more. Can you guess what the Index would be?

## RBS: RISE AND FALL

My second story is how the systemic crisis of 2008 destroyed one of the oldest UK banks (founded in 1727). Or maybe we should not blame the crisis?

For the first 270 years of its history, RBS used to be an old fashioned conservative bank, a regional player in the Scottish financial market. But everything changed in this millennium. Sir George Mathewson, the CEO and then the Chairman, started the process of an ambitious national and international expansion in 2000, acquiring the National Westminster Bank (NatWest). Next year, the 42-year-old Fred Goodwin, a former consultant with a diploma in law, was appointed as the Group CEO and he continued to transform a regional bank into a global financial giant.

Under Goodwin's management, in seven years RBS grew from a mid-sized UK bank to the world's fifth largest bank. How was it possible? A miracle of mergers and acquisitions. RBS bought some 26 banks in seven years and ruthlessly cut costs through staff reductions. As a result, between 2000 and 2007 the bank's total assets increased six-fold from £320 billion to £1.9 trillion (Figure 1.7). This made a compound annual growth rate of total assets of 71 per cent! Yet the shareholders' equity grew at a much slower rate – 19 per cent compound annual growth rate (CAGR).

While such 'acquisition fever' might sound like a deadly disease, it was highly praised by the society and the investors' community. In 2004, Fred Goodwin was knighted by the Queen for his services to the banking industry. By 2007, the empire built by Sir Fred reached the top of its power. Together with Fortis and Santander, RBS made a mega-acquisition of the Dutch financial giant ABN Amro. RBS bosses were very optimistic about the deal:

> It was, and remains the Board's view that the acquisition of ABN AMRO
> will deliver good, long-term value enhancement to shareholders. The
> businesses which the Group has secured will enable us to accelerate the
> implementation of our growth strategy and also provide the Group with

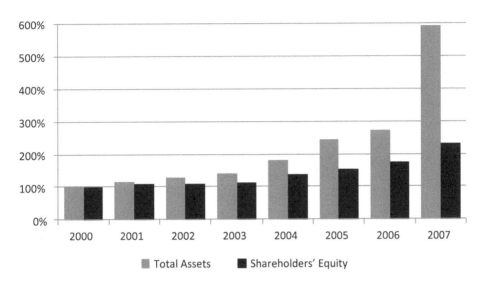

**Figure 1.7    RBS total assets and shareholders' equity growth (2000=100%)**
*Source*: Author's own figure using data from RBS annual reports.

> *a significant presence and options for expansion in the world's most*
> *rapidly growing economies.*
>
>                                                          *(RBS 2007: 8)*

In 2007, RBS ran operations in more than 50 countries and had 226,000 employees. The Group remained strongly capitalised with a Tier 1 capital ratio of 7.3 per cent and a total capital ratio of 11.2 per cent. Needless to add that in 2007 RBS generated a record before-tax profit of £9.9 billion. RBS was named Global Bank of the Year 2007 by *The Banker* magazine.

It was no surprise that in spite of a serious deterioration of the global macro-economic environment at the beginning of 2008, RBS's Chairman Tom McKillop insisted on their growth strategy:

> *We have a great deal to do in 2008. Markets will continue to be*
> *demanding and we have a major integration to deliver. But we also have*
> *an unparalleled set of opportunities and their realisation will allow us*
> *to continue on the impressive growth trajectory that has characterised*
> *RBS over the past decade.*
>
>                                                          *(RBS 2007: 8)*

The optimistic message from top RBS bosses: we are still dancing...

The growth trajectory suddenly changed direction. In April 2008 (just two months after the publication of the report above), RBS warned about £6 billion write-downs on its credit market exposure and raising £12 billion from a rights issue. In August, for the first half of 2008 RBS reported a pre-tax loss of £691 million – the first RBS loss in 40 years and the second largest loss in UK banking history. After the Lehman collapse, the value of RBS assets fell and its shares dropped dramatically. On 13 October 2008, RBS announced that as a £20 billion capital raising agreement, HM Treasury would buy 58 per cent of the bank. RBS's Chairman and the CEO stepped down.

The biggest surprise awaited the investors at the beginning of 2009 when the bank announced their 2008 results. RBS reported a pre-tax loss of £24 billion, of which £16.2 billion related to write-downs arising from the ABN-Amro acquisition together with huge losses on collateralised debt obligations (CDOs). The trajectory indeed changed dramatically (Figure 1.8).

The largest loss in British corporate history forced the UK government to launch a bail-out plan. Overall, the UK government provided RBS with £45 billion direct support and the bank is now 86 per cent owned by the British taxpayer. Later, in its 452-page report, the UK regulator – the Financial Services Authority (FSA) – characterised the ABN Amro acquisition as 'the wrong price, the wrong way to pay, at the wrong time and the wrong deal' (FSA 2011: 54). But time revealed that RBS had more skeletons in the closet than just ABN Amro and CDOs. One of these skeletons was the loan portfolio. Over the 2007–10 period, loan impairments amounted to £32.5 billion, significantly exceeding the £17.7 billion of losses on credit trading activities. FSA clarified that 'the full extent of those losses would not have been clear to the market in autumn 2008' (FSA 2011: 24).

The RBS story – one of the most spectacular 'rising stars' in the British corporate history – ended suddenly and sadly. To complete this story, I would like to mention that starting from 2005, the RBS management conducted the Employee Opinion Survey. In its 2007 annual report, the management team led by Sir Fred Goodwin proudly said that once again they outperformed the Global High Performance Norm with 71 per cent of employee job satisfaction and engagement. Unfortunately, in 2008 the annual report was modestly silent about the employee satisfaction figure. In February 2012, Fred Goodwin's knighthood was 'cancelled and annulled' by the Queen on the advice of her government and the Honours Forfeiture Committee.

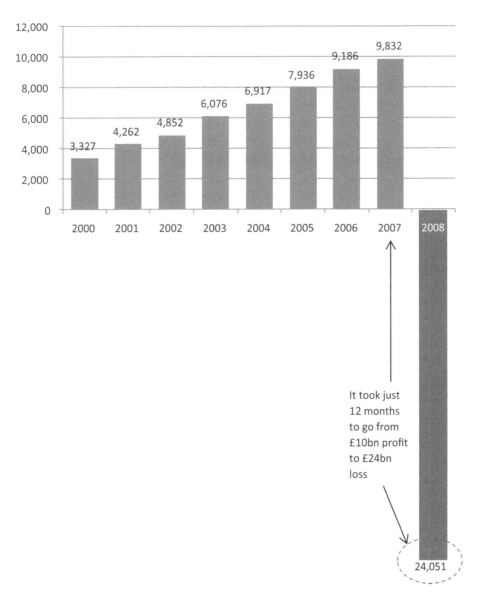

**Figure 1.8    RBS profit before tax (£ million)**

*Source*: Author's own figure using data from RBS annual reports.

To conclude this chapter, I would like to summarise several learning points from the stories above:

- A systemic extreme event like the global financial crisis represents a huge distractive power which can change the economic landscape beyond recognition. This power can easily wipe out not only small start-ups but global players with hundreds of years of experience and almost invincible market position.

- This power is not blind. The 'perfect storm', when it occurs, affects firms in different ways. Some of them can face difficulties; others suffer losses, but some have almost no chance of survival.

- The victims of the last systemic crisis like HBOS and RBS were not innocent victims of a blind destructive power of the systemic crisis. Similar to a vast majority of other 'innocent victims', in the years preceding the fiasco, their top managers made a huge effort to warehouse as much extreme risk as possible. The time bomb was waiting for the right moment.

- The management of failed firms ignored numerous warning signals and focused on its ambitious plans and good news, maintaining the culture of blind optimism. Even when the crisis was in its full swing, they were dancing ...

- For the top managements of failed companies, the failure of their firms has been absolutely unexpected and the speed that their 'ships' went underwater was shocking. How was it possible that these smart and experienced people equipped with modern risk management models and tools overlooked the key risk drivers and did not see the weaknesses of their business until it was too late? In the next chapter, I will give you my answer to this question.

# 2

# Models, Experts and Extreme Events

In this chapter, the analysis of the contemporary risk management approach from the standpoint of its effectiveness against tail risk is provided. The analysis reveals substantial limitations of current methods, tools and models used in risk management practice. This includes both judgemental risk models, Basel-type models and sophisticated internal models like economic capital models and early warning tools. Basel III enhancements are also analysed here and its limited anti-tail risk efficiency and unintended consequences are described. While the modern risk tools, models and methods can be very effective in the measurement and mitigation of normal day-to-day risk, they typically are misleading and unhelpful when applied to the area of the tail. The chapter provides insight into why it happens and why this risk 'rocket science' is inappropriate for extreme risk areas.

## Applying the Meat Grinder Principle

I spent several years of my career leading a team of quantitative risk analysts. My task was to build various risk models to address Basel requirements. When I discuss risk models and other quantitative tools with people outside risk analytics, I find that quite often people have a vague understanding what risk models can and cannot do, how models work and how assumptions used in the model algorithm can affect the model output.

It is important to understand that models do not produce any new knowledge. They can help systemise raw data, filter records and extract and assemble valuable pieces of information from noisy and low structured databases. They can produce a summary from a large volume of information. Yet models only operate within the boundaries of the data, algorithms and assumptions predefined by the model developers.

To explain risk models in simple terms, I usually use the analogy of a meat grinder. I compare models to the meat grinders that most of us have in our kitchens. What comes out of a grinder does not fundamentally differ from what you put into it. If you insert chicken, you don't expect to have a beef mince as the output. If one key ingredient of the mince recipe is missing, the grinder will not add it even if this is a state-of-the-art grinder with advanced automated cutting modes. Like a meat grinder, a risk model cannot make miracles happen, or create something from nothing. Therefore, we need to critically analyse what we put into our 'grinder'.

If we simplify the situation slightly, all models that we currently use in risk management can be divided into three broad categories:

1.  Statistical models: these models are based on established statistical relationships between particular risk drivers and modelled risk values. It is clear that this type of model can only be applied in areas where a sufficient quantity of statistical data is readily available. For example, market risk models and credit risk models for retail portfolios are often purely statistical.

2.  Expert models: these models are driven mainly by expert judgement and use quantification provided by experts. This does not mean that these models ignore any empirical evidence or historical data, but the model output is to a large extent driven by parameters based on the experts' judgement. These models are used for risk assessment for portfolios or business areas where principal risk drivers are unquantifiable or historical data is limited, which impedes building the full scale statistical models. In banking practice, credit risk models for low default portfolios often represent expert type models.

3.  Hybrid models: these models widely utilise statistical methods which are underpinned and enhanced by expert judgement. Most rating models for wholesale portfolios belong to this class (e.g. rating models for banks and other financial institutions).

Each class of models has its own advantages as well as weaknesses. While there is no ideal solution, the priority is often given to statistical models. If sufficient historical data is available, the choice can be straightforward – build a statistical model. Model developers' first choice is to use the power of quantitative methods and build statistics-driven models which range from simple deterministic models to complex stochastic models.

Regulators encourage financial institutions to build statistical and/or hybrid models where historical data is used as a backbone of the models' algorithm. At the same time, if models used for regulatory purposes (e.g. calculation of risk-weighted assets and capital ratios), regulators are not willing to accept judgemental models: 'Estimates should be derived using both historical experience and empirical evidence and not be based purely on judgemental considerations' (FSA 2005: 4).

## Statistical Models: Success Factors

What are the main advantages and drawbacks of statistical models? In general, the statistical model approach is based on the formalisation relationship existing between input variables on the one hand, and output estimates on the other. Model developers need to decide what input variables influence the parameters that need to be estimated. For risk assessment, these variables can include macroeconomic factors, various market parameters and benchmarks, financial products or borrower's characteristics, etc. Then the model needs to be 'trained' on historical data to use statistical relationships between input and output. And then the model can be used to make ex-ante estimates, applying the established ex-post formalised relationship for the future period.

There are several 'ingredients' of success for statistical models. The level of expertise of model developers to a large extent explains the success or failure of any model. Expertise should include not only knowledge of quantitative methods and techniques, but also probably, in the first instance, a deep understanding of the real economic processes that they try to model. Developers should have a clear view on what fundamentally drives the economic processes, for example, what factors predetermine and influence the creditworthiness of borrowers. They need to be able to drill down into the processes to find out key cause–effect relationships between driving forces and estimated parameters. They must select the most fundamental drivers and include these relationships in the model. This ensures that the model has a relevant and complete set of drivers, both economically and statistically. In other words, this determines the 'shape' of the model: what factors the model takes into account and what has been left outside the model's realm.

Another ingredient of success is data used for the model development. If the data is of poor quality or insufficient, the model will fail to provide an accurate and reliable prediction of estimated parameters regardless of the model design. The development data must meet the criteria of relevance, completeness, consistency and correctness. Should data satisfy these requirements, the developers can be proud of having decent raw material at hand to prepare a robust statistical model.

Going forward, the formalisation process comes as the next important ingredient of a good model. Usually model developers have a choice of how they can formalise the relationships between the model's input and output. The choice of the algorithm predefines not only the predictive power of the model but also the way in which the model can be implemented. A simple, intuitive and user-friendly design has always been an important factor in model success.

When a model is built and implemented in the real business environment, it starts to live its own life independent from its 'parents' – model developers who did everything that they could to ensure a good life for their 'child'. What is often underestimated is the importance of how the model is used after its implementation. I have seen many cases when a good model performed unsatisfactorily after its implementation. As a model developer, I monitored the model performance after implementation to ensure that models were working as expected and to find ways of enhancing their performance. For example, for probability of default models, which are used to assess the creditworthiness of borrowers and generate credit ratings on a master scale (or sometimes the probability of default percentage on a given day), the important 'fit for purpose' indicator is the percentage of overrides. When model users run the probability of default model, they need to do a 'sense check', to ensure that the credit rating generated by the model looks reasonable. If they disagree with the rating produced by the model, they can override it using their own judgement and established override procedures. For model developers each override case provides food for thought: why the model was wrong in this assessment and what factors were ignored, underestimated or overestimated.

Surprisingly, when I analysed overrides of ratings produced by new models, I found that up to 30 per cent of overrides would not have been necessary if models had been used correctly! Model users simply violated some key model requirements. Most often, they input wrong data into the model, which led to incorrect outputs. Quite often, model users input incomplete data, while the full set of required data was readily available, and this also affected the model output. In some cases, a model was used to assess the creditworthiness of borrowers who did not belong in the target portfolio (e.g. applying the model to borrowers from a different industry or from a different geographic area or of different size).

To use the meat grinder analogy, model users simply put the wrong ingredients (or wrong proportion of products) into their grinders or forget some important ones. It is not surprising that the mince has a strange, unexpected taste. However, consumers come back to the meat grinder experts and blame them for the unsatisfactory results.

To conclude, statistical models have several key success factors (Figure 2.1). During the model development and implementation, the experience and skills of model developers matter, as well as the availability of sufficient quantity and high quality of statistical data, sensible assumptions and intuitive algorithms. The bottom line is that these models are only as good as the underlying data and assumptions. When models are implemented and incorporated into the decision-making process, the role of model users and decision-makers, who use the model output for making strategic and tactical decisions, becomes crucial for the model's success or failure. Success at this stage depends on how the model is understood and applied and how the model output is interpreted by decision-makers and top executives (Figure 2.2).

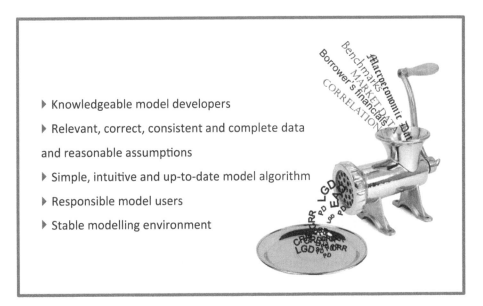

▶ Knowledgeable model developers

▶ Relevant, correct, consistent and complete data
and reasonable assumptions

▶ Simple, intuitive and up-to-date model algorithm

▶ Responsible model users

▶ Stable modelling environment

Figure 2.1    Key ingredients of success for statistical models

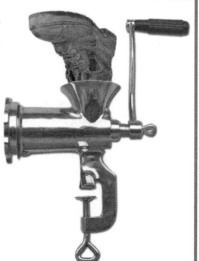

The important element of model success or failure is how the model is understood, applied, managed and used in the decision-making process:

▶ Input data: how to ensure that input data meet all development requirements.

▶ Model users' knowledge: model users have to be fully aware of models' assumptions, limitations and weaknesses.

▶ Model output: interpretation of model output by model users, decision makers and top executives.

**Figure 2.2     Model success factors after the implementation**

## Why Statistical Models Often Fail

The global financial crisis of 2008–9 became a good test for the efficiency of risk models. Most statistical models performed satisfactorily in the pre-crisis period, which created the impression that risk can be measured correctly via a set of statistical models. However, the industry's track record with model performance during the crisis period has been poor. The crisis highlighted the known weakness of statistical models once again – they are inherently backward looking. The whole idea of statistically driven models is to determine ex-post relationships via historical data analysis and replicate them for ex-ante analysis. Therefore, the models' function is to extrapolate past relationships to the future period. If the relationships hold, then model predictions are normally reliable. However, if the market conditions change abruptly, models struggle to generate accurate predictions. Not only risk models, but also the whole class of statistically driven models suffer from this weakness.

### MODELLING FUTURE PRICES

A good illustration of how statistical models can fall short in predicting events when circumstances defy the past pattern/trend is the oil price forecasts produced by the Energy Information Administration (EIA), the independent statistical and analytical agency within the US Department of Energy.

The EIA publishes annual analytical reports called 'International Energy Outlook' (Energy Information Administration 2001). Amongst other things, the reports contain the analysis of oil prices and the long-term forecast of the oil price trend. The 2001 EIA report has the projection covering a 20-year period from 2001 to 2020 – quite an ambitious task to provide a projection for such a long period. The report concludes: 'World oil prices are expected to reach $22 per barrel in 1999 dollars ($36 per barrel in nominal dollars) at the end of the projection period' (Energy Information Administration 2001: 2). According to the report, the oil price, for example, for 2013 was forecasted at the level of about $20 per barrel in 1999 dollars.

Today, this forecast looks odd. We are already used to living in a world where oil prices stand above $100 per barrel. If we combine two graphs – the International Energy Outlook 2001–20 and the actual oil price trend for 2001–12 (Figure 2.3), then we can see that the forecast was more or less reliable only for the first year or so. Then the market conditions changed dramatically and the world entered a new oil price era where $20 per barrel became no more than a dream.

Being a statistical and analytical agency, the EIA used advanced analytical tools to produce their forecasts. I am sure that it is not too difficult for them to ensure that the key success factors for statistical models are in place. As I already explained in the previous chapter, such factors include the knowledgeable model developers, sufficient quantity and high quality historical data, as well as intuitive model algorithms. I have no doubt that the people who developed the forecasting model for the oil price were highly qualified. Ample historical data for the oil market is also available: not only the long history of oil prices per se, but also various historical data reflecting oil market drivers and trends (e.g. detailed oil demand and supply data). Nevertheless, in 2001 the model failed to produce a meaningful forecast even for five years ahead.

We should not blame the model developers. It was not their fault that the predicted oil prices were way below the actual prices. Statistical models can only operate within the boundaries of past relationships. They cannot see beyond the historical trends. The oil price rise, which started at the end of 2002, turned out to be not just a temporary jump, but rather a fundamentally new state of the oil market. The oil price growth accelerated and skyrocketed in 2008 in a way that has not been evidenced since the 1973 OPEC (Organization of the Petroleum Exporting Countries) embargo. This fundamental change in the market state led to substantial changes of key relationships between the market prices and their drivers. The statistical forecasting tool, which was built in 2001 and utilised historical data, could not predict the tectonic shift of the oil market.

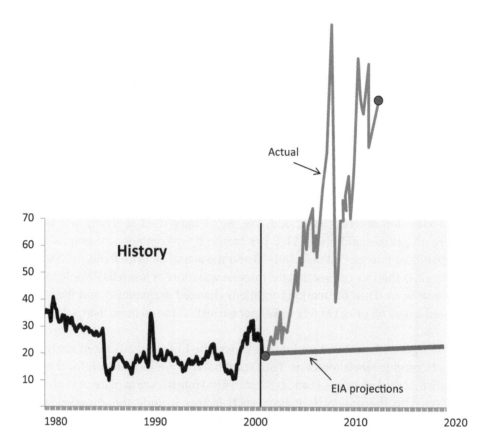

**Figure 2.3    Long-term forecast and actual oil price (US$ per barrel)**

*Source*: Author's own figure using data from Energy Information Administration,
Bloomberg.


One can argue that price forecasting is an extremely difficult or even
impossible task as prices are often driven by 'irrational behaviour' of market
participants. Well, we can look at how statistical models can predict the 'next
big thing' in the more predictable areas such as macroeconomics. I have been
curious about how well macroeconomic models performed during the last
global financial crisis. For example, did models predict a substantial contraction
of the economic output in 2008?

## MODELLING MACROECONOMIC PARAMETERS

I propose to look at two highly respected organisations which produce their
macroeconomic forecasts on a regular basis and whose predictions play an

important role in strategic decisions made not only for private businesses but also for government policies. The International Monetary Fund (IMF) and the Bank of England (BoE) are the two respected institutions I am referring to. To predict the main macroeconomic parameters, both organisations use sophisticated econometric models and plentiful historical data. In April 2008, the IMF published their semi-annual analytical report called 'World Economic Outlook' (IMF 2008a). In the report, the IMF provided their GDP growth projections for 2008 and 2009. As the report was published in April 2008, in the midst of the impending crisis, it was clear that this was a short-term forecast covering less than two years. Also, it is important to stress that by the time the report was published, the growing economic concerns were apparent. Simon Johnson, the Economic Counsellor and Director of the IMF Research Department rightly said in the Foreword:

> *The world economy has entered new and precarious territory. The U.S. economy continues to be mired in the financial problems that first emerged in subprime mortgage lending but which have now spread much more broadly. Strains that were once thought to be limited to part of the housing market are now having considerable negative effects across the entire economy, with rising defaults, falling collateral, and tighter credit working together to create a powerful and hard-to-defeat financial decelerator.*
>
> *(IMF 2008a: 11)*

Therefore, the IMF already included the key negative trends of the world's economy in their projections. The growth projections have been revised and reduced substantially compared with the projections done six months earlier. Nevertheless, when we look at the projections and compare them with actual figures, especially for the counties which have been the most affected by the crisis, the only conclusion we can draw is that macroeconomic predictions were noticeably outside the actual range of GDP growths (Table 2.1).

It is apparent that the results generated by the macroeconomic models were wrong even for 2008, in spite of the fact that the predictions covered just a little longer that six months. For 2009, the difference between actual GDP growth numbers and predictions is astonishing. For countries like the USA, Japan, the UK and Italy the forecast was not only incorrect numerically, but the overall forecasted trend was also wrong. For example, for Japan, the models suggested that modest GDP growth in 2008 (+1.4 per cent) would accelerate to +1.5 per cent in 2009. The reality was a deep downward trend: –1.2 per cent in 2008 and –5.2 per cent in 2009.

**Table 2.1**    World economic outlook: GDP growth projections vs. actual
(annual percentage change)

| | Projections as of April 2008 | | Actual | | Difference (actual – projection) | |
|---|---|---|---|---|---|---|
| | *2008* | *2009* | *2008* | *2009* | *2008* | *2009* |
| World output | 3.7 | 3.8 | 3.0 | −0.6 | −0.7 | −4.4 |
| | | | | | | |
| Advanced economies | 1.3 | 1.3 | 0.5 | −3.2 | −0.8 | −4.5 |
| USA | 0.5 | 0.6 | 0.4 | −2.4 | −0.1 | −3 |
| Euro area | 1.4 | 1.2 | 0.6 | −4.1 | −0.8 | −5.3 |
| Germany | 1.4 | 1.0 | 1.2 | −5.0 | −0.2 | −6 |
| France | 1.4 | 1.2 | 0.3 | −2.2 | −1.1 | −3.4 |
| Italy | 0.3 | 0.3 | −1.3 | −5.0 | −1.6 | −5.3 |
| Spain | 1.8 | 1.7 | 0.9 | −3.6 | −0.9 | −5.3 |
| Japan | 1.4 | 1.5 | −1.2 | −5.2 | −2.6 | −6.7 |
| UK | 1.6 | 1.6 | 0.5 | −4.9 | −1.1 | −6.5 |
| Canada | 1.3 | 1.9 | 0.4 | −2.6 | −1.9 | −4.5 |
| Other advanced economies | 3.3 | 3.4 | 1.7 | −1.1 | −1.6 | −4.5 |
| | | | | | | |
| Central and Eastern Europe | 4.4 | 4.3 | 3 | −3.7 | −1.4 | −8 |
| Commonwealth of Independent States | 7.0 | 6.5 | 5.5 | −6.6 | −1.5 | −13.1 |
| Russia | 6.8 | 6.3 | 5.6 | −7.9 | −1.2 | −14.2 |
| Excluding Russia | 7.4 | 7.0 | 5.3 | −3.5 | −2.1 | −10.5 |

*Source*: Author's own table using data from IMF World Economic Outlook 2008, 2010.

Probably the most striking gap between the projected and actual numbers was Russia's GDP growth for 2009. While the IMF's model projected a robust 6.3 per cent growth, the actual growth was −7.9 per cent. The gap between the actual and projected growth reached −14 percentage points! The comparison of IMF predictions and actual GDP growth figures is depicted in Figure 2.4.

It is true that the global economic crisis had not yet revealed its maximum force at the time when the research was published (April 2008). But there were clear signals that the 'financial hurricane' was approaching (e.g. the collapse of Northern Rock in the UK and Bear Stearns in the USA, the deep dive of the US housing market, growing problems with the sub-prime mortgage sector and derivatives linked to this market). The task for the forecasters did not look so unachievable: predict how deep the crisis over the next 1.5 years would be. Yet the macroeconomic models failed to provide reliable numbers.

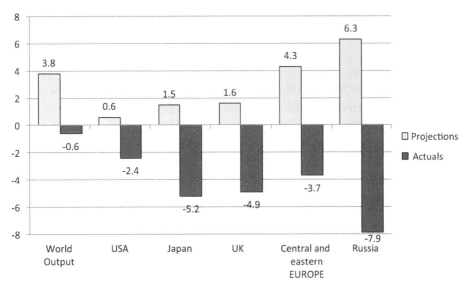

**Figure 2.4    IMF projected and actual GDP growth for 2009 (annual percentage change)**

Another forecast that is also worth discussing here is the GDP forecast produced by the Bank of England in 2007. The Bank of England publishes the Inflation Report – a bi-annual analytical report, which contains a comprehensive mid-term outlook for the main macroeconomic indicators for the UK. The report published in May 2007 provided the projections for the 2007–10 period (Bank of England 2007). In the section of the outlook for the GDP growth, the main message was given as follows: 'The central projection is for output to grow roughly in line with its average rate over the past decade, slowing a little over the course of the forecast period as business investment and public spending decelerate' (Bank of England 2007: 6).

The report contained a fan chart depicting the GDP projections. It would be fair to say that, unlike the IMF, the Bank of England has been more cautious in their forecast approach and allows some degree of uncertainty in their projections by giving the range of possible outcomes rather than solid forecast numbers. The fan chart covers different possible future outcomes ranging from the base case – the most likely scenario – to less probable outcomes. As the fan chart's footnote describes, GDP growth was expected to lie somewhere within the entire fan chart on 90 out of 100 occasions. In other words, even if the predicted fan chart shape was completely different from the actual GDP trend, technically we would not be able to say that the prediction completely failed.

Nevertheless, it seems important to compare the range of projections with actual GDP growth in the UK for the 2008–9 period.

We can combine the fan chart with projections and the actual GDP growth trend in the UK for 2007–10 (Figure 2.5). What we can see now is that the actual GDP trend departed from the projected base case almost immediately after the report was published and the gap was widening for the second to fourth quarters of the forecast horizon. Moreover, in the second half of 2008 and 2009, not only did the actual trend move materially compared to the base case, but it also turned to fall beyond the scope of the entire forecasted range and stayed outside the range until the end of the forecast horizon.

To conclude, the fan chart demonstrates that in May 2007, the BoE did not expect any downturn for 2008–9. There were no signals from the BoE that the UK economy was approaching the most turbulent period in the past 40 years.

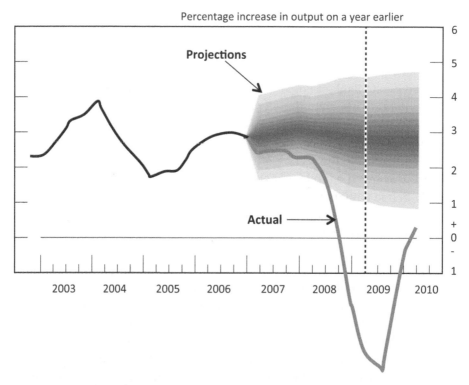

**Figure 2.5**    **Bank of England's projection of UK GDP growth vs. actual GDP growth**

*Source*: Bank of England, Inflation Report, May 2007; Bloomberg.

Its analysis showed no more than an extrapolation of the stable economic growth that the UK economy experienced in the period of 2000–2007.

Would it be realistic to expect the BoE's statistical models to have the power to predict extreme events such as the collapse of economic output of 2008–9? No, the models cannot do that. Even the collective effort of econometric modelling and human judgement appeared to be insufficient. What we see in the fan chart was much more than just a blind output of the statistical model. The model output was overlaid with expert judgement. The BoE report called it 'Committee's best collective judgement'. The Committee was referring to the BoE Monetary Policy Committee (MPC) chaired by the the BoE Governor, as well as Deputy Governors responsible for monetary policy and financial stability and several other great minds of the BoE. If these people couldn't predict the forthcoming financial disaster one year in advance using the power of their sophisticated econometric models, then who could?

Interestingly, the prediction of extreme changes for even more controllable macroeconomic parameters than GDP remains a challenge. Take inflation. Obviously, the BoE has a much stronger control and greater visibility of inflation than GDP. At the end of the day, the prime responsibility of the Bank is to maintain the monetary stability which is based on inflation control. The BoE has an array of means to control inflation and should be in a better position than anyone else to predict the future inflation trend. Can we rely on their inflation forecast?

In February 2009, the BoE published their Inflation Report (Bank of England 2009). At the time of publication, the Consumer Price Index (CPI), the widely accepted measure of inflation, was on a downward trend (about 3 per cent) and the BoE expected the trend to continue. In particular, commenting on a three-year projection the report highlighted: 'In the central projection, CPI inflation falls well below the 2 per cent target in the medium term, as the drag from a substantial margin of spare capacity more than outweighs the waning impact on import and consumer prices from the lower level of sterling' (Bank of England 2009: 5). Unfortunately for them, the inflation trend changed direction and went outside of the projected range as soon as the end of the fourth quarter of 2009 (Figure 2.6). In 2010, CPI growth accelerated and reached 5.6 per cent in the third quarter of 2011 – materially above the BoE's projections.

Again, the BoE projections for CPI were not just based on the model output. They were a result of quantitative assessment adjusted judgementally by the MPC. The report clarifies the approach as follows: 'Although not every member

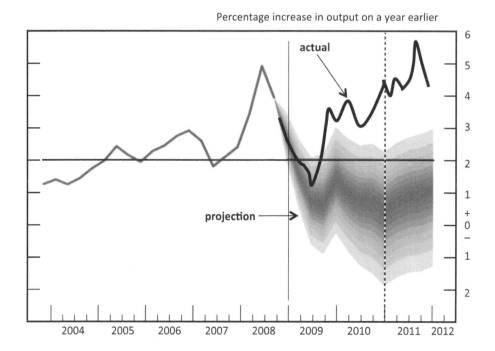

**Figure 2.6    CPI inflation projection as of February 2009 and actual CPI**
*Source*: Author's own figure using data from Bank of England, Inflation Report,
February 2009; Bloomberg.

will agree with every assumption on which our projections are based, the fan
charts represent the MPC's best collective judgement about the most likely
paths for inflation and output, and the uncertainties surrounding those central
projections'. Yet the best collective judgement underpinned by powerful
modelling did not result in a reliable prediction of the inflation trend.

An important factor of success or failure of statistical models and hybrid
models (when the quantitative modelling is supplemented with human
judgement) is the level of stability of the system. In a slow-moving world with
stable trends, statistical models do a very good job. However, if the system
enters a volatile stage, the statistical modelling approach loses its predictive
power. The above examples from the EIA, IMF and Bank of England practices
illustrate this rule of thumb. There is no need to blame the model developers.
They operate within the natural limitations of statistical models and cannot
breach these boundaries. Statistically driven models are inherently backward
looking, while by definition any extreme event is defined by a rare and material

departure from the past trend and norm. That is why statistical models struggle to predict or measure risk associated with extreme events.

Next time, when the economy is hit by the 'perfect storm', will statistical models let us down again? Yes, they certainly will. We cannot rely on these models in predicting extreme and tail risk events. It is beyond the models' capability. We can comfortably apply them in a stable environment and trust their output. What is important to remember is that in the event of the environment changing abruptly, these models do not have the capability to give us a warning signal of the upcoming shift and reliably forecast what will happen after the system moves to its new state.

## Expert Judgement and Tail Risk Event Predictions

Statistical models are locked into their backward looking world and cannot be reliable tools for predicting future extreme events. Can the expert-judgement-driven models and tools help look ahead and give a trustworthy signal of upcoming extreme events?

When answering this question, I have more reasons to be optimistic. At least expert-judgement-driven tools are free from their dependence on historical data which drags statistical models into the past. Strictly speaking, the expert approach does not need historical data at all. Experts can solely use their knowledge and expertise to make assumptions about the future and assess future trends, completely ignoring what happened in the past. Moreover, experts can use their intuition – the cognitive apparatus which is not available to any sophisticated models. Therefore, theoretically, we can expect a stronger predictive power of judgementally driven tools when we focus on future extreme events.

However, one dependency needs to be considered with care. The success or failure of the expert approach is purely determined by experts' skills, knowledge and ability to make correct assumptions regarding the future changes. For the sake of fairness, it has always been a difficult task to find experts fit for this challenging task.

I tried to understand how well experts can predict extreme events. For example, what was the proportion of correct predictions of the 2008 financial disaster? After the event, many experts, market analysts and academics claimed that they correctly predicted the 2008 market crash. I am not sure if anybody has done a comprehensive research regarding correct predictions of the global financial crisis. I have not found any so far. However, there are facts that can help to draw a picture of what experts predicted in 2006 or 2007 (Appendix 1).

My conclusion is far from optimistic. Most gurus, with rare exceptions, failed to predict correctly the global financial crisis. When an extreme event hits the industry, there are some experts who correctly predicted it and provided a warning signal. I personally know several specialists whose opinions I respect and who correctly predicted the crisis of 2008–9. At the same time, the market is awash with all sorts of predictions. Each day, hundreds of specialists forecast different extreme events which never materialise. The large number of 'false alarms' dilutes our ability to select the right alarm and to react to it.

The key problem with predicting extreme events resides in our limited understanding of the mechanics of extreme events in the financial sector. We do not understand the practical 'equation' that links risk drivers and their devastating consequences. A French American mathematician, Benoit Mandelbrot, once said: 'The basis of weather forecasting is looking from a satellite and seeing a storm coming, but not predicting that the storm will form. The behavior of economic phenomena is far more complicated than the behavior of liquids or gases' (Solman 2008).

At best, we can talk about some theoretical concepts of the crisis, but we struggle to bring it to a practical level. Each crisis tends to have a different scenario. We have not defined a clear cause–effect relationship concept that can explain a 'black swan' event in the financial markets. Without the practical concept, we are forced to operate by 'the best guess' or 'gut feeling'.

## GURUS VS. DART-THROWING MONKEYS

I don't want to present several examples of successful and unsuccessful predictions that I describe in Appendix 1 as comprehensive scientific research about the reliability of expert judgement. This is just an illustration that the ability of experts to make a forward-looking view and correctly predict the next extreme event is rather limited. One success does not guarantee that the same expert will make a string of other successful predictions.

Now, let us look at the academic studies on the accuracy of expert predictions. There were several comprehensive research projects focused on the ability of experts to predict future extreme events. Philip Tetlock, a Professor of Business Administration, Political Science and Psychology at the University of California at Berkeley, made possibly the most comprehensive research on expert judgements to date. In 2005, he published *Expert Political Judgement. How good is it? How can we know?'* (Tetlock 2005). Tetlock managed to collect an impressive statistical database: over the course of 20 years he worked with 284 experts who offered advice on political and economic trends, asking them to assess the probability of occurrence of different events in geopolitics, political life and economy. There were 82,361 subjective probability estimates derived from responses to 27,450 forecasting questions. It is important to mention that Tetlock worked with experts, with many of them being deemed top calibre. Characterising the level of expertise, Tetlock highlighted that most of the experts (52 per cent) had doctoral degrees and almost all had postgraduate training (96 per cent). Approximately 80 per cent of experts had served at least once as formal or informal consultants on international political or economic issues to the government, private sector, international agencies or think tanks.

What conclusions can we make based on Tetlock's research? For the subject of this book, the most important conclusion is that the overall accuracy of expert predictions for extreme events is very poor and not materially better than guesses of non-experts. Louis Menand compared the forecasters with dart-throwing monkeys:

> *On the first scale, the experts performed worse than they would have if they had simply assigned an equal probability to all three outcomes — if they had given each possible future a thirty-three per cent chance of occurring. Human beings who spend their lives studying the state of the world, in other words, are poorer forecasters than dart-throwing monkeys, who would have distributed their picks evenly over the three choices.*
>
> (Menand 2005)

In the long run, arbitrary rules such as 'always predict no change' deliver more accurate forecasts than the best forecasters.

Another conclusion that can be important for us is that famous experts do not necessarily perform better in predicting future extreme events than their less famous colleagues. In this book I will provide many examples when top executives made terrible decisions based on their predictions of the future market situations which appeared to be wrong. One of the explanations why famous experts and top executives are weak in their forecasting resides in their overconfidence. They often have self-belief that they understand the market better than other people and, therefore, rely on their 'gut feel' rather than on external facts and market signals.

Another possible explanation has been provided by Tetlock. He found that experts can be divided in two groups: 'hedgehogs' and 'foxes'. Hedgehogs are experts 'who know one big thing' and they apply their big theory boldly in the forecasts. Foxes are experts 'who know many small things'. They are usually much more flexible in using different theories than 'hedgehogs' and adjust their forecasts based on information they receive from different sources. 'The most consistent predictor of consistently more accurate forecasts was 'style of reasoning': experts with the more eclectic, self-critical and modest cognitive styles tended to outperform the big-idea people (foxes tended to outperform hedgehogs)' (Lehrer 2011).

I guess that many famous experts and top executives of large and global financial institutions belong to the class of 'hedgehogs'. No surprise then that they often are wrong in their bold predictions.

## SEARCHING FOR THE PERFECT EXPERT

Overall conclusions regarding the accuracy of expert judgement could be discouraging. However, we cannot say that human judgement is absolutely hopeless. Rather, we believe that good forecasters are a rare species in the concrete jungle of Wall Street. But it is definitely worthwhile searching for a guru in the crowd of mediocre experts whose accuracy of prediction does not differ from tossing a coin. In particular, we need to focus on the prediction of extreme events and identify those experts who are able to make it correctly. If we can find a way to identify these rare top-notch experts who consistently outperform their peers, then we stand a good chance of enhancing our judgement-driven tools for assessing tail risk and predicting extreme events.

Priority should be given to objective scientific methods rather than self-assessment of experts as people often have a short memory regarding their failures and a long one regarding their successes. This is why we often observe a situation when experts claim to be correct in more past predictions (especially about large events like economic crises) than they actually were. One academic study is particularly interesting because the authors set a task to identify those experts who are able to predict extreme economic events correctly. Oxford economist Jerker Denrell and Christina Fang of New York University built an analytical model to test experimental and field data (Denrell and Fang 2010).

As field data, scientists used the data from the *Wall Street Journal's* Survey of Economic Forecasts, which is produced every six months by about 50 renowned economists. Experts predict key macroeconomic parameters such as GDP, unemployment rate, CPI, exchange rates and interest rates. The analysis covered seven surveys from July 2002 to July 2005.

Denrell and Fang identified those experts who successfully predicted some extreme events and compared their overall performance with those who have been less successful in predicting the next big thing. Surprisingly, their analysis suggests that those who had a better record of predicting extreme events had a worse record in general.

> *The explanation for this pattern is that poor forecasters made more extreme predictions ... Because poor forecasters were more likely to make extreme forecasts, they are also more likely to make extreme forecasts that turn out to be accurate. Thus, an ability to call many extreme events correctly was an indication of poor judgement. In fact, the analyst with the largest number as well as the highest proportion of accurate and extreme forecasts had, by far, the worst forecasting record.*
> *(Denrell and Fang 2010: 20)*

For us, this is bad news. The strategy of identifying a group of experts who can successfully predict extreme events and following their advice is unlikely to be viable. In addition, the consistency of experts to predict extreme events correctly comes into question. The story of Gary Schilling, an economist and the President of A Gary Schilling & Company, can be a good illustration of how difficult it is to be consistently successful in predictions. Schilling was one of the few people who correctly predicted the global financial crisis. He made 13 predictions about the economic situation in 2008 and all of them appeared to be correct. After this astonishing success, he made 12 predictions for 2009 (e.g. S&P 500 index would drop to 600 points). But this time all his predictions were wrong (Roth 2010).

In his article 'Gary Schilling's 2009 Predictions – What Went Wrong?', Alan Roth concluded: 'Schilling's incredible accuracy in 2008 was nearly matched by his incredible inaccuracy the following year. Thus those that became aware of Mr. Schilling at the end of 2008, and followed his advice for 2009, experienced the full pain of the 2008 collapse without getting any of the rebound' (Roth 2010).

Unfortunately, one spectacular success with extreme event prediction does not guarantee the accuracy of the following predictions. Experts who correctly predict extreme events are more likely to be 'hedgehogs' (using Tetlock's terminology) as they tend to make bold predictions. Consequently, by making extreme predictions, they choose to be wrong most of the time, which is reflected in their poor overall forecasting results.

So, how successful could the search possibly be for the perfect expert who can correctly assess tail risks and consistently make correct predictions of the next big thing? Knowing the results of the academic studies and assuming that their conclusions truly reflect the reality, I hesitate to express a lot of optimism. There were and will always be correct and spot-on predictions of extreme events. Yet correct predictions look more like a matter of luck or occasional success of some theoretical concepts which appear to be wrong in the long run.

What conclusions can we draw from the analysis of expert judgements? There is no effective way of ex-ante selection of judgements about future extreme events. Experts with good track records of successful forecasts ('foxes') will most likely miss the next big thing. Poor forecasters have a tendency to make extreme predictions and could be right on one big prediction, but are unlikely to repeat the success next time round. The best strategy in this situation is to use expert judgement with caution. We should not ignore expert opinions when discussing tail risks. However, at the same time, we should not fully rely on expert predictions. Knowing the limited ability of experts to foresee future extreme events, I would not take the risk of basing a material business decision (like a major investment or a large change of the business model) on the prediction of an expert, even if this expert has successfully predicted previous tail risk events.

## TIME FACTOR IN FORECASTING

How many times have you heard people say: 'See, this is exactly what I predicted'? More often than not, we live with the illusion that we can predict the future well. Maybe in our day-to-day life we are good at predicting and can, indeed, rely more on our forecasting ability and gut feel, but in the socio-economic area, expert judgement does not demonstrate the level of accuracy that everyone expects from skilled and often highly paid experts. The problem is that to claim a successful prediction, the expert needs to be correct in two elements:

1.  The event: exactly what will happen. This should include the event and its main characteristics. For example, seismologists can predict a major earthquake in Northern California with a magnitude of 8.0 or higher. Or an economist can forecast a collapse of the commercial real estate market in the UK with a price drop of more than 40 per cent from the current level. If seismologists predict a major earthquake with a magnitude of 8.0 or higher but in reality a light earthquake occurs (say magnitude 3), we would not give credit to these experts for their prediction as the exact event that was forecasted did not occur. Instead, an event with different characteristics took place.

2.  The timing of the event: when exactly the event will occur. The timing is an equally important part of any prediction as the predicted event per se. An expert has to give a reasonable time scale in his or her forecast, otherwise the forecast becomes meaningless. For example, you do not need a PhD to predict a recession in USA. In the last 40 years, the USA saw five different recessions and, undoubtedly, more will happen in the future. The timing of the next recession is paramount. Similarly, everyone can predict a major earthquake in California. But if you are not able to provide an exact timing (e.g. within a few weeks), this forecast is absolutely worthless. Everybody can predict a drop of China's economic growth to 1 per cent (China cannot grow its GDP with an annual rate of 10 per cent forever). But the crucial question is: When will it happen?

The importance of timing is often either forgotten or underestimated. When people ignore the timing, they not only substantially inflate their ability to make an accurate forecast but also overestimate the value of this forecast for business.

I have a good real-life example demonstrating the importance of timing in prediction. Some time ago, one of my friends moved from abroad to the UK. He settled down in London and rented an apartment. In 2000, when I visited London, we met in the pub for drinks. I asked him if he was going to buy an apartment. He gave me an interesting answer. He spent some time doing a comprehensive analysis of the UK housing market including different drivers of the house price and their trends. Based on this analysis he identified a housing 'bubble' in the UK. He concluded that it did not make any economic sense to buy a property at that time, but wait for the 'bubble' to burst and prices to re-adjust before acquiring an apartment.

It was difficult to argue with him. The residential property market was experiencing a boom. Since 1996, the average house price had grown by 40 per cent. The growth was especially fast in 2000 (Figure 2.7). I think that my friend was right in spotting the property 'bubble' and predicting its burst. Where he was wrong was the timing. He expected that the 'bubble' would burst within the next one or two years and his decision to continue renting a property looked like a sensible business strategy.

However, in reality it turned out to be easier to identify the problem and predict the event per se than its timing. The UK residential property market boom continued until the end of 2007! In these seven years, the average house price adjusted for inflation grew from £115,000 to £216,000 (i.e. 87 per cent)! At the end of 2007, the market collapsed in the way that my friend predicted. Prices dropped by about 15 per cent. My friend claimed to have made the correct prediction. When we met in 2008, he said: 'Remember, I told you that this was a "bubble" and I told you that the market would collapse.' Indeed, he was right. Yet even after the drop, the property prices remained 50–60 per cent (inflation adjusted) higher than they used to be in 2000. As you can see, the correct prediction of the event does not spell a successful prediction at all if the timing is wrong.

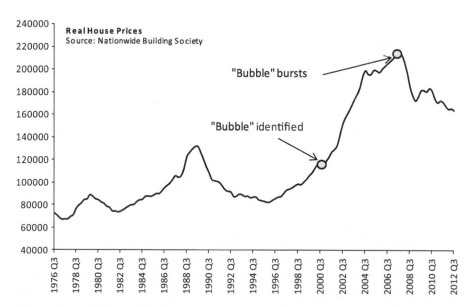

**Figure 2.7    UK real house prices**
*Source*: Author's own figure using data from Nationwide.

You most probably want to know whether my friend bought an apartment or still lives in the rented one. Yes, he bought a property. He monitored the housing market closely, waiting for the price correction to come. It did not happen in 2001, 2002 or 2003 ... and prices kept on climbing. Finally, he ditched his forecast and bought an apartment in London. It happened at the beginning of 2007!

Regardless, if we use statistical models or judgemental tools to assess future events, we need to understand the limitations not only in the correct prediction of the future extreme events but also of the timing and forecasting horizon. To be wrong in timing means to be wrong in the overall forecast. The further we try to extend the forecasting horizon the less accurate the prediction is.

## EFFECTIVE FORECAST HORIZON AND UNFILLED AMBITIONS

Each model, tool or human judgement has an effective forecast horizon, beyond which the accuracy of the forecast diminishes. Everyone who is planning on using forecasts in his or her decision-making process needs to clearly define the level of uncertainty attributed to different forecast horizons. It is important to remember what Winston Churchill said: 'It is always wise to look ahead, but difficult to look further than you can see'.

Macroeconomic models, for example, can technically generate long-term forecasts for key macroeconomic indicators. The forecast can cover several years ahead (normally between three and ten years) but in some cases macroeconomic models are used to generate forecasts for 15 years and beyond. However, there is a huge difference in accuracy of the forecasts for between, say, three and ten years. The accuracy of macroeconomic predictions starts to deteriorate substantially beyond a one-year horizon. Macroeconomic models have very little or no predictive power beyond a five-year time scale. In the current dynamic economic world, long-term predictions have, strictly speaking, only theoretical worth and hold no practical value. Remember the 20-year oil price forecast provided by EIA that I discussed earlier in this chapter? Beyond several months, the prediction of oil prices becomes almost impossible, taking into account numerous factors (many of them are inherently unpredictable, like geopolitical events) that influence the oil price market.

The forecast horizon is one of the crucial factors in risk modelling. Most credit risk models such as probability of default (PD) or loss given default (LGD) have a forecast horizon of 12 months. The extension of the horizon beyond this period, for example, to three years would substantially undermine the models' predictive power and make them ineffective, if not useless. The timing factor impedes the building of reliable risk models for some asset classes such as project finance. The very idea of risk assessment for project finance requires making a cash flow projection for a project. As most projects have a long-term nature (e.g. major infrastructure or industrial projects with a long completion time), it becomes necessary to forecast the main variables (e.g. costs, revenue items, interest rates, inflation, market prices) for a period of 10–25 years or further. This length of the horizon relegates the analytical task to the level of 'best guess' made under heroic assumptions.

I think that the overestimation of the effective forecast horizon is responsible for the lion's share of inaccurate forecasts. It is the natural ambition for each expert to become the person who is able to correctly predict what will happen in many years' time. Everybody wants to know the future. We hate uncertainty and praise everyone who can stand out from the crowd and tell us what the future will be in many years to come. This creates the wrong incentives for experts to claim that they can look further than they actually can see.

When the stock market gurus take courage to predict S&P 500 for the next 12 months (see Appendix 1), they simply overestimate their predictive power at the horizon of that length. Taking into account the dynamic nature of the stock market, the effective time horizon for such forecasts is probably several trading days at best. However, there has always been a demand from investors to have more certainty about the stock market performance for longer periods ahead (for one year and beyond). And experts put them forward and offer their forecasts even when the forecast horizon substantially exceeds their effective range.

The correct estimation of the effective forecast horizon for economic variables is not a straightforward task. Clive Granger, the winner of the Nobel Prize in Economics, who did a thorough research of economic forecasting, described the problem with the effective economic forecast horizon: 'In some sciences there seems to be a horizon beyond which useful forecasting is not possible; in weather forecasting this seems to be four or five days, for example. It is unclear if economics has similar boundaries as variables differ in their forecastability' (Granger 2001: 483).

Several studies on this subject suggest that the effective forecast horizon varies substantially for different economic variables (Brisson et al. 2003, Oller 1985).

Particular macroeconomic variables can be predicted better due to their high autocorrelation and overall stability. On the other hand, some variables are very difficult to forecast. For example, John Galbraith and Greg Tkacz found that 'data series such as growth in industrial production and growth in real GDP are difficult to forecast beyond the shortest horizon' (Galbraith and Tkacz 2007: 10). According to their study, the GDP could only be effectively predicted within one or two quarters. They compared the derived effective horizons with typical horizons used in practice and concluded:

> Forecasts are being produced at horizons which are sufficiently long that only the unconditional mean (or the partial sum of unconditional mean growth rates, for example) serves as a reliable guide to the outcome. That is, some published forecasts are given at horizons for which the content, or forecast skill, is approximately zero.
>
> (Galbraith and Tkacz 2007: 13)

They also found that for some macroeconomic variables, which were inherently unforecastable, experts kept on producing forecasts on a regular basis: 'The change in an exchange rate (appropriately transformed), being an asset return, typically has a forecast content horizon close to zero (literally zero under the strong form of efficient markets hypothesis), but is nonetheless a popular variable of interest for forecasters'.

Investment gurus should know better than the others as to how inherently unforecastable asset returns are and should refrain from providing long-term forecasts and advice on the asset returns. Yet they keep on providing forecasts, stretching the horizon far beyond what they can see and later put themselves in embarrassing situations. Remember the survey of USA Today conducted in January 2008 (see Appendix 1)? In addition to the forecast of S&P 500 for 12 months ahead, the newspaper asked the financial gurus to share their investment ideas for 2008. Tobias Levkovich, Chief US Equity Strategist in Citigroup, also known as the 'best market seer' and the person from the '30 smartest people in investing' list gave the following advice: 'Buy General Electric (GE). Why? Multiyear laggard can post double-digit profit growth' (USA Today 2008). Well, in 2008, General Electric's shares dropped by 55 per cent. This was much worse than S&P 500, which lost 37 per cent (Figure 2.8).

I know that the general public and investors' community have a short memory and after several months they do not remember exactly what the investment advice was. However, it would be better not to give any advice at all as far as the long horizon is concerned.

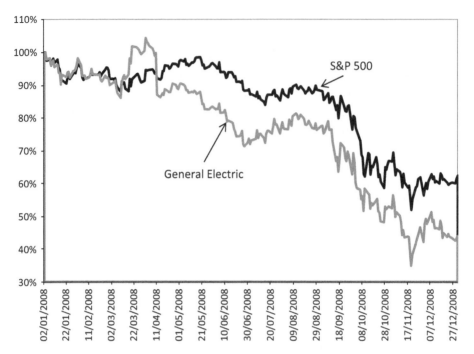

**Figure 2.8    General Electric's share price performance vs. S&P 500 Index (1 January 2008 = 100 per cent)**

*Source*: Author's own figure using data from Bloomberg.

Indeed, attempts to stretch a forecast horizon far beyond its effective limit could lead to unacceptably large forecasting errors. For example, the effective horizon for economic output (GDP) is likely to be six months. But the BoE's standard projection horizons for GDP growth and inflation cover three years. In two examples of forecasts discussed earlier in this chapter, the BoE's projected base case scenarios did not deviate very far from the actual numbers for the first two quarters. Then the gap grew rapidly and after six months, the gap between the base cases and actual trends became embarrassingly large.

Yet business, investors, governments and other stakeholders are desperate for a long-term certainty. They would like to know whether or not the economy will grow, stagnate or shrink next year, in three years or even in five years. An army of forecasters rushes to meet this demand and make their forecasts extend to a much longer time horizon than the effective forecasts could possibly reach.

Since the academic research discussed above provides evidence that the accuracy of expert predictions appears to be surprisingly low, I think that experts should blame themselves for using self-defeating forecasting practices that relegate highly skilled folk to the level of dart-throwing monkeys, as Louis Menand wrote. Experts need to be honest about the effective forecast horizon. If somebody requires a projection for a time horizon which is much longer than the effective one, the expert should not try to fool himself or herself and the others and give the following answer: 'I can give you my forecast for the next quarter and guarantee that this forecast will certainly be accurate enough. But if you need a forecast out to three years, please toss a coin.'

## Portfolio Models: Rocket Science without a Rocket

In the previous chapter, I explained why statistical models and expert judgement tools often fail to provide a reliable risk assessment for the majority of extreme events. The last global financial crisis was not an exception. It became yet another proof that these models can perform satisfactorily only in relatively stable environments free of tail risk events. How about the most sophisticated state-of-the-art portfolio risk models? Portfolio models, like economic capital models, were built to specifically address tail risk. They strive to calculate unexpected loss under the most extreme situations. Did they work reliably during the 2008–9 crisis? Well, the crisis became a moment of truth for these models. And the truth was that many economic capital models failed. It is necessary to analyse and understand why it happened, what went wrong and what we need to do to change the situation.

### ERA OF PORTFOLIO RISK MODELS: FROM HERO TO ZERO

From a risk management perspective, one of the most important lessons of the global financial crisis of 2008–9 was the weakness of risk models. The decade preceding the crisis can be called the era of quantitative methods in risk management. Never before have the financial institutions spent so much effort and money developing and implementing quantitative risk solutions. Basel II (International Capital Adequacy Accord), undoubtedly, gave a main push to the process of risk quantification.

Based on a survey of banks in Europe and North America, Accenture estimated the costs of Basel II implementation and the associated cost of compliance to be around £2.5 billion for the UK alone. Most European banks expected to spend more than €50 million each on implementing Basel II, with one particular UK bank expecting to spend more than €200 million (Campbell 2005). McKinsey & Co. provided their own estimate of Basel II related costs.

According to their assessment, for large diversified banks, the cost was typically in the region of $100 million, but can increase to as much as $250 million. For diversified regional banks, the cost was between $25 million and $50 million. (Buehler et al. 2004). Regardless of what the exact figures of the Basel II bill might be, we know that Basel II was a very expensive project and the lion's share of the costs is attributed to the improvement of risk infrastructure and enhancements related to risk quantification (e.g. data collection and data management, model development and implementation, risk reporting).

During the years of robust growth preceding the 2008 bust, the overall attitude towards risk modelling remained quite positive. Banks built thousands of different risk models and started actively using them in the decision-making processes. In addition to the relatively simple 'plain vanilla' risk models assessing different risk parameters for different asset classes (PD, LGD, EAD, expected loss), the banks started to develop and implement a special class of sophisticated models – portfolio risk models – which were used to calculate the aggregated risk for multiple asset classes. I call this category of portfolio models 'rocket science without a rocket' because portfolio models represent an impressive and complicated solution combining the economic theory framework, statistical methods and heroic assumptions. This creates a lot of fire and smoke, but nobody cares that the rocket is missing.

Although the first portfolio risk models were introduced in the 1970s in some financial institutions, the period of 10–15 years before the global financial crisis (mid-1990s to 2008) was a period of proliferation of complex risk portfolio models. Initially, portfolio models focused on one specific risk area such as traditional credit risk (credit VAR or credit risk economic capital models) or market risk (VAR models). Then, the new generation of portfolio models attempted to accomplish the ambitious task of aggregating several risk areas. The most sophisticated economic capital models were thought to provide a comprehensive enterprise-wide risk calculation by aggregating not only the three traditional 'Basel II-type' risks (credit, market and operational) but also the less tangible risk areas like liquidity risk and even business risk. As such, economic capital is supposed to be the ultimate measure of risk. It represents the maximum loss that the firm may be exposed to at a given confidence level and time horizon, and subsequently the amount of capital that firms need to set aside to offset this loss and remain solvent.

The whole idea of having the ultimate measure of risk was so attractive that the majority of large and global banks in Europe and North America developed their economic capital models and many of them started to use economic capital as the primary risk measurement. Economic capital became more than just a portfolio risk characteristic. It became a 'common risk currency' and a strategic measure which was used for optimising asset portfolios, setting the risk appetite, making strategic business decisions, pricing commercial transactions and assessing performance. Economic capital, VAR and RAROC (risk adjusted return on capital – a return measure calculated using economic capital or VAR) were included in all risk reports and annual business plans.

The euphoria regarding risk models in general, as well as economic capital models, abated quickly after the crisis hit the industry. The sub-prime mortgage crisis revealed that many banks noticeably underestimated their risks under stress conditions. When the market environment was benign, the actual default rates and losses were within portfolio model predictions. Economic capital and VAR models looked robust enough. But when the 'perfect storm' started, financial markets crashed, liquidity evaporated and, subsequently, losses for certain asset classes rocketed to a level that has never been previously considered possible. As the risk was miscalculated initially, all risk-adjusted parameters (e.g. RAROC, risk adjusted performance) appeared to be severely inflated.

It triggered a revision of portfolio risk models used for various asset classes to bring the estimated risk parameters in concordance with reality. Economic capital models began to be heavily scrutinised. The disappointment with economic capital models' failure resulted in the situation of many financial institutions revising the role of economic capital in their risk and business practice. Many banks made decisions to relegate economic capital related measures from the 'premier league' of strategic risk measures. They substantially reduced the area of application of economic capital measures.

Yet the following question needs to be answered: How come the models, which were built based on the most advanced analytics ideas, cost the financial institutions a fortune to develop/implement and were supposed to calculate risk with a very high confidence level, failed to pass the first serious real life test?

## WHAT IS HIDDEN BEHIND CONFIDENCE LEVEL

We can start from the confidence level. Economic capital models report the maximum loss at the very high confidence level. Normally the confidence level exceeds 99.9 per cent, but the typical level for large financial institutions is 99.95 per cent and above. Figure 2.9 illustrates the confident level of economic

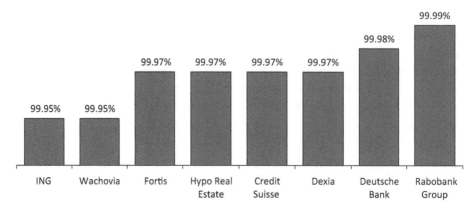

**Figure 2.9    Confidence level for economic capital reported by some banks in 2007**

*Source*: Author's own figure using data from annual reports.

capital reported in 2007 by some banks. What does it mean – X amount of loss in the next 12 months at 99.95 per cent confidence level? Some people interpret this in layperson's terms that the total loss can exceed X amount in only one year out of 2,000. This is not the correct interpretation. We are not talking about years, but about the probability. Based on the model output, there is only one chance out of 2,000 that the loss can exceed X. In other words, if we can imagine 10,000 different scenarios for the next 12 months, from the most benign to the most severe, only in five scenarios would the loss be higher that X (or a 1: 2,000 chance).

As you can see, we are stepping on very thin ice. We move from reality to an imaginary world. If you look a year ahead, you can imagine an indefinite number of hypothetical scenarios. However, real life knows only the one scenario, which materialises. We are not able to come back and restart the same the year again and again. Historical experience, which we can work with, is not extensive enough to be a solid ground for generating such a large number of 'real life' scenarios. Therefore, here we don't talk about statistical probability. We talk about the hypothetical probability of the occurrence of hypothetical scenarios.

Yet, the typical 1:2,000 confidence level for economic capital sounds very high. Many banks use even higher confidence levels, which can be as high as 1:10,000. In other words, economic capital at this confidence level becomes a measure of tail risk. This is the principal difference between economic capital models and other Basel-type models. The latter calculate risk under normal circumstances, for example, the probability of default models or loss given default models estimate long-term though-the-cycle parameters, not extreme ones.

## Confidence level and credit rating

It might be interesting to investigate the logic behind the choice of such a high confidence level for economic capital models. Normally, the confidence level reflects the firm's target credit rating. Suppose the firm's target credit rating is AA on the S&P rating scale. The historical one-year default rate for AA-rated firms is approximately 0.05 per cent (the exact probability depends on which historic period has been chosen). This means that an AA-rated firm on average has a 99.95 per cent chance of surviving the next 12 months. To be consistent with the AA-rating survival rate, the firm needs to ensure that for the next 12 months it can sustain all possible scenarios, save for only the 5 most drastic out of every 10,000. Therefore, the firm should estimate its unexpected losses with the confidence level of 99.95 per cent and keep a capital buffer sufficient to cover the highest loss within this range. If the target credit rating is AAA as for Rabobank, economic capital should be calculated at a 99.99 per cent confidence level, which is consistent with the historical default rate for AAA-rated companies (circa 0.01 per cent probability of default in the next 12 months).

I found this logic a little bit weird. In order to default or fail, a company does not necessarily need to make a loss exceeding its own capital. Although there are many cases when a firm fails due to unbearable losses which fully wipe out its capital, defaults can occur for many other reasons (e.g. liquidity problems or substantial reputational damage). If a market panic develops and customers suddenly decide, rightly or wrongly, that the bank has big problems, they start a run on the bank, which can end up in bank's collapse. For example, by 2008, HBOS had shareholders' equity of £21.8 billion and during the year made a loss of £7.4 billion (HBOS 2008). While the loss was much smaller than the available capital and the capital buffer remained substantial, it was enough to undermine the confidence and the bank had to be rescued. A similar story happened with the Icelandic bank Landsbanki, which collapsed over the course of several days and defaulted in October 2008.

Therefore, it could be important to know the maximum loss at the confidence level of, say, 99.95 per cent and keep the respective amount of capital buffer, but it does not guarantee a 99.95 per cent probability of survival. It does not even guarantee a 90 per cent probability. The capital buffer is only one factor supporting the firm's chances of survival out of many others. So I found the idea of linking a probability of survival (credit rating) to a capital buffer and the confidence level of economic capital extremely naïve.

### Price we pay for a high confidence level

I fully understand the desire to obtain loss estimation at a very high confidence level. This is necessary for addressing the tail loss problem and economic capital model users can set the confidence level as high as they wish to. However, a desire per se is not sufficient to achieve reliable calculations. From reading statistics text books, everyone knows that the price we have to pay for a high confidence level is a less accurate estimation of the parameter value.

Suppose our task is to estimate the potential loss for your credit portfolio in the 12-month period. If we choose a 50 per cent confidence level (to derive the expected loss), we can reach a relatively small error margin in our loss estimation (provided our data sample is sufficient and variation of losses is pretty normal). Now if we decide to increase the confidence level to 99 per cent, with all other things being equal, the estimated unexpected loss error margin becomes huge. And here we have two options:

- accept this huge error margin as an inevitable price we pay for the high confidence level;

- substantially enlarge our data sample and re-estimate the parameters.

If we choose the second option, we need to answer the following question: how many annual observations do we need for our credit portfolio to reduce the margin of error to a tolerable level?

In order to obtain a flavour of how confidence level, margin of error and sample size are linked, we can use a simple statistical calculator to generate a normal distribution (e.g. Raosoft calculator). Suppose we set a confidence level of 50 per cent. With the sample size of 40 observations, we can calculate the value of the parameter of the whole population with a margin of error of 5.35 per cent (or roughly plus or minus 5 per cent). Now if we decide to increase the confidence level to 90 per cent with the same sample size, the margin of error will rise to 13 per cent. At a confidence level of 99 per cent, the margin widens to 20.34 per cent based on Raosoft calculations. With the confidence

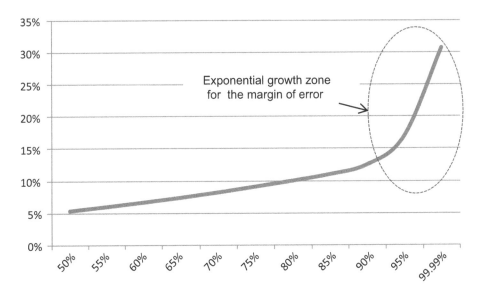

**Figure 2.10    Margin of error (per cent) at different confidence levels
              (per cent)**

*Source*: Author's own figure using data from Raosoft calculator.

level increasing, the error is growing exponentially, accelerating at the tail of
the distribution. The relationship is shown in Figure 2.10.

At the highest end of the confidence levels (99.95 per cent or higher), the
margin of error becomes noticeably large. For example, for a 99.99 per cent
confidence level, the error margin will be at ±31 per cent.

Obviously, such a large margin error cannot be acceptable. Therefore we
need to find a way to reduce it. How can we do it? We need to enlarge the
sample size. We will face the same exponential relationship: as we increase
the confidence level, the necessary minimum sample size grows exponentially.
Suppose we would like to keep a 5 per cent margin of error. For a 50 per cent
confidence level, our sample size of 40 observations was sufficient to reach this
level of accuracy. If we increase the confidence level to 80 per cent, in order
to stay within the 5 per cent margin of error we are required to more than
triple the sample size (143 observations). For a 99 per cent confidence level, the
minimum sample size should be 564. However, for 99.95 per cent and higher,
we need more than 1,000 observations or 25 times more than we need at the 50
per cent confidence level (Figure 2.11).

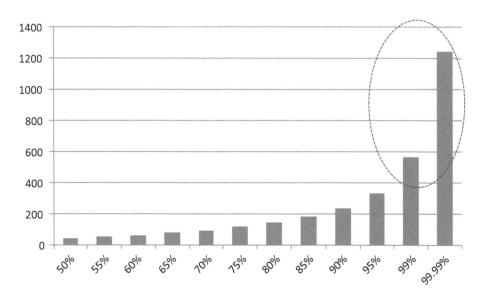

**Figure 2.11    Minimum sample size at different confidence levels (per cent) for targeted margin of error of 5 per cent**

*Source*: Author's own figure using data from Raosoft calculator.


Keep in mind that this hypothetical example is a very rough approximation provided here to illustrate the issue. It assumes a normal distribution. In real life, losses do not follow a normal distribution. Instead, they have unknown and skewed distributions with a fat tail. This means that relationships between the confidence level, the margin of error and the sample size are much more extreme: migration to a higher confidence level leads to an even greater error margin and a reduction of error margin requires a substantially greater sample size compared to what we would otherwise need under the normal distribution assumption.

### Simulation and five 'ifs'

Now back to the real world. We need to assess how large samples can normally be obtained by firms when they estimate, for example, the credit risk economic capital figure for their credit portfolio. Model developers would be lucky if they obtain the historical portfolio loss data for the last 15–20 years (let's assume that the credit portfolio was relatively stable so that its loss data 10–15 years ago still remains relevant to the current portfolio). But this sample is not enough to obtain the estimation of the potential losses with an acceptable margin of error at the confidence level of 99 per cent (unless the credit portfolio performance is almost free from any variability, which is hardly possible in reality). If we raise the confidence level to 99.95 per cent, even the history of the last 100 years is nothing compared to the minimum sample size required! We need thousands of annual observations. It sounds like an unsolvable task.

How have economic capital models solved this problem? How do they manage to operate with naturally limited historical data samples when portfolio loss distribution is unknown and has a fat tail?

Quantitative analytics found the 'genius' way out: if real historical observations are not large enough, hypothetical observations can be created. We can simply model different future scenarios. Luckily, thanks to the efforts of mathematicians, physicists and other science researchers, stochastic methods have already been developed and modern computers provide enough computation power. From this point, the economic capital modelling moved from the real world to virtual reality. Using Monte Carlo simulations, the model can generate as many 'observations' as required.

To estimate unexpected losses, the economic capital models apply multiple iterations. Each simulation generates one hypothetical scenario with a calculated portfolio return. The reference document for CreditMetrics™, one of the most popular portfolio models, provides the following description of the approach:

> the mean and standard deviation may not be the best measures of risk in that, since the loss distribution is not normal, we cannot infer confidence levels from these parameters. We can however estimate percentiles directly from our scenarios. For example, if we wish to compute the 5th percentile (the level below which we estimate that 5 per cent of portfolio values fall), we sort our 20,000 scenarios in ascending order and take the 1000th of these sorted scenarios as our estimate ... Here we see the advantage of the simulation approach, in that we can estimate arbitrary percentile levels, where in the analytic approach, because the portfolio distribution is not normal, we are only able to compute two statistics.
>
> (Gupton et al. 2007: 125)

This is where magic happens: the sample size is not a problem any more. We can generate millions of scenarios, which cost us nothing but computer processing time. Normally, when economic capital is calculated, the model performs from 20,000 to 2,000,000 simulations using the random number generator. This means that we can reach a high level of accuracy for any confidence level, regardless of whether it is 99.95 per cent or even 99.99 per cent. Is this true? Not really.

There is one problem and this problem is very serious. By accepting the framework described above, we move from the real world of historical observations and start to operate hypothetical scenarios. How can we be sure that the model-generated hypothetical scenarios correctly represent the real life processes? Well, we cannot.

The hypothetical scenarios of portfolio performance, and therefore overall loss estimations provided by the model, can be a good reflection of what would really happen only if:

1.   all portfolio data are complete and correct (e.g. basic characteristics of portfolio assets);

2.   all macroeconomic parameters (e.g. exchange rates, interest rate curves) are perfectly correct;

3.   all risk characteristics of individual assets (e.g. probability of default, LGD, etc.) are right;

4.   all assumptions regarding portfolio performance, market behaviour and risk drivers are correctly and comprehensively reflected in reality;

5.   the simulation logic and computational algorithm are flawless.

The above five points I have called the five 'ifs'. You can try to answer the question on how realistic it is to expect that all 'ifs' – all five conditions – can be met. If you are struggling to answer, in the following sections I will describe some key assumptions used in the economic capital modelling framework in detail. But to conclude the discussion about the confident level, I would like to stress the following:

•   Reporting economic capital numbers at a very high confidence level creates an illusion for non-quants (among them are most of the top executives, investors, regulators, etc.), that unexpected losses can be calculated with high certainty in the area of its tail.

•   People who make decisions in financial organisations do not necessarily need to be quantitative experts and understand all particularities of quantitative analytics. However, they must understand the limitations of risk models and tools. If they use for their decision-making process economic capital and its derivations (e.g. RAROC), they have to be aware of how economic capital numbers have been derived and what assumptions have been applied.

- Quants need to clearly communicate all possible limitations and weaknesses of the models that they build to model users and decision-makers. While in many financial institutions quantitative analysts provide training to model users and circulate model documentation, I do not believe that it is sufficient.

## Should we blame quants?

I remember a conversation I had with one of the top risk people of a large international bank. He explained to me a problem that he regularly faces when dealing with the economic capital team:

> *Each time, they give me sets of economic capital numbers and their recommendations regarding transactions that would optimise the return on economic capital. But I don't understand how they calculate all these numbers and how reliable their conclusions are. Even when I have doubts regarding their optimisation recommendations, I can't challenge them.*

After the global financial crisis occurred and it became clear that the risk of many asset classes had been materially underestimated, people started to blame the quants. Of course, some models failed miserably during the crisis. However, the problem was not only in poor risk modelling. For people outside quantitative analytics, many complex models, including economic capital models, remained 'black boxes'. Even when model documentation was available, people without quantitative backgrounds found it very difficult (or even impossible) to understand 200–300 pages of technical text full of long formulas with Greek symbols and abracadabra, such as the orthogonal systemic risk factor, single-factor Gaussian normal copula model and the two-sided Kolmogorov–Smirnov goodness-of-fit test for uniform distribution.

I think that quants have to take the blame for failing to clearly explain their complex models such as portfolio risk models to non-quant users in lay terms. This education process should specifically include a discussion about the weaknesses and limitations of the model. This discussion is absolutely vital for the proper education process. When the model builders present to the non-quants a framework of economic capital model and solutions used for unexpected loss estimations, it can be not so obvious for non-quants as to what might be the weaknesses and limitations of the approach. A broad understanding of the model framework does not guarantee that the person also clearly sees the weaknesses of the framework and the limitations of using the model.

Unfortunately, model developers do not always bother to mention the weaknesses and limitations of their models in their presentations and model documentations. Usually model documentation for portfolio models provides a lot of technical details (most of them are not comprehensible to the average model user). To make things worse, you will very rarely find a chapter there called 'Model weaknesses and limitations'. There is a possibility that you may find many pages where the model developers describe the advantages of solutions that they used in the models, but there is no guarantee that at the same time you can find a page where the authors give you a warning about the model drawbacks. For example, refer to the quote from the reference document for CreditMetrics™ that I previously provided (see page 65). When the authors describe how the model generates hypothetical scenarios and uses them for portfolio return estimation, they talk about the advantages of the approach ('Here we see the advantage of the simulation approach'). Yet they do not give readers their analysis on potential drawbacks, which also exist.

To conclude, the motivation to use a very high confidence level for portfolio risk models is understandable. We need models to estimate tail risk and the portfolio risk models strive to deliver it. Yet the choice of specific confidence levels does not sound reasonable and quite naively links it to a firm's targeted survival probability. When model developers fell into the high confidence level trap, they faced a problem of huge error margins of their estimations. This could be solved by expanding the data sample size. However, for such high confidence levels, all available historical data that we can think of is still insufficient. When portfolio data remained scarce, economic capital modelling developed in a new direction – generation of hypothetical scenarios by applying Monte Carlo simulations. While the problem with the sample size per se has been resolved, another problem arises: how to ensure that model-generated hypothetical scenarios really reflect the real life situations. Only when the five 'ifs' – five conditions – are met, can we talk about the robustness of economic capital models. Otherwise this nicely built portfolio risk framework with millions of scenarios generated by the model algorithm will remain no more than a theoretical concept. Model developers should communicate these issues better to model users, top managers and other stakeholders. It will help eliminate the illusions that we are able to calculate tail risk with high precision. People who make strategic decisions need to be fully aware of all uncertainties around the reported economic capital numbers and models' weaknesses and limitations.

## LARGE, LARGE MEAT GRINDER

In the previous section, I formulated five 'ifs' – five conditions that we need to ensure that an economic capital model generates reliable unexpected loss numbers. The list of five 'ifs' is not exhaustive and can be expanded further. But I believe that these five points are the most vital. How realistic is it to expect that all conditions have been met?

Before answering this question in detail, I prefer to have a look at the economic capital model framework. I am not going to provide any technical details (readers who are interested in technical details can read the model documentations, provided they have a quantitative background), but rather give the big picture.

Do you remember when I figuratively described risk models as meat grinders? We put some ingredients into the 'grinder' (different historical and judgemental input data), turn the handle and get ready mince (risk parameters estimated based on input data). Now we can present the economic capital model as a meat grinder as well. Imagine a very large industrial meat grinder. Unlike a simple small home grinder, this one can produce 'mince' with a much larger quantity of 'ingredients' to follow a very sophisticated recipe. The recipe of this mince could surprise anyone including Gordon Ramsay, Anthony Bourdain and Jacques Pepin. What are the main ingredients? We can separate all input data necessary for a generic economic capital model into three categories:

1.  General portfolio data and macroeconomic data: this is data that can be received at spot, does not require any extra calculations or derivation and, in most of cases, is either readily available or can be collected relatively easily. This information includes basic data on customers: type of customer, Standard Industrial Classification (SIC) code, country of incorporation, etc. Portfolio asset data also belongs to this category: type of asset, a coupon, maturity, collateral type, etc. We can also add macroeconomic data to this category: exchange rates, interest rate term structure, etc.

2.   Data derived from other models and tools: the economic capital model requires information derived from other models. For example, this can be the probability of default for credit assets derived using internal models, external models (e.g. KMV EDF) or rating agency assessments.

3.   Assumptions: to assess portfolio risk, economic capital model requires assumptions reflecting different aspects of risk. For example, this can be assumptions on risk free rates or assumptions on default correlations of different asset classes.

Four of the 'ifs' formulated in the previous section focus on quality of data and reasonability of assumptions. Data categories above cover these 'ifs'. I specifically separated all required input information into three distinctive categories because of different accuracy and reliability issues.

## Portfolio data quality

Information from the first group in most cases is readily available or, at least, can be obtained reasonably easily. The high quality of this data should be an achievable task subject to proper information systems. The systems should allow extracting necessary data from databases or source required data from external data providers such as Reuters, Bloomberg, Data stream and external rating agencies.

Of course, in the real world, sometimes people have to spend a lot of time refining even the most basic data to ensure acceptable quality. We know that data quality has never been perfect and, probably, will never be. In most financial firms, data quality has been separated in a special management area. Some organisations have even introduced the role of Chief Data Officer. A large number of dedicated specialists do nothing but clean and verify data. Yet perfect quality remains a distant target. Even the most basic portfolio information quite often contains numerous errors. Consider that a credit portfolio of a large bank can have thousands and millions of different customers and millions of credit facilities. For each facility, the economic capital model requires the user to enter dozens of different parameters such as type of facility, exposure, maturity, currency, collateral type, etc.

While simple errors remain a common occurrence and are likely to happen in the future (for example, databases can contain some wrong country codes, industry codes, currencies, dates of maturity, etc.), the most common issue for this data category is missing data. Firms often have to use a manual search to look for missing data to complete the model input. Overall, while we do not expect perfect quality of this data, we can live with some errors and missing pieces. Provided that errors affect only limited data samples, this normally does not undermine the integrity of the whole data input.

## Second order input

The second category provides more trouble for those who would like to ensure high data quality. I call this category the 'second order' input. It means that this category is exposed to two sources of errors. Similar to the previous group, the first source of data non-integrity comes from errors in databases and missing data. For example, for credit assets, the economic capital model requires probabilities of default (PDs), loss given default (LGDs) and exposures at default (EADs). When we source this information for many thousands of credit assets, we can probably discover that for some, these parameters are missing or erroneous. But this is just a sourcing issue – a technical issue. As with any technical issue, it can be solved relatively easily provided data specialists have enough capability to enhance their information systems.

The second source of errors for this category is stemmed from the model risk. All these parameters are not given; they are not solid facts. They have been calculated by models and tools and cannot exist outside models. Therefore, the quality of these estimated parameters is as good as the models and tools that generate them. What if the models systemically overestimate or underestimate the values of these parameters? If we input biased risk parameters into the economic capital models, then this will undermine the integrity of the economic models' results. While the firms spend a lot of effort improving their models and tools, the problem of model risk remains a big concern.

Consider the accuracy of PDs and LGDs estimated by internal banks' models or by rating agencies. For fairness, ratings produced by rating agencies are not model generated outputs, but expert judgement estimates. However, in its assessment each rating agency applies its formalised methodology which prescribed rating drivers and benchmarks. Therefore, we can talk about judgement model principles.

To assess the model risk, starting from 2007, UK regulators (Financial Services Authority, FSA, renamed to The Prudential Regulation Authority) run bi-annual peer model comparison exercises on a regular basis. They call it a hypothetical portfolio exercise. Regulators ask several large UK banks to provide PDs and LGDs for selected sovereigns, banks and large corporates for comparison. Unlike the benchmark approach (Standard & Poor's (S&P) rating), peer comparisons aim to understand to what extent key risk parameter predictions (PDs and LGDs) differ across financial firms. While the FSA does not expect that individual models generate identical PDs and LGDs, they want to assess the variability of model outputs. The comparison of PDs across participating banks suggested that 'firms' sovereign, banks and large corporate PDs are broadly consistent with the external data. However, there are examples of estimates that are significantly lower or higher than the median PD for a given rating' (FSA 2012: 11).

Indeed, the PDs assessed by different banks for the same companies differ significantly. For example, for one obligor (a bank), which had a 'B' rating from S&P, the minimum PD assessed by participating firms was 0.5 per cent, while the maximum was 10.7 per cent. Another striking example is a large corporate rated 'BB' by S&P. Its minimum PD based on the firm's internal models was 0.16 per cent and its maximum was 2.6 per cent (FSA 2012: 9). This means that PD variations across different internal models for the same obligor can vary by 10–20 times! While we cannot say which estimate was correct and which one was wrong, we can see how different firms assess default risk and how large the model risk could be.

Traditionally, financial firms have much more advanced PD modelling techniques, and their estimates of PDs look much more robust than estimates of LGDs and EADs. The FSA hypothetical portfolio exercises confirmed this observation. After performing comparisons of LGD estimates, the FSA concluded:

> The 2011 HPE (hypothetical portfolio exercises) is the first to collect LGD estimates that can be compared between firms and this has shown a large variation in firms LGD estimates. The FSA is currently discussing approaches to wholesale LGD and EAD modelling with the industry – with the aim of improving the consistency of the estimates used by different firms. The collection of PD and LGD values allowed the FSA to approximate RWA estimates for the three portfolios. The results suggest that there might be a significant difference in the RWAs (risk weighted assets) being held by firms against the same obligors.
>
> (FSA 2012: 11)

The hypothetical portfolio exercises help us to see how significant the potential data quality problem for the 'second order' data could be. We cannot fix this problem easily. Unlike the first data category where improvement of data sourcing and data cleaning normally provides a viable solution, for the second order data we need to assess the accuracy of models and tools and recalibrate or even rebuild some of them if necessary. This is not a data maintenance problem, but rather a methodological problem of risk drivers estimation.

## How reliable are assumptions?

And finally, the third category of inputs required for portfolio models represents the assumptions used for the calculation of unexpected losses. They can be relatively narrow assumptions which are applied for a particular asset class or for a particular risk driver. For example, the model users can make an assumption on how collateral losses of structured instruments will affect the value of different tranches. Or model users make an assumption on reinvestment of the portfolio's cash flow received within the modelling horizon.

At the same time, the model requires fundamental assumptions that will affect the entire process of loss calculations. While the list of such assumptions can be quite long, I would like to mention some of them:

- Assumption on risk-free rates. For example, the Moody's Analytics economic model RiskFrontier assumes a credit-risk-free term structure of interest rates called the zero–EDF curve.

- Assumption on discount factors which are used to account for the time value of money and calculation of present value of future cash flows.

- Assumptions on credit quality migration and defaults. For example, the CreditMetrics model uses assumptions that all firms tagged with a given rating will act alike, meaning that the full spectrum of credit migration likelihoods – not just the default likelihood – is similar for each firm assigned to a particular credit rating (RiskMetrics Group 2007: 68).

- Correlation assumptions. Assumptions on correlation of credit quality migration, defaults and market values of assets stay at the heart of economic capital modelling. The very idea of the portfolio approach is based on the understanding that we can reduce risk if we build a portfolio of assets which are not perfectly correlated. In other words, the sum of risk associated with individual assets is greater than the overall risk of the portfolio of these assets due to a diversification effect. As assets do not correlate perfectly with each other, the overall risk (hence, economic capital) depends on the exact level of correlation. For most of the assets classes, correlation cannot be easily calculated due to the absence of required data or a statistically insignificant sample size available to model developers. Therefore, model developers have to make assumptions to resolve the issue. In addition, correlation changes constantly, which again requires further assumptions to simplify the calculations.

Looking from a data quality standpoint, I call all information belonging to this category the 'third order' data. This is because the potential data quality issues reside at three levels. The first level includes traditional technical issues (simple data and sourcing errors). The methodological problems (second level) could also affect the quality of data. For example, the correlation model is used for deriving correlation coefficients for different assets which then feed into the economic capital model. Any modelling issues would affect accuracy of correlation coefficients and hence accuracy of economic capital estimates. And the final level represents potential issues with reasonability of assumptions per se. In other words, if any of the material assumptions applied in the process of economic capital calculation appeared to be wrong, then we have a serious problem.

Think about the very basic assumptions on credit quality migration. As we do not know what might be the future credit quality migration for each individual obligor in our portfolio, we have to make an assumption. We can assume that all obligors with the same rating will experience the similar pattern of credit quality migration. Then we need to calculate this pattern using historical data and apply it to all our obligors. But what if this assumption does not correctly reflect true real-life relationships? We know that in real life, the credit quality of obligors with the same rating very rarely moves in fully synchronised way, yet we can accept this assumption if the overall picture remains relatively truthful. But if we realise that multidirectional credit quality migration for similarly rated obligors not only happens often but also substantially affects the potential portfolio loss distribution, then this assumption threatens the integrity of economic capital estimations. I am not challenging this particular credit quality migration assumption, but rather using it as an illustration of the problem.

More broadly speaking, I fully understand that there are no assumptions that perfectly reflect realty. Each assumption contains an element of simplification. We drift from reality, but accept it as an unavoidable evil. These simplifications are necessary to overcome the immeasurable or, sometimes, incomprehensible

**Table 2.2    Potential data/input problems for economic capital modelling.**

| Data/input category | Examples | Data problems |
|---|---|---|
| General portfolio data and macroeconomic data: readily available data, does not require any calculation or derivation. | Customer name, customer type, SIC code, country of incorporation, asset type, facility type, coupon data, maturity, collateral type, currency type, exchange rates, interest rate term structure. | Technical problems: Data sourcing issues, missing data problems. |
| The 'second order' input: data derived from other models and tools. | PDs, LGDs, EADs derived using internal models, credit quality data derived from external models (e.g. KMV EDF, credit ratings from rating agencies). | Technical problems: As above. Methodological problems: Potential model quality issues that result in model risk. |
| The 'third order' input: Assumption used for estimation of input data and for economic capital framework and calculations. | Assumptions used for estimation of risk-free rates and a credit-risk-free term structure of interest rates, default correlation, credit quality migration, assumptions on reinvestment of portfolio cash flow. | Technical problems: As above. Methodological problems: As above. Conceptual problems: Assumptions fail to correctly reflect the fundamental relationships of risk drivers and losses and materially distort the true picture. |

complexity of real life. However, if an assumption stretches too far from the real world, then this inadequacy becomes a conceptual issue which undermines the whole approach. Needless to say, in this case the error in economic capital estimation becomes massive.

Unfortunately, normally there are no quick-fix solutions for conceptual problems linked to assumptions. If an assumption is not central to the economic capital framework (e.g. affects a single input parameter) then we can change an assumption and relatively easily recalculate the results. However, when we deal with central assumptions, their reconsidering could lead to the need to make fundamental changes in the whole model framework. In the next section, I will explain in detail an issue that I have with one of the central assumptions.

To conclude, the bottom line is that quality of data and information used in the model development and model use predetermines the accuracy of estimations. The large 'meat grinder' called the portfolio model requires a massive volume of data. For economic capital models the data quality problem becomes acute since the models aim to measure not only normal everyday risk, but also tail risk (a traditionally very high confidence level of 99.9 per cent and higher). Measurements of normal risk are based on the principle of averaging, hence we can tolerate some data imperfection. For extreme risk measurements each bit of information can become crucial as we search for uniqueness. After looking at potential data issues discussed above, you can answer the question that I formulated at the beginning the section: How realistic is it to expect that conditions regarding accuracy of general portfolio data, asset risk characteristics (the 'second order' data) and assumptions (the 'third order' data) can be met? To me, the answer is obvious.

Nevertheless, I believe that the story about portfolio risk models will not be complete without more detailed discussions about the correlation assumption – the central assumptions behind the portfolio risk concept. The analysis of correlation provides a clue to why many economic capital models failed during the recent crisis. In addition, it helps to understand where we are now in our tail risk measurement and where we should be going to.

## POTATOES AND SOPHISTICATED MODELLING

Before I share my thoughts on complex risk portfolio modelling and correlation assumptions, I would like to tell a story from many, many years ago which took place in a country that no longer exists. When I was a university student in the Soviet Union, it was a very well known Soviet tradition each September to send students to work at collective farms to help peasants collect crops. As I was born and lived in Siberia at that time, the most popular task that students were assigned during their compulsory collective farm duty was to collect potatoes (potatoes were and remain the main agricultural product of Siberia). The task of some students was to follow a tractor, which ploughed the upper layer of the soil, and collect the potatoes from the ground as they became exposed. They then put the potatoes into large wooden crates, which were loaded into trucks once they became full.

Some other students worked at a warehouse where they unloaded the boxes from the truck and sorted potatoes by size and quality. I remember our very first day at the warehouse. Dozens of students, including myself, were very busy sorting potatoes by size. Suddenly, a local farmer walked into the warehouse. He was wearing dirty grey clothes and mud-covered rubber boots. He was noticeably intoxicated, despite the early hours of the day. He watched how we sorted potatoes for a couple of minutes and then said: 'If you keep sorting in this manner, you will be here until tomorrow morning.' Then he picked up a full box of potatoes and shook it forcefully. Half a minute later, we saw a 'miracle' develop in front of our eyes: all small potatoes shifted to the bottom of the box, while the large potatoes moved to the top and the medium-sized potatoes stayed in the middle. Even for us, people who studied at university and were fully aware of what the law of gravity was, the result of this 'hands-free' sorting looked truly impressive.

Now imagine that there is a group of people who have no idea about the law of gravity (e.g. aliens who just landed on Planet Earth). They have been asked to find out if it is possible to sort potatoes 'hands-free' by shaking the box. To answer the question, they decide to build a mathematical model which can describe the processes happening when the box is shaken. As the law of gravity is the 'unknown unknown' to them, they would probably assume that the movement of potatoes in the box can be described by the Brownian motion theory of random movements (a very popular approach used to explain various market movements, for instance). Based on the outcome of such a model, they would conclude that, assuming the Brownian movements, it was not possible to sort potatoes by shaking the box. Why? Because the process could take years and years before potatoes, moving randomly, reach the desirable positions in the box.

And now, the drunk farmer comes along and demonstrates to them how he can sort the potatoes 'hands-free' just by shaking the box of potatoes. He does it with three boxes in three minutes. What would be the reaction of these people? They would conclude that what they have just seen was a coincidence that can happen once in 10,000 years. In addition, they would insist that what has happened was an extreme outcome and their model fully supports this conclusion.

I told this story to highlight the following important aspects of risk modelling:

- The knowledge and application of advanced theoretical concepts (even the Brownian motion theory) do not guarantee the model's success.

- If the central assumption is wrong or an important driver of the process is missed, overlooked or misinterpreted, the model will fail to provide the correct reflection of the reality.

- Model outcomes should always be treated with exceptional care, especially if some outcomes are challenged by the reality.

## CORRELATION: A MAN UNDER A LAMP POST

Portfolio risk models differ from most single asset risk models not only by their complexity but also by their ultimate goal. Portfolio models aim to deliver estimates not only of the long-tem average risk parameters but also of tail losses including those triggered by systemic events like economic busts or financial crises. Economic capital models strike very high confidence levels (99.9 per cent and above) so that firms could get an estimation of how much capital they need to cover unexpected losses in case of an extreme risk event occurring. However, this is the aspiration of model developers. In reality, the ability of measuring the tail risk correctly is a problematic one.

### *From a problem of quantity to a problem of quality*

The traditional ways of risk measurement in the financial industry are not fully applicable to tail risk. As was demonstrated earlier, statistical models that are widely used by financial firms in their risk management practices have a very limited ability to capture the tail risk. As extreme risk events are, by their very nature, very rare, the statistical data that can be used contains very few data points representing tail risk events, if any at all. Consider systemic events like deep economic recessions. In the USA, in the last 65 years there have been only nine quarters when the GDP growth dropped below –2 per cent. From a statistical standpoint, this 'recession' historical sample represents only 3.4 per cent of the total sample (Figure 2.12).

In the UK, deep recessions happened even less frequently: since 1955, the GDP growth below –2 per cent has been reported only in four quarters, which represents 1.7 per cent of the historical sample (Figure 2.13). These tiny historical samples do not give model developers enough data to build something meaningful. In any case, historical data on tail risk events that can be at the disposal of model developers, by the very definition of an extreme event, is never statistically significant.

Struggling with data paucity, quants finally found an elegant solution. As described earlier, they proposed to use the Monte Carlo simulation to generate hypothetical scenarios of portfolio returns. Modern computer power allows the production of an almost unlimited number of scenarios in a relatively short period of time. Having millions of hypothetical scenarios at their fingertips, risk analysts have solved the problem of quantity – but created a problem of quality. The quality of hypothetical scenarios and to what extent these scenarios reflect the reality has become a concern.

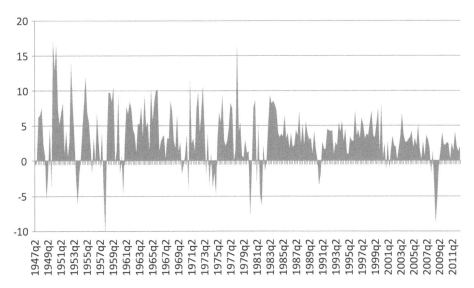

**Figure 2.12    US GDP percentage change based on current dollars (seasonally adjusted annual rates)**

*Source*: Author's own figure using data from US Bureau of Economic Analysis.

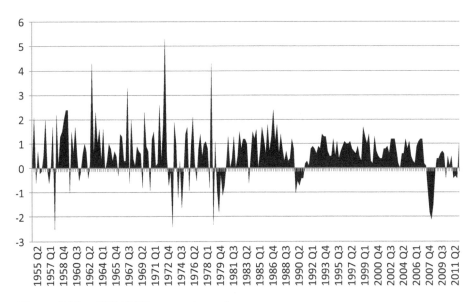

**Figure 2.13    UK GDP percentage change**

*Source*: Author's own figure using data from UK Office for National Statistics.

Indeed, model developers borrowed the Monte Carlo simulation approach from the realm of natural science (where it had been developed and successfully used) and applied it to economic capital calculations.

Yet we need to recognise how big the difference is between, for example, physical processes and economic processes. When physicists use Monte Carlo simulations to model the movements of neutrons or other elementary particles, they deal with certain processes. The main parameters of particles like velocity, mass and energy can be described by the laws of physics and calculated with high certainty. Where Monte Carlo simulation can help is to model how processes would run when numerous particles move and collide randomly.

When we apply the Monte Carlo simulation for portfolio risk tasks, the asset performance does not exactly follow set laws or principles as elementary particles do. We do not have formulae or precise equations. Nobody knows the full list of factors and risk drivers that can affect the performance of a single asset as well as the whole portfolio. In this sense, the system that we try to model remains open. Human behaviour plays a great role in the economic processes and influences the asset return. Unlike elementary particles, each human being is unique. Elementary particles do not have fear, greed, ambition and moral values. Each banker, risk manager, investor and any decision-maker included in the economic system, which we try to simulate, has his or her own world. What equations do we have to describe human behaviour and decision-making processes in different economic situations?

The task of realistically modelling portfolio risk looks too broad for the Monte Carlo method in spite of all the impressive computational abilities of the stochastic simulation. As I mentioned before, we can get robust results only if five conditions regarding data, assumptions, and simulation logic are met.

## Joint default probability

One assumption is central for the entire portfolio approach when we think of systemic risk. To assess a portfolio's unexpected losses we need to make an assumption on asset default correlation. The existence and the power of default correlation can be observed in a period of economic turmoil, depicted by the number of default spikes which lead to substantial portfolio losses. When the benign business cycle phase arrives, the number of defaults goes down (Figures 2.14 and 2.15). What we can see is a correlation where either many highly correlated obligors default together or none of them (or very few) defaults.

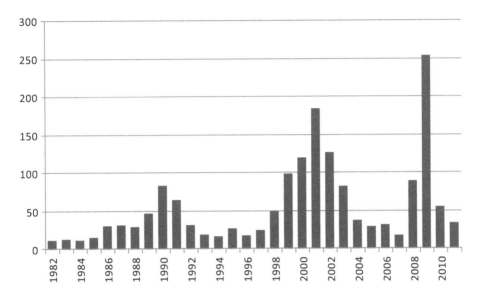

**Figure 2.14    Global speculative grade corporate issuer default counts**

*Source*: Author's own figure using data from Moody's Investors Service.

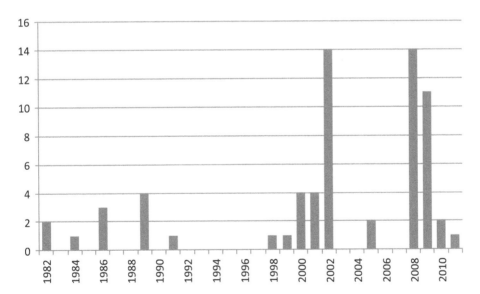

**Figure 2.15    Global investment grade corporate issuer default counts**

*Source*: Author's own figure using data from Moody's Investors Service.

With such a high annual variation of default counts, the default correlation plays a significant role in the portfolio performance. If the obligors in the portfolio are highly correlated, a default of one obligor might directly or indirectly trigger further defaults of correlated obligors creating a chain reaction. We observed this situation in 2001, when hundreds of 'dot com' companies defaulted in a very short time period. In 2008, the Lehman Brothers' collapse opened the floodgate of financial failures. On the other hand, if the obligors' correlation in the portfolio is immaterial, one default does not lead to further defaults. Obligors default in an independent, uncorrelated manner. Therefore, for future loss estimations we need to determine the joint credit quality change likelihood or, in a more narrow sense, joint default probability.

Can we calculate joint default probability using historical data? Unfortunately not.

Stephen Kealhofer, founder of the company KMV and one of the pioneers of portfolio risk modelling, and his colleague Jeffrey Bohn, formulate the problem:

> The historically observed joint frequency of default between two companies is usually zero. Exxon and Chevron have some chance of jointly defaulting, but nothing in their default history enables us to estimate the probability since neither has ever defaulted. Grouping firms enables us to estimate an average default correlation in the group using historical data, but the estimates so obtained are highly inaccurate. No satisfactory procedure exists for directly estimating default correlations. Not surprisingly, this has been a major stumbling block to portfolio management of default risk.
>
> (Kealhofer and Bohn 2012: 9)

The main problem of calculating joint default probability is the insignificancy of historical data. If we look at the period since the Second World War, based on Moody's statistics, the maximum annual corporate default rate was 5.3 per cent and the minimum stayed at 0. On average, each year less than 1 per cent of the firms defaulted. This is a very low number from a statistical standpoint. Most of the companies never defaulted in the past (individually or jointly), giving us no statistical observations to work with.

Moreover, even this scarce pool of default data cannot be fully utilised in the analytical process. Most of the defaulted companies vanished forever and all this historical data became worthless. For example, we know that in 2002,

WorldCom Inc. defaulted. At the same time, British company Marconi plc also defaulted. The good news is that now we have one data point to calculate the joint default probability of these obligors. But there is also bad news: firstly, it is clear that one data point is not enough to make any meaningful statistical analysis, so we need more observations and more WorldCom and Marconi defaults. Secondly, soon after their defaults both companies disappeared and all historical observations became useless.

Of course, there are some companies which defaulted in the past, but then re-emerged from bankruptcy and continued their operations. For example, in 2009 General Motors, Ford Motor Company and Chrysler defaulted. They also have previous default track records. Yet for calculating joint default probability these data points are still not enough. Indeed, we can use some heroic assumptions and calculate some numbers anyway, but these numbers will reflect our assumptions, not the real historical experience.

The only solution is to use direct historical default data to calculate joint default probability to group the obligors and calculate correlation for groups rather than for individual obligors. However, the data aggregation inevitably leads to the loss of information. Each company is unique. Even companies that operate in the same sector, in the same country and have the same credit rating continue to be different. They have different management teams, different businesses, different risk cultures, different organisational structures, etc. If we had aggregated several companies in a large group, we would kill the individual uniqueness and this would lead to an unacceptable drop in accuracy of future loss estimations.

## *Asset correlation instead of default correlation*

I can agree with the portfolio risk modelling pioneers: there is no satisfactory approach to directly estimate default correlations. The historically observed frequency of the joint default of two companies is usually zero or, in very rare cases, insignificant to derive correlation numbers. To overcome the data paucity issue, risk management and analytics had to move from empirical study to theoretical concepts. While it does not mean that historical data and empirical analysis are not to be used at all, the approach for the portfolio risk assessment relies now on theoretical concepts and assumptions that can help connect dots and fill gaps. A substitution of the statistical approach for theoretical concepts comes at a cost. As these assumptions become central for the whole loss estimation approach, portfolio risk models exhibit high sensitivity to assumptions that they use.

The first assumption that was adopted was from the Merton model, which assumes that a firm will default when its market asset value falls below the face value of obligations (the 'default point'). Overall this assumption is reasonable and has been supported by empirical studies for non-financial firms, but for the finance sector the Merton approach looks too narrow. Banks can default much earlier than reaching the 'default point', when for some reason a market panic is developing and creditors run on the bank. In spite of some criticism, I can accept the Metron assumption in general.

The next assumption paving the way to the estimation of joint default probability is that this probability can be implied from asset price correlation. The logic behind this is as follows: if a firm defaults when its asset values drops below the face value of its obligations, therefore two firms would default together if both firms' asset values simultaneously fall below their respective liabilities' values. Unlike the unsolvable task of directly calculating the historical probabilities of joint defaults, the mission of estimating simultaneous asset value change looks quite doable.

Kealhofer and Bohn elaborate on the approach:

> The derivatives approach enables us to measure the default correlation between two firms, using their asset correlation and their individual probabilities of default. The correlation between the two firms' asset values can be empirically measured from their equity values ... The correlation between two firms' asset values can be calculated from their respective time series ... By knowing the individual firms' default probabilities, and knowing the correlation of their asset values, the likelihood of both defaulting at the same time can be calculated.
>
> (Kealhofer and Bohn 2001: 10)

The assumption is that by knowing the asset correlation, we can derive joint default probability. This eliminates the necessity to rely on historical default data, which are not sufficient for statistical analysis in any case. Instead, we can use the historical share price to calculate equity values, then to calculate asset values and estimate pair-wise correlation between asset values of two firms.

Therefore, model developers proposed and applied different 'indirect' ways of default correlation estimations. In the absence of historically observed frequency of joint defaults, other available data is heavily used (e.g. share prices). While this or similar approaches look statistically driven (indeed, tonnes of historical data are processed), in reality these approaches are to a large extent assumption driven.

I admire the creativity of people who 'solved' the default correlation problem by using asset correlation derivatives. However, all this reminds me of an old joke about a man under a lamp post. Late at night, a really drunk man is walking home from the pub. On the dark street, he suddenly realises that he lost his keys. He goes to a lamp post, drops to his knees and starts looking for his keys. A policeman sees the drunk man, approaches him and asks: 'Are you OK? What are you doing?'. 'I am looking for my keys', was the answer. 'Where did you lose your keys?', the policeman asks. 'Over there, near the pub.' 'Why are you looking for your keys here?' 'Because it is dark over there near the pub.'

With joint default correlation, model developers used the drunk man's logic: to calculate joint default probability we need historical default data, which are not available in the quantity necessary for an analytical solution. Thus there is no point in looking for 'keys' in the dark. The solution should be under a lamp post – the place where different historical data is available. And now the quants are on their knees and are looking for a solution under the lamp post. And a miracle happens: they find tonnes of share price data, which are what they are actually looking for, but with this 'key' they are hoping to unlock a door leading to the default correlation mystery solution.

Unfortunately, I have many doubts about the trick with asset correlation. Let's start with a simple question: suppose we can use asset value correlation to derive joint default probability. Asset correlation appears to be dynamic rather than static. If we calculate the asset correlation of two firms in different time periods, we discover that correlation varies with the large range. For example, in the period between 2006 and 2009, for six leading UK banks (Lloyds TSB, Barclays, HSBC, HBOS, RBS and Standard Chartered), the pairwise asset correlation (measured by R-squared) moved from high positive numbers (0.7– 0.8) to low ones (0.1–0.15). To tell you more, there have been periods when the asset values of some banks moved in the opposite direction, signifying negative correlation. Which number are we going to use for deriving joint default probability?

There is no definite answer. For example, CreditMetrics proposes to use the last 190 weekly returns to estimate asset correlation. The technical document explains the choice:

*we weight all of the returns in each time series equally. The motivation for this is that we are interested in computing correlations which are valid over the longer horizons for which CreditMetrics will be used. Note also that the correlations we compute are based on historical weekly returns. It is therefore an assumption of the model that the weekly correlations which we provide are accurate reflections of the quarterly or yearly asset moves which drive the CreditMetrics model.*

*(RiskMetrics Group 2007: 97)*

Yet it is not clear why the last 190-week data would predict the future correlation better than, for instance, the last 52-, 208- or 26-week data. Note that default correlation per se does not influence the expected loss at all, but plays a key role in the estimation of unexpected loss. The higher the confidence level, the more sensitive the results are to the choice of default correlation. In other words, calculated tail loss figures are determined by our choice of correlation to a large extent. If we strike a very high confidence level (say, 99.95 per cent), to calculate tail loss with a one in 2,000 chance, why do we use 190-week data to calculate correlations 'which are valid over the longer horizons', as CreditMetrics suggested? As correlation is dynamic and has a large range of variation, it would be more logical to choose extreme correlation values for calculating extreme unexpected losses. In any case, whatever period we choose, by choosing the observation period, we make heroic assumptions regarding a factor which will drive estimations of tail losses.

If some people really like the idea of using the Monte Carlo simulation to generate a bunch of hypothetical scenarios with respective portfolio returns (I do not belong to this fun group and have a very sceptical view on the usefulness of this approach), then why do they not also extend this approach to correlation simulation? Variability of asset correlation can be modelled via simulation to emulate the dynamic nature of this parameter. This would be more logical than the current approach when fixed average correlation numbers are used to calculate tail losses. During crises, the asset correlation experiences large volatility and often moves to its extreme boundaries. That could be simulated in the same way as economic models simulate future hypothetical scenarios. While I do not like the idea of Monte Carlo simulations of unexpected losses in its current form, I would find the approach of asset correlation simulation more consistent with:

- the whole economic capital framework;

- the probabilistic and dynamic nature of asset correlation.

When economic capital models ignore the dynamic nature of asset correlation, I consider it as a serious weakness. But when joint default correlation derives from asset correlation, I consider it as a fundamental flaw. Looking for a key under a lamp post does not sound to me like an acceptable solution. I would like to demonstrate it by using the following simple example.

## Default correlation examples

Suppose we need to calculate the joint default probability of two obligors of our credit portfolio. The first obligor is Tata Motors, an Indian automotive company, one of the largest car manufacturers in the world, with headquarters in Mumbai. The second obligor is a small Indian company producing car components. Let's call it Mumbai Motors. This company specialises in the production of spare parts for ignition systems (e.g. an ignition switch and a distributor). Mumbai Motors has a long-term contract with Tata and is one of several hundred dedicated auto part suppliers to Tata. Almost all their production goes to the Tata factory, which produces the Tata Iris (you probably never heard about this exotic model). Both companies have never defaulted in their histories and we have no options to directly derive their joint default correlation from historical default data.

We can then use the derivative approach discussed above to estimate the default correlation from asset correlation. Suppose that both companies are publicly traded, so we can obtain historical data of share price and calculate asset return on Tata Motors and Mumbai Motors. Then we can estimate the asset correlation and finally calculate its joint default correlation (let's say that we resolved the issue with the historical period of asset return data necessary for correct estimation of the dynamic default correlation). Suppose we find that pairwise joint default correlation of Tata Motors and Mumbai Motors is, for instance, 20 per cent. The job is done and we can use this number to calculate our economic capital.

However, let's think about this correlation number. It tells us that there is a 20 per cent probability that both companies will default together. Imagine that Tata Motors would face economic difficulties and defaults. What is the probability that Mumbai Motors would default at the same time? It would be, probably, close to 100 per cent. Being a dedicated Tata supplier and selling almost all its products to Tata, Mumbai Motors would be unable to sell the same spare parts to any other car manufacturer, since nobody else can produce Tata's Iris model. The company would be in the deep trouble and have almost zero chance to muddle through.

Now imagine that Mumbai Motors experiences financial problems and default. What would be the probability that Tata Motors would default at the same time in this case? Probably very low (0 per cent or close to that). Mumbai Motors' default would not jeopardise Tata Motors' sustainability and Tata would be able to find another ignition part supplier for its Iris model very quickly. So depending on the scenario, a pairwise joint default probability of Tata Motors and Mumbai Motors would move from 0 per cent to 100 per cent. A question arises about a 20 per cent pairwise joint default probability derived from historical share price data: what does this number tell us? If this number just reflects an average correlation, then it does not make sense because it does not truly describe possible default scenarios: Tata Motors and Mumbai Motors either default together or Mumbai Motors defaults alone.

Let me give you one more example. Suppose there are the two largest UK food retail companies among other borrowers in our credit portfolio. UK top grocery retailer Tesco faces tough competition from Sainsbury's, the number two grocery chain. We need to estimate joint default correlation of Tesco and Sainsbury's. They have never defaulted before in their history, but we can estimate their default correlation using the commonly accepted derivative approach by using their asset correlation and their individual probability of default. Both companies are listed on the London Stock Exchange, so we can easily obtain their historical share price data as well as liability structure data. Suppose we derive their joint default probability of 30 per cent.

Now imagine a situation where Tesco suddenly defaults. What is the probability that Sainsbury's defaults at the same time? Tesco has been the main rival for Sainsbury's. If Tesco goes out of business, Sainsbury's would not only become the largest supermarket chain but would also have a good chance to seize Tesco's share of the market. People need to buy food every day and even Tesco's most loyal customers would shift to other food retailers (most probably to Sainsbury's). In this situation, the probability that Sainsbury's would default at the same time becomes very small. As a result, the creditworthiness of Sainsbury's would improve due to its leading market position after Tesco's default.

Imagine a situation where Tesco defaults and straight after, two other leading supermarket chains – Asda and Morrisons – also default. What would be the joint default probability for Tesco and Sainsbury's? Well, it is likely that in this case, Sainsbury's would be in trouble and likely to fail together with Tesco. In other words, it would be reasonable to estimate joint default probability of 100 per cent or close. This is because the scenario above represents a UK supermarket sector crisis which would result in failure of leading grocery chains. The survival of Sainsbury's in this situation would be problematic.

From the example above, we can see that the joint default probability of two companies is conditional and often depends on the scenario chosen. It could be a very low probability in the case of one rival's default. On the other hand, the joint default becomes almost unavoidable under the scenario where a rival defaults together with peers. Note that Asda and Morrisons could be not part of the reference portfolio, so we should not necessarily calculate any pairwise default correlation for these specific obligors when estimating the economic capital, yet their defaults can be indicative for one of tail risk scenarios for our credit portfolio.

To conclude the discussion about default correlation, the fundamental flaw of the current approach used in economic capital models resides in ignoring the following:

- Default correlation is highly dynamic. Using one fixed number for a joint default correlation sounds like a naïve approach to me and an unacceptable simplification of the reality.

- Default correlation is not only dynamic but also conditional. The actual correlation depends on what exact scenario unfolds. The dynamic correlation also means that we deal with more than a small fluctuation of joint default probability number around its median value. The range of probability can change abruptly and vary laterally from 0 to 100 per cent driven by different scenarios.

- Default correlation cannot be derived from asset value correlation. The 'search for the key under the lamp post' does not sound like a good idea to me. Historical asset value correlation is driven to a large extent by share prices. Therefore, the implicit assumption behind the idea to derive default correlation from asset value correlation is that financial markets can price default risk correctly. I am not sure that we can rely on this assumption. The main problem with estimation of joint default correlation has a similar nature as a problem of estimation of tail risk losses. It resides in our inability to provide clear cause–effect relationships and formalise them. If we fully understood all the complexity of forces that push firms into joint defaults, we would be able to propose equations, formulas or other formal expressions that connect all dots in the puzzle of default correlation. However, the driving forces of default correlation remain too complex for us, often immeasurable and invisible.

## *Default correlation and sensitivity of tail losses*

We could turn a blind eye to the issue with the estimation of default correlation and accept some simple approximation if default correlation was not a material driver of unexpected portfolio losses. Yet the reality is different. Due to the highly non-linear impact of correlation on the extreme loss estimation, relatively small changes in default correlation numbers lead to significant impacts on estimated tail losses. If I use my analogy again and compare an economic capital model with a large meat grinder and insert the data as meat that we use to prepare mince, then the correlation numbers would be spices that we add to the meat when preparing mince. As you know, while being a small substance in terms of weight compared to the other mince ingredients, spices play an extremely important role in the future taste of the end product. Should you make a mistake and put slightly more or slightly fewer spices than the recipe requires, the taste of the food utterly changes. If you use the wrong spices, you can completely spoil the meal.

The high sensitivity of a portfolio's unexpected losses to default correlation is very well known. For example, McNeil (2008: 30) illustrates the impact of correlation to the credit loss distribution of a hypothetical portfolio consisting of 1,000 homogenous loans with a default probability of 1 per cent under two correlation assumptions:

- zero default correlation (independent defaults);

- a default correlation of 0.5 per cent (dependent defaults).

Even a 0.5 per cent increase of default correlation leads to a substantial change of the distribution shape. While the number of expected defaults remains unchanged (10), the probability of unexpected defaults (20 or more) more than triple due to the fat tail of the distribution in the case of default dependency.

The high sensitivity of such models to correlation assumptions means that a change in the assumptions leads to substantial shifts in economic capital figures. But this shift is not linear. While default correlation has an insignificant impact on the results close to the area of expected loss, sensitivity increases greatly for the tail of loss distribution. When economic capital is estimated at a very high confidence level, the very small variation in default correlation numbers means a large shift in economic capital.

I can even say that portfolio tail losses are driven more by correlation than the portfolio composition per se. In real life, after changing the correlation numbers, the economic capital figures for typical models (targeting a 99.95 per cent confidence level or so) can easily rise or fall multifold depending on underlying portfolio composition and the confidence level used. Therefore, tail risk models become assumption-driven tools and the process of tail risk calculation appears to be more of an arbitrary one. To mitigate this risk, we need to be right in our correlation assumptions and absolutely precise in correlation numbers to obtain the reliable tail risk estimates. Yet the assumptions (and the derivative approach) used by various model developers to estimate correlation look too heroic to me.

Typical correlation assumptions used in economic capital models ignore a dynamic and conditional nature of correlation that I have described above. Brandon Davies nicely formulates the mystery of the dynamic and conditional nature of correlation:

> *Dynamic conditional correlation demonstrates that extremely bad outcomes can be much more likely than would be the case if the assumption were made that the correlations between different asset portfolios in the overall balance sheet were stable. It also shows that the correlations between individual asset portfolios change (are dynamic), and change differently, depending on circumstances (are conditional).*
>
> *The tail risk ceases to be static and becomes dynamic. To put this statistically, we might find in our dynamic world that a seven-standard deviation event is almost inevitable given that a five-standard deviation event has happened, whereas looking at a static distribution in similar circumstances the seven-standard deviation event is still very unlikely. There are challenges for those looking to use this measurement tool, including describing the event or events which trigger this dynamic correlation process, and measuring how the correlations will change given a certain set of – often evolving – events.*
>
> (Davies 2012: 21)

I would even say that at the current stage of our rather superficial understanding of tail risk processes, changes in asset correlation can hardly be predicted with certainty. I deliberately omitted the discussion about an even more complex correlation problem here – estimation of inter-risk correlation used in economic capital models (correlation between credit, market, operational, business and liquidity risks). This area remains a territory where assumptions (often very bold ones) completely dominate the analytical process. Overall, the correlation dynamic has been and will remain a 'black swan' for us until we uncover all driving forces of correlation.

## CONCEPTUAL PROBLEM OF BACK-TESTING

There is one more issue with economic capital models and measuring tail risk that we need to take into account. All models that are used for decision-making should go through a rigorous validation process. Traditionally, all risk models should be back-tested. Back-testing is a necessary but insufficient procedure to prove the validity of a model. However, when tail risk is going to be assessed, back-testing becomes an unachievable task as we deal with events having a very low likelihood of occurrence and, by definition, for these extremely rare events historical data are either scarce or even not available at all. Indeed, for example, to perform a back-test of the economic capital model which estimates a portfolio loss over a 12-month horizon at the confidence level of 99.96 per cent (or loss with a 1 in 2,500 chance) a model reviewer needs to have access to historical data covering an unrealistically long observation period. Even if the reviewer had data covering a 100-year history, this would not be sufficient to validate the models targeting losses with 1:2,500 probability. And of course data which is 100 years old becomes less relevant or even completely irrelevant for the current situation due to the high dynamism of the economic transformations. For proper back-testing, the reviewer needs thousands of historical observations yet up-to-date and fully relevant to the portfolio in question. This sounds like a mission impossible in truth. There are some tricks that developers try to use to overcome this difficulty. The BIS document suggests some approaches:

> For portfolio credit models, the weak power of backtesting is noted in BCBS. As has been suggested by some authors, there are variations to the basic backtesting approach which can increase the power of the tests. Examples include: performing backtesting more frequently over shorter holding periods (eg using a one-day market risk backtesting standard versus the 10-day regulatory capital standard); using cross-sectional data by backtesting on a range of reference portfolios; using information in forecasts of the full distribution; testing expected losses only; and comparing outcomes against the expected values of distributions as opposed to high quantiles.
>
> (BIS 2008: 35)

Yet these tricks can only create an illusion of data sufficiency. We can slice and dice the data at hand (e.g. cut 10-day periods into one-day periods), yet we remain stuck with the same information. We can keep back-testing expected losses, but it would give us no information about the robustness of the model in tail loss estimation.

Moreover, in addition to the historical data paucity problem, I see here a conceptual problem with back-testing of tail risk models.

Even when substantial historical data is available to back-test the model (let's imagine this miracle) and the model performs satisfactorily on the test sample, it will not be a sufficient 'fit for purpose' test for the tail risk model. This statistical validation is normally acceptable for risk models that estimate regular risk (e.g. through-the-cycle probability of default). But for tail risk assessment, the validation against the past history alone is not enough. Events that have no precedents in the past also have to be considered. As the model targets events with a probability close to zero (e.g. 1 in 3,000), coverage of events that happened in the past will not suffice. For the evolving world, we cannot assume that all risk drivers that we observed in the past stay unchanged. As they are constantly evolving and influencing each other, it can create a new dynamic which leads to a sudden 'transformation' of the system (e.g. cliff effects) that has not been around in the past. In the normal day-to-day risk assessment, these rare 'transformations' can be neglected, but they cannot be ignored when assessing the tail risk. This is because the risk driver transformations often conceal the tail risk itself and it needs to be modelled.

Only if the model fails this limited back-testing do we receive a definite result. Passing the back-test for the tail risk does not remove the uncertainty: it can be equally probable that the model is good or the tail event sample was not complete (and, by definition, the tail event sample can never be complete).

To summarise, due to complexity of tail risk estimations, a large number of assumptions are mixed with historical data when portfolio risk models are developed. This leads to the creation of quasi-statistical models, which look very scientific but are driven by assumptions. As model outcomes are very sensitive to assumptions, the arbitrary element plays a significant role. In addition, there are no reliable methods of validating tail risk models. The back-testing normally is either not possible due to tail risk data scarcity or where limited data is available, the back-testing is not sufficient for confirming that the model is reliable.

The Monte Carlo simulation for economic capital models does not save the situation. Models generate thousands and millions of hypothetical scenarios in the absence of sufficient historical data, yet these scenarios and the distribution of unexpected losses are not necessarily consistent with the reality. Don't get me wrong – I am not saying that the Monte Carlo simulation is a useless approach. Overall, the Monte Carlo simulation can be a powerful tool when key processes are known, properly formalised and correctly described, but a few random factors remain in the system. These random factors create a multivariation that Monte Carlo can simulate. Hence, the Monte Carlo simulation is widely and successfully used in physics, engineering and weather forecasting. The situation with extreme losses and economic capital estimation targeting tail risk is fundamentally different. We simply do not fully understand the main drivers and logic of the processes. We try to simulate the situation while we do not understand all of the drivers. But simulation cannot solve this task. In the previous section, I told the 'potato story': if we try to simulate the process of 'hands-free' sorting of potatoes but do not include an equation of the gravity forces in our model, regardless of how powerful the computer is and how many millions of outcomes we simulate, the picture that the model creates will never be realistic.

## THE PROOF OF THE PUDDING

The sub-prime financial crisis was the first crisis during which the vast majority of large financial institutions were measuring their portfolio risk using quantitative models. Most of the banks from developed countries used Basel II models and regulatory rules for estimating credit, market, operational risk and regulatory capital. By coincidence, when the final Basel II accord was issued in 2001, the implementation data was set for 1 January 2008. Therefore, by 2008 global and large financial institutions in Europe and North America already deployed the full array of Basel II tools and embedded them in their decision-making process. More sophisticated institutions applied their internal economic capital models in addition to the Basel II models. Regulators checked risk models, tightly oversaw risk management processes and prescribed the quantity capital each financial institute should have held with respect to the risk taken to ensure solvency. This created a false sense of security. Many financial institutions sincerely believed that they were very well capitalised and fully understood the risk that they had been exposed to. Not very often did financial firms ask the question: what if we are actually holding more risk than our portfolio risk models estimated?

I have been very curious about the industry perception of economic capital models before the crisis and how the models behaved (and how subsequent perception changed) during the crisis. The pre-crisis euphoria was apparent in the survey on economic capital carried out for the IFRI/CRO Forum in 2007. The survey concluded:

> *There is significantly increased experience in using Economic Capital across the whole financial services sector (e.g. for banking, frameworks have been in place an average of over 6 years and for insurance 4) and firms now feel broadly comfortable with the accuracy of outputs (75 per cent+ for both insurance and banking). This in turn has meant that far more institutions feel sufficiently comfortable with their Economic Capital results to use them in discussions with external stakeholders, and there is increased use in business applications, albeit often as supplementary information rather than as a core driver.*
>
> (McNeil 2008:7)

In general, before the crisis, banks were comfortable with the accuracy of economic capital models and started to expand the area of economic capital application. The situation changed very quickly when the global financial crisis hit the industry. Suddenly many banks faced tail losses which exceeded their estimations of extreme unexpected losses. This raised a question about the robustness of economic capital models and other risk models that banks had been and remained exposed to.

## Fortis

My first example of a real-life test comes from Fortis NV. Fortis was a large Benelux financial group with headquarters in Brussels and Utrecht. Before the crisis, Fortis used to be in the list of the world's Top 20 largest financial institutions. In 2007, Fortis had a market capitalisation of €40 billion. The company operated in more than 50 countries and had a workforce of more than 85,000. Fortis' operations included four financial businesses: retail banking (over 6 million customers), merchant banking (corporate business for large and medium-sized companies), asset management and private banking (investment business and service for high net worth individuals) and insurance (with a wide range of insurance products in the portfolio). The company had a very strong position in private banking, being one of the top three private bankers in Europe. Yet in September 2008 Fortis faced severe turmoil and found itself on the brink of default and was bailed out by the Dutch and Belgian governments.

As with most top European financial institutions, Fortis developed and implemented its economic capital model. We can find some details in Fortis' 2007 annual report, which had an optimistic slogan, 'Solid foundation, exciting perspectives' (the slogan suggests that Fortis' top management probably did not expect that in just nine months' time, the company would collapse and would have to rely on the governments' lifelines to stay afloat). The report explained Fortis' approach:

> We have developed 'economic capital' as a consistent and comparable measure of risk across all risk types and geographies at Fortis. It serves as an indicator of Value at Risk (VaR) to a confidence interval of 99.97 per cent and with a horizon of one year, which represents extreme events. The methodology is refined and improved on an ongoing basis. The economic capital is calculated separately for each risk type per business. We then determine the total economic capital at business level, at banking/insurance level and for Fortis as a whole. The figures obtained in this way are used for a range of internal monitoring and management purposes.
>
> (Fortis 2007b: 60)

The report provides some economic capital numbers and their breakdown (Figure 2.16). In particular, at the end of 2007, Fortis' total economic capital was €17.6 billion at a confidence level of 99.97 per cent. The economic capital number is broken up into six components reflecting the estimated unexpected loss in all main risk areas: credit risk (46.5 per cent of total economic capital), trading (6.1 per cent), ALM (asset-liability management – 39.3 per cent), business (5.6 per cent), insurance (0.1 per cent) and event risk (2.4 per cent). From first glance, Fortis' approach looks quite impressive. The economic model does not even provide unexpected loss estimations at the extremely high confidence level of 99.97 per cent (or a maximum loss with a chance of 1 in 3,300) for all geographies, but also covers all main risk types including the most intangible and unquantifiable, such as business risk and event risk.

The economic capital model, however, failed to pass the real-life test. What the model estimated was that Fortis' maximum loss in 2008 (on a 12-month time horizon) cannot be higher than €17.6 billion and there were only three chances out of 10,000 that the loss would exceed €17.6 billion. In September 2008, the growing financial difficulties forced Fortis to seek government support. On 28 September, Fortis was partially nationalised, with the three Benelux countries investing a total of €11.2 billion to save the bank. At the end of 2008 Fortis

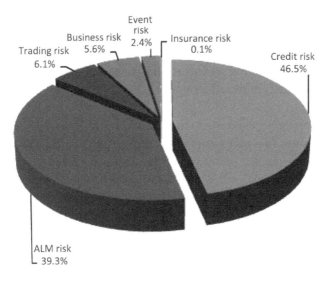

**Figure 2.16    Fortis' economic capital structure after diversification (year-end 2007)**

*Source*: Author's own figure using data from 2007 Annual report (Fortis 2007b: 61).

reported an €18.5 billion net loss which was higher than its estimated economic capital. What a nasty surprise!

There are two possible explanations as to why actual net loss exceeded the model estimated one: either the economic capital model failed or Fortis was knocked down by a 1 in 3,300 chance event. My personal view is that the model failed to correctly estimate the tail risk that Fortis was exposed to at the end of 2007. It's a little bit of a theoretical argument as to whether or not the actual scenario of September–December 2008 was outside of a 99.97 per cent confidence level. But my gut feeling tells me that the probability of the occurrence of this adverse situation is somewhat higher than 0.03 per cent.

I have strong grounds to think that the economic capital model that Fortis implemented and relied on did fail. While the 2007 annual report provided a very high level of information about the model per se and its outcomes, there were some numbers provided that we can analyse. Take, for example, the economic capital number for credit risk. According to the report, credit risk accounts for 46.5 per cent of the total economic capital of €17.6 billion, i.e. €8.2 billion. In Fortis' financial statements, we can find the total credit risk exposure, which represents the principal amount of on-balance-sheet claims

and off-balance-sheet potential claims on customers and counterparties. As at
31 December 2007, this exposure was €839 billion (Fortis 2007a: 62).

The comparison of the economic capital number for credit risk and the total
credit risk exposure is depicted in Figure 2.17.

One disproportion strikes me when I look at this figure. Theoretically, the
absolute maximum loss that Fortis could face was €839 billion (a very extreme
scenario when the value of its entire credit exposure becomes 0). This represents
a 100 per cent confidence level, which is shown as the large circle in Figure 2.17.
At the same time, Fortis said that, based on their model outcome, the maximum
credit loss at a confidence level of 99.97 per cent should not be more than €8.2
billion or less than 1 per cent of their total credit risk exposure (the small circle).
In other words, the economic model estimated that Fortis was not going to lose
more than 1 per cent of their credit exposure under any of the 9,997 scenarios
out of 10,000. For the remaining three scenarios, the loss could be anywhere in
the range from €8.2 billion and €839 billion.

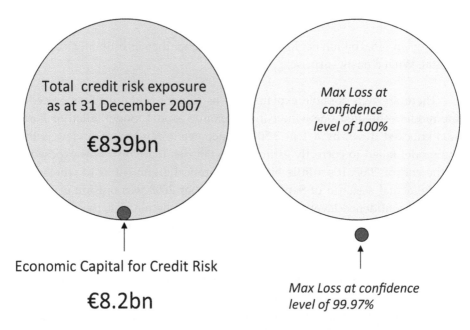

**Figure 2.17    The economic capital for credit risk and total credit risk
                exposure**

*Source*: Author's own figure using data from 2007 Fortis Annual Report and Financial
Statements.

Here, I can see a huge underestimation of actual risk: realistically, the bank should expect to lose more than 1 per cent of its credit exposure, even in a relatively mild adverse situation. And this can happen much more often than once in 3,333 chances. A huge difference between the size of the large circle (total credit risk exposure – 100 per cent confidence level) and the small one (estimated maximum credit loss at 99.97 per cent) looks odd to me.

Another indirect piece of evidence that Fortis' economic capital model simply failed was the fact that the economic capital section completely disappeared from the 2008 annual report. Moreover, the term 'economic capital' was not mentioned in the 2008 report at all!

## Hypo Real Estate AG

Another dramatic economic capital story happened with the German bank Hypo Real Estate AG. Hypo Real Estate specialised in financing property deals with diversification to commercial real estate, public sector and infrastructure projects, assets management and capital markets. The bank was the second largest commercial property lender in Germany and had operations in several European countries, the USA and Asia.

Hypo Real Estate used its economic capital model to assess enterprise-wide risk and ensure that the bank had sufficient capital to withstand extreme risk events. Its 2007 annual report provides an insight into the model:

> *Economic Capital serves as the main measure for the assessment of the Group's aggregate risk position and capital base. The Group's policy is to maintain a level of common equity and other equity type instruments with loss absorption features that exceed Economic Capital with a comfortable cushion. Economic Capital is calculated by taking into account a greater number of risk types than are used in calculating regulatory capital.*
>
> *(Hypo Real Estate 2007: 87)*

Indeed, the model that Hypo Real Estate used embraced six main risk areas: credit, market, operational, business, real estate and equity risks. Similar to Fortis' economic capital model, Hypo Real Estate reported that their model was able to assess business risk – the risk of loss of profit due to changes in the external business environment that damage the underlying economics of the bank. A really ambitious statement!

The annual report also stated that

> *each risk type is quantified using a quantitative approach and the*
> *aggregate Economic Capital is estimated using benchmarked inter-*
> *risk correlation. Risk types are scaled to a one year time horizon in*
> *like with market standards … Methodologies are constantly evolving to*
> *ensure that the Economic Capital framework is comprehensive as well*
> *as consistent. The methodologies are benchmarked to industry practices*
> *through participation in surveys, reviews and industry interactions.*

It sounds like Hypo Real Estate's top management was fully satisfied with the
model and its output.

The annual report contains the overall economic capital number and its
breakdown by risk area. As at the end of 2007, Hypo Real Estate reported a
total economic capital of €4.9 billion after taking into account the diversification
benefits. The model used a 99.97 per cent confidence level. The highest risk area
was credit risk, which accounted for 60 per cent of total economic capital or
€2.9 billion (in the 2008 annual report, the bank provided a different credit risk
number of €4 billion on an undiversified basis) (Figure 2.18).

Assessing the Group's enterprise-wide risk, the bank made the following
conclusion: 'For year end 2007, Hypo Real Estate Group has a comfortable capital
buffer. Applying a 99.97 per cent confidence level, the capital buffer for the Group

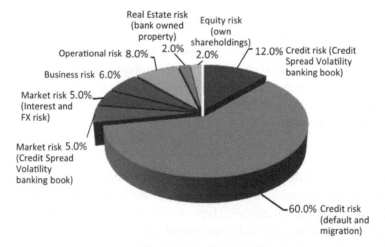

**Figure 2.18    Hypo Real Estate: Group economic capital structure (year-end
2007)**

*Source*: Author's own figure using data from 2007 Annual report (Hypo Real Estate 2007: 87).

amounts to approx 26 per cent of the total available financial resources of €6.6bn' (Hypo Real Estate 2007: 87). In other words, Hypo Real Estate stated that as of 31 December 2007 there were only three chances out of 10,000 that their loss in the next 12 months would exceed €4.9 billion, while their financial loss absorption resources amounted to €6.6 billion. Nothing to worry about!

Less than 10 months later, Hypo Real Estate asked for urgent financial help from the German Government and a consortium of banks. In September 2008, Hypo received a €35 billion credit line. In October, the bank asked for another lifeline and received the bail-out package of €50 billion, of which €20 billion was contributed by Bundesbank and €30 billion by other German banks. This was not enough to stop Hypo's slide to insolvency as the bank reported new problems and asked for more help. By April 2009, government support for Hypo reached €102 billion! In October 2009, the bank was nationalised. The government paid Hypo's investors €1.3 per share, which was about 2.5 per cent of what investors paid in Hypo's shares in 2007 (Figure 2.19). For 2008, Hypo Real Estate Group reported a €5.5 billion net loss, which was higher than

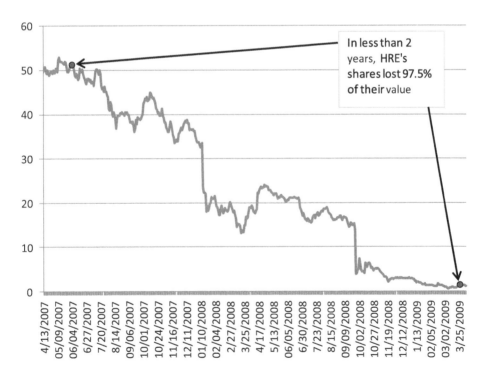

**Figure 2.19    Hypo Real Estate Group share price (€ per share)**

*Source*: Author's own figure using data from Bloomberg.

their economic capital of €4.9 billion at a confidence level of 99.97 per cent! (Figure 2.20).

Again, I am convinced that in 2008, Hypo did not experience any extreme scenarios carrying a probability of less than 0.03 per cent, which stayed beyond the model's confidence level. I suspect that the answer, unfortunately, is simple: the economic capital model failed. Yes, 2008 was a very difficult year for all financial firms with substantial exposure to the real estate market. However, I cannot believe that we can say that what happened in 2008 had a one in 3,333 chance of occurrence.

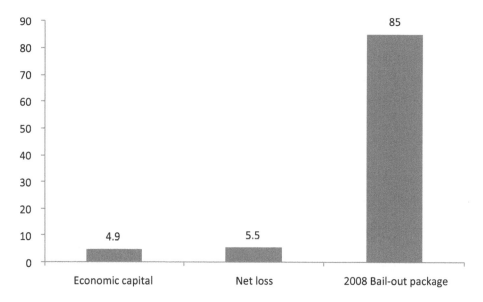

**Figure 2.20    Hypo Real Estate Group economic capital (31 December 2007), net loss and bail-out package in 2008 (€ billion)**

*Source*: Author's own figure using data from HRE annual and interim reports.

## Wachovia

I would like to tell one more economic capital model failure story. This is the story about Wachovia, which used to be the fourth largest US bank by total assets. Wachovia ran a diversified financial business, providing a very broad range of financial services including retail and corporate banking, private banking, asset management and investment banking.

Wachovia was one of the pioneers of using the economic capital models. The 2007 annual report informed: 'We employ an economic capital framework developed to measure the declines in economic value that a transaction, portfolio or business unit could incur given an extreme event or business environment' (Wachovia 2007: 24). The report claimed that the economic capital model employed by Wachovia estimated the enterprise-wide risk covering key risk types including credit, market, operational, business risk and other risk. Again, like Fortis and Hypo Real Estate Group, Wachovia claimed that its economic capital model calculated business risk, which represented the potential losses that the business lines could suffer from and that have not been captured elsewhere (such as losses from a difficult business environment).

Economic capital had been widely used by Wachovia not only as a direct measure of risk but also as a strategic tool:

> We use RAROC and economic profit measures in a variety of ways. They are used to aid in the pricing of transactions such as loans, commitments and credit substitutes in each of our business segments. These transactional measures are aggregated to provide portfolio, business unit, business segment, and ultimately company-level RAROC and economic profit amounts. Incremental activities such as new product analysis, business line extensions and acquisitions are also measured using these tools.
>
> (Wachovia 2007: 24)

At the end of 2007, Wachovia reported that their total economic capital for the next 12 months was $25.6 billion at a confidence level of 99.95 per cent. At that time, Wachovia's performance already experienced severe pressure. Net profit was declining throughout the entire year starting from an impressive $2.3 billion in the first quarter and finishing marginally breaking even in the fourth quarter ($51 million only). In the first quarter of 2008, the company reported a $350 million net loss, which was the bank's first quarterly loss since 2001. Wachovia blamed Golden West Financial's portfolio performance (a bank that Wachovia acquired in 2006). But this was just the start. In the second quarter, the bank made its free fall, reporting a record quarterly loss of $8.9 billion. In this situation, the CEO Ken Thompson resigned. Yet the free fall continued.

The third quarter turned to a full scale disaster. In October 2008, Eric Dash, the *New York Times* correspondent, described the situation that Wachovia found themselves in:

> *The Wachovia Corporation announced a $23.9 billion third-quarter loss on Wednesday as it prepared to be taken over by Wells Fargo. The bank took an $18.7 billion charge to write down the value of good will and wrote off $6.6 billion in credit losses tied largely to its disastrous purchase of Golden West Financial in 2006. And the red ink is unlikely to end soon. Wachovia projected an additional $26.1 billion in mortgage-related losses in 2009. And it wrote down only a tiny portion of its $219 billion commercial real estate and corporate loan portfolio.*
>
> *(Dash 2008)*

To avoid a disaster, the US Government forced Wells Fargo to step in and acquire Wachovia. By the end of 2008, the merger was completed and Wachovia, a bank with a 120-year history, disappeared forever.

We still do not know how much Wachovia lost during the 12-month period starting from 1 January 2008. We only know Wachovia's results for the first three quarters of 2008. The consolidation with Wells Fargo in the fourth quarter made the exact calculations cumbersome. According to the *Washington Post*, Wells Fargo estimated that Wachovia lost an additional $11.2 billion during its final three months of 2008 (Appelbaum 2009) (Figure 2.21). If this number were correct, then the overall loss for Wachovia in 2008 should be more than $44 billion. According to Eric Dash from the *New York Times*, Wells Fargo estimated that it would absorb about $74 billion in losses (not necessarily all losses were

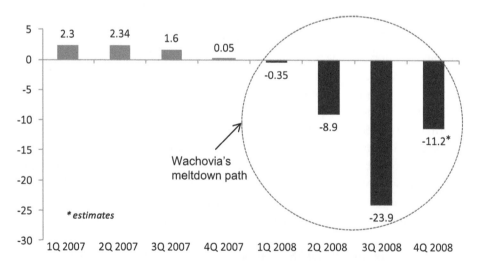

**Figure 2.21    Wachovia's quarterly profit/loss (US$ billion)**

*Source*: Author's own figure using data from Annual report, the *Washington Post*, the *New York Times*.

due in 2008). In any case, it is absolutely clear that Wachovia's net loss in 2008 did exceed its economic capital calculated at the end of 2007. The comparison of numbers can lead to jaws dropping (Figure 2.22).

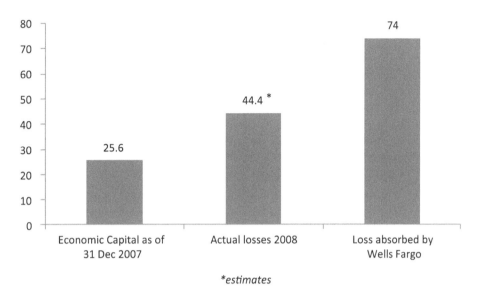

*estimates*

**Figure 2.22    Wachovia's economic capital, actual loss and Wells Fargo's estimated loss at the merger deal ($ billion)**

*Source*: Author's own figure using data from Annual report, the *Washington Post*, the *New York Times*.

Wachovia's economic capital model calculated that in 2008 the unexpected loss should not exceed $25.6 billion in 1,999 chances of out of 2,000 (the confidence level of 99.95 per cent). Yet in the first three quarters Wachovia lost more than $33 billion and the total annual loss likely exceeded their economic capital by at least 70 per cent!

It looks like Wells Fargo has not been at all impressed by Wachovia's economic capital framework and the model. At least Wells Fargo never mentioned the economic capital in their annual reports published after the Wachovia acquisition.

## THE END OF THE BEGINNING

At the end of the day, I need to clarify my position regarding portfolio risk models. While I believe that single-asset risk models (e.g. probability of default models or loss given default models) can provide relatively reliable risk estimates under normal conditions, I am much more sceptical about the ability of portfolio risk models to deliver robust estimates. This is because of three distinctive elements of portfolio risk models that I explained already in this chapter:

1.  Portfolio models such as economic capital models attempt to address the tail risk, which makes the model developers' task immensely more difficult compared to that for single asset risk models focusing on normal risk.

2.  Portfolio risk models are much more complicated than single-asset risk models and have many 'moving parts': massive input data, numerous assumptions (e.g. asset correlation) and the simulation engine. Any small error in any of these 'moving parts' translates into a large (often an unacceptably large) estimation error at the tail of the loss distribution.

3.  Reliable back-testing of portfolio risk models addressing extreme risk losses is problematic or, using more colloquial language, impossible. At best, using all tricks of data enhancing (yet we never have enough data for proper back-testing), we can spot the deficiencies of the model and reject it. However, if the model passes the tests, we will still remain uncertain if the model generates reliable estimates for the tail losses. In this situation, the decision to use the model for risk and business purposes becomes an act of belief rather than an analytical verdict.

Sometimes when I express my scepticism about economic capital models, people ask me the same question: 'So you want to say that we need to stop all economic capital modelling projects, cut the budget and re-deploy model developers to different tasks.' Actually, my conclusion from what I said about portfolio risk model is exactly the opposite. My key message is that we need to be honest when we discuss the weaknesses of economic capital models. Portfolio models strive to solve an immensely complicated task – to estimate large systemic and tail risk losses, one of the most difficult tasks that financialanalytics has ever had. After the 20 years or so that the industry had to solve this task, we have passed a period of euphoria and proliferation of portfolio models. The global financial crisis has revealed the weaknesses of the models and reminded us that some people started to celebrate the success too early. Now we have entered a period of great disappointment since it has become clear that the nice portfolio risk theoretical framework and an impressive computational array could not deliver reliable tail risk estimations.

While it can sound frustrating that the goal remains unachieved, it is not a reason to give up right away. We are where we are. Twenty years of developments, trials and errors is a relatively short period for a task of this complexity. Therefore, my view is that tail risk modelling should be treated as a high priority for risk analytics. Financial institutions should consider allocating extra resources to the enhancement and redevelopment of their economic capital projects.

We have ended the initial phase in portfolio risk modelling. Rather than axing all portfolio risk projects, we need to learn our lessons from past experience and continue to work hard to reach the long-term goal. Otherwise, the reliable tail risk models will remain an unachievable dream.

How can we run a business if reliable tools to measure extreme risk do not exist? We often say: if you can't measure it, you can't manage it. For me, this logic is no more than a stereotype. In real life, we manage a lot of things around us (and manage successfully) without the existence of any measurements. In fact, areas where human society has developed and used robust quantification methods are not as large as you might think. The next time you go to a restaurant, ask the chef about how he manages to prepare tasty food without any food tasting quantification. Does he really need a 'taste-o-meter'? If you go to an exhibition or a museum, ask artists how they manage the business and quality of the paintings without using any quantification methods. In fact, the whole area of art in its wider meaning (e.g. music, visual art, dancing, design, fashion, etc.) belongs to a world where quantification does not play any substantial role. People can easily manage this without measuring.

In terms of measurement, the risk management in the financial sector is currently in the middle of the road to completion. We actively manage everyday 'normal' risk using risk quantification which is pretty reliable. However, the tail of the loss distribution remains challenging for reliable quantification. How can we manage tail risk then?

Well, firstly we need to be clear that our portfolio risk models are still a work in progress and not yet state-of-the-art measurement tools as many people might think. Removal of the illusion per se puts us in a much stronger position. At least it should no longer be like flying an aeroplane, blindly relying on the dashboard gauges which are likely to often be wrong.

Secondly, while quants are struggling to design a robust extreme-risk-measurement approach, risk and business people should learn how to manage and mitigate extreme risk, applying more non-quantitative methods and 'soft' skills. The second and third parts of this book shed some light on one of the possible approaches of managing extreme risk.

# 3

# Anti-Basel: How Modern Regulation Missed the Point

*There is nothing that is a more certain sign of insanity than to do the same thing over and over and expect the result to be different.*

(Albert Einstein)

## Aristotle and the Common Housefly

Before I start to talk about modern regulation, I would like to go back more than 2,000 years to the human history in the times of ancient Greece. I would like to tell a story about Aristotle, a Greek philosopher, scientist and the teacher of Alexander the Great. Aristotle was, possibly, the greatest scientist who has ever lived on the planet. He is one of the founders of Western philosophy, as well as the person whose interests covered many scientific areas (from physics, geology, mathematics and logic to biology and linguistics).

One of the areas where Aristotle made a unique contribution was zoology. He wrote the *History of Animals*, the fundamental zoology research where he described and classified living organisms. Amazingly, his classification became the foundation of zoology and was used for more than 2,000 years until Charles Darwin's evolution theory was released. Therefore, it could be the longest ever survival of widely accepted scientific classifications.

When Aristotle classified living creatures, among others he provided a description of a common housefly, an insect of the order Diptera. Everyone knows this insect. We can see a lot of these flies in gardens or in homes during spring and summer. When Aristotle gave his description, he wrote that the fly had eight legs.

Aristotle's authority in the Western scientific world in general, as well as in zoology in particular, was so high that, for many centuries, in all zoology manuscripts European scientists repeated what Aristotle wrote: 'a housefly has eight legs'. It continued until the Renaissance period, when a curious scientist decided to catch a fly and count its legs. To his and everyone's surprise, he discovered that flies actually have six legs!

I decided to include this story because it shows sometimes how important it can be to question things that are commonly accepted for ages and sound unarguably correct to everyone. Yet the scientific scepticism remains an important element of human progress. We have to challenge the postulates from time to time even if they were formulated by one of the greatest thinkers like Aristotle. There is a chance that even Aristotle could be wrong.

Of course, the modern regulatory principles for the financial industry were formulated by very smart people, although probably not of Aristotle's calibre. It is unlikely that their names will be remembered 2,000 years from now. Therefore, it would be prudent to analyse and challenge some of the regulatory principles now, rather than wait for several centuries. Even though these principles have already been commonly accepted to some extent, we need to be clear on what these regulatory measures can and cannot deliver to make the financial service industry stable and what their unintentional consequences could be.

## Basel I, Basel II, Basel III – Sold!

Today, we can no longer imagine how the financial industry existed without Basel regulations produced by the Bank for International Settlements. People who work in the financial sector and deal with regulatory issues on a daily basis might have an impression that this regulation has been around forever. However, Basel is still very young.

### DAYS WHEN IT STARTED

A quarter of a century has passed since the original Basel Accord (currently known as Basel I) was agreed and put forward for implementation. The 1990s became the period of initial acceptance of Basel principles. Today, people treat Basel as a regulation addressing the key elements of risk management and risk reporting. Yet the initial idea and focus of Basel was quite narrow and only covered the capital adequacy of 'internationally active' banks. The framework included only credit risk and prescribed a simple approach to calculate risk-weighted assets and the minimum required capital to cover this risk.

I remember many, many years ago, when I did my MBA degree, attending the course of Banking and Risk Management. Our professor was enthusiastic about the Basel Accord. In particular, he criticised the non-risk-adjusted leverage ratio that banks used in the pre-Basel era. He told us: 'It doesn't make sense to look at the pure asset/equity ratio because if a bank has exposure to low risk assets such as AAA-rated government bonds, it can afford to maintain a higher financial leverage without jeopardising the financial stability and vice versa,' Indeed Basel opened an era of risk-adjusted measurement which at that time was a large step forward. However, my professor also criticised some elements of Basel I. He pointed out that from a capital adequacy perspective, the level of risk differentiation in Basel I was not sufficient. 'We need to clearly differentiate assets by their risk in each large asset group', he suggested. 'If we do not do this and place, let's say, all corporates in the same risk bucket and, hence, need to allocate the same amount of capital, then we are providing wrong incentives for credit decisions.' Seems like God has heard his voice.

In the 2000s came the era of Basel II, which is substantially more detailed than the initial Basel approach, where market and operational risks are embraced in addition to credit risk. While it was still the capital adequacy act, the new edition covered areas outside the narrow capital perimeter such as risk disclosure. I am not going to describe the Basel II framework in detail. This falls outside this book's scope and there are a lot of very good textbooks dedicated to the Basel II approach. What is worthwhile to mention is the level of complexity of Basel II compared to Basel I. One interesting fact that I noticed can tell you more than one hundred words about the difference in complexity of these two accords. Have you ever checked how long the main Basel I document is? The whole approach is described in just 16 pages (excluding annexes)! (BIS 1988).

So how long is the Basel II framework document? The answer is 242 pages excluding annexes (BIS 2006). But this is not the end of the story. The Basel II framework has been emulated on an international level in a number of documents such as the EU Capital Requirements Directive (CRD). In addition, national regulators produced their interpretations of the Basel II framework. For example, the UK regulator, the FSA, published the General Prudential Sourcebook ('GENPRU') and the Prudential Sourcebook for Banks, Building Societies and Investment Firms ('BIPRU'). Each document contains hundreds of pages.

The introduction of Basel II materially changed the regulatory and risk management landscape. How has the financial world changed since then? Well, we have moved on to an era of total risk quantification. In the countries which adopted Basel II, banks employed thousands of quants that built hundreds of risk models, extending the risk quantification to all key business areas. The implementation cost a lot of money and brain power. By 2008, the majority of large and global financial institutions in Europe and to some extent the USA had already adopted Basel II and managed their risk and capital based on the most advanced and complex regulatory framework that the financial sector had ever had. But then came the crisis ...

## NEW REGULATION

The global financial crisis, which unfolded suddenly, revealed that the whole industry with all its risk models and capital management tools was ill prepared for this challenge. Did we really spend our money and intellectual resources as effectively as we hoped? If Basel II, the most advanced regulatory framework, did not protect us from collective failure, then what was it put in place for?

While the crisis was still in full swing and specialists were having hot debates on what actually happened and what caused the crisis, regulators started to revise the key elements of Basel II. They started to develop new rules that were supposed to ensure that the 2008–9 disaster would not repeat itself in the future. The regulators came up with new proposals, consultations and reached an agreement incredibly fast, which surprised many people, taking into account how much time it took to develop and approve the previous Accords. In 2010, a new set of regulatory rules commonly known as Basel III was announced (BIS 2010a).

I must confess that I was anxiously waiting for the new regulation. For me it was absolutely clear that what happened in 2008–9 was not the failure of just some financial institutions. It was an acid test for the entire Basel ideology and architecture built over many years. Basel failed the test. Not just some of Basel's architecture components but the fundamental Basel principles appeared to be flawed. I was anxiously waiting for regulators to re-conceive the principles and propose a new concept free of traditional Basel weaknesses.

The new regulation announced in 2010 surprised, confused and disappointed me.

Let me explain my thoughts. The first surprise came when I printed the Basel III document: it was long, too long for a document that is meant to focus on fundamental principles. 162 pages long! The American regulators went even further. The final text of the Dodd–Frank Act (the American version of the new Basel regulation) includes 849 pages (Dodd–Frank Wall Street Reform and Consumer Protection Act 2010). When British Prime Minister Winston Churchill once received a large document, he said: 'The very length of this document defends it well against the risk of being read.' I am sure that the authors of Dodd–Frank Act have almost eliminated this risk. I remember when I participated at one of the banking forums in the USA in 2011, one of the participants at the plenary session asked who had managed to fully read the Dodd–Frank Act. Out of 60 people (most of whom were American risk and regulation practitioners) in the room, only two raised their hands.

What confused and disappointed me even more than the length of the new Basel proposal was the content per se. The obvious conclusion that one can reach reading Basel III is that the new regulation, to a large extent, continued the Basel II trend on detailed risk quantification, even more deeply than Basel II. It looks like the regulators came to a conclusion that severe underestimation of risk at the pre-crisis period was attributable to either some errors in risk calculations or insufficiently deep quantification of risk. Was it not clear enough that tight regulatory prescriptions and the expansion of quantification to all possible areas of risk (Basel II framework) did not provide better protection from systemic and large losses? Do we really believe that by changing some regulatory formulae or risk weights we can solve the problem of risk quantification and, most importantly for the future financial stability, the systemic and tail risk quantification? I am convinced that the Basel II failure during the crisis was not attributable to just a technical issue that can be corrected by 'tweaking' and adjusting existing tools. I am sure that the Basel II framework and subsequently Basel III are suffering from a conceptual problem, which I will describe below.

So what is the essence of Basel III? I will summarise this lengthy document on banking regulatory reform in a few sentences. The Basel Committee provide three keystone messages:

1.  financial institutions will need more capital

2.  financial institutions will need better liquidity

3.    financial institutions have to maintain a prudent level of financial leverage.

With regards to banks' capitalisation the Basel Committee introduces the higher capital requirements than it was under Basel II regime.

The main direct capital enhancement measures include:

- an increase of minimum common equity capital ratio to 4.5 per cent from 2 per cent;

- the procyclicality approach, which requires to maintain capital conservation buffers driven by macro-economic adjustment: this will limit a bank's ability to reduce capital (above minimum capital requirements) below a certain threshold;

- an additional capital buffer for systemically important financial institutions (called the 'too big to fail' solution).

The main indirect capital enhancement measures include:

- a new definition of a bank's capital; in particular, more strict criteria for Tier 1 and Tier 2, which will push banks to raise more capital with higher loss absorption ability;

- the introduction of stressed exposure at default (EaD) and downturn probability of default (PD), which aims to make the calculation of risk-weighted assets more conservative and, therefore, will result in higher capital requirement;

- an increase in correlation factor for large financial institution exposures by 25 per cent, which again will result in more conservative estimation of risk-weighted assets and, subsequently, in higher capital requirement.

While the capital requirements remain at the heart of Basel I and II, the introduction of liquidity rules becomes a new element of the regulatory framework. Basel III introduced a 30-day liquidity coverage ratio requirement underpinned by a longer-term structural liquidity ratio.

The third proposal includes the non-risk-adjusted maximum financial leverage. The leverage ratio and liquidity coverage ratio should play the role of safeguarding against underestimation of risk to supplement risk-based requirements. Therefore, higher capital, better liquidity and the prudent financial leverage become the three silver bullets that the Basel Committee hopes will stop future systemic crises.

## BASEL III COSTS

It is difficult to argue that, with all things being equal, a bank with a higher capital base, ample liquidity and a conservative leverage would be more stable during financial stress. Therefore, it seems perfectly reasonable to propose these enhancements. However, these 'silver bullets' are not cheap. They come at high costs, both direct (for each financial institution) and indirect (for banks' customers and the economy).

Since the Basel III final document was published, there have been several studies done to estimate the costs of the new regulatory regime. McKinsey & Co. estimates that there are several areas where the impact of the new Basel rules on the banking sector will be substantial, in their paper called 'Basel III and European banking' (Härle et al. 2010):

- US and European banks will need about €1.7 trillion of additional Tier 1 capital, €1.9 trillion of short-term liquidity and about €4.5 trillion of long-term funding.

- The capital need is equivalent to almost 60 per cent of all European and US Tier 1 capital outstanding, and the liquidity gap equivalent to roughly 50 per cent of all outstanding short-term liquidity.

- Implementation costs (excluding capital, funding and balance sheet management) will be €45–70 m for a mid-size European bank.

- Return of equity for European banks would decrease by between 3.7 and 4.3 percentage points.

There are quite a few studies on the global impact of Basel III on economy. The estimated impact numbers here deviate quite substantially from each other. It is not a surprise that the Basel Committee maintains the most optimistic view among others. Its Macroeconomic Assessment Group (MAG) came up with the conclusion that the negative impact will be hardly visible at all:

*Taking the median across the results obtained by group members, the*
*Interim Report concluded that a 1 percentage point increase in the*
*target ratio of tangible common equity (TCE) to risk-weighted assets*
*would lead to a maximum decline in the level of GDP of about 0.19*
*per cent from the baseline path, which would occur four and a half*
*years after the start of implementation (equivalent to a reduction in*
*the annual growth rate of 0.04 percentage points over this period) ...*
*A 25 per cent increase in the holding of liquid assets relative to total*
*assets implemented over four years, combined with an extension of the*
*maturity of banks' wholesale liabilities, was estimated to be associated*
*with a median decline in GDP in the order of 0.08 per cent relative to*
*the baseline trend after 18 quarters.*

(Macroeconomic Assessment Group 2010: 1)

On the opposite side of the spectrum, the Institute of International Finance (IIF)
provided a study where conclusions were not as rosy as the Macroeconomic
Assessment Group predicted. Philip Suttle, IIF Deputy Managing Director and
Chief Economist, summarised findings of their assessment (Suttle 2011: 2):

'Implementing the current reform agenda fully will have a meaningful
impact on the global economy:

- reduce (GDP-weighted) average level of GDP by 3.2 per cent by
  2015;

- level of employment about 7.5 million lower by 2015.'

I would refrain from judging whose opinion sounds more plausible. I am
sceptical about anyone's ability to predict the exact economic impact of
complicated matters such as the global regulatory reform. In this battle of
opinions it is unlikely that someone can claim victory. I do not believe that we
are able to calculate all direct impacts and unintended consequences of Basel
III. We just do not have any means of assessing the high complexity of how the
regulatory reform in reality will affect different areas and how it will influence
behaviour and reactions of key parities affected by the reform. But I can share
the view that Basel III will be a very expensive journey for the financial industry.
Some of these costs (maybe a substantial part) will be passed to customers and
even to the wider economy.

In addition, the implementation of proposed measures could create some
unintended consequences for the economy. Two consequences are clearly visible:

1.  Boost of 'shadow banking': new restrictive measures will undermine a balance of supply and demand for banking credit, which will likely lead to expansion of unregulated 'shadow banking'.

2.  Regulatory arbitrage: as the Basel III implementation will not be fully synchronised by time and geographies, many financial institutions will undoubtedly use financial innovations that can exploit advantages of regulatory arbitrage.

To conclude, if the three 'silver bullets' were to come at no cost, I would have supported the proposals without a doubt. However, the price is going to be substantial and negative, unintended consequences are likely. Therefore, we need to ensure that Basel III measures will prevent the financial industry from the collective disaster similar to what we saw in 2008–9.

## The Three 'Silver Bullets' of Basel III

When the sub-prime mortgage crisis unfolded and developed to the global financial crisis, regulators found them under severe political pressure. G20 started to shape the agenda of regulatory reform and regulators had no choice but to deliver their proposals quickly to remedy the situation. This can explain the way in which regulators set the new Basel rules. The whole Basel III approach appeared to be a direct response to the crisis (Figure 3.1):

*   During the crisis, financial institutions faced a shortage of capital due to its depletion under heavy losses and write-downs. Hence, regulators proposed to increase minimum capital requirements (directly and indirectly).

*   When the crisis unfolded, the liquidity crunch stormed the financial industry, forcing Central Banks to step in and provide liquidity facilities to save the industry from a complete collapse. Hence, Basel III specifically addressed the liquidity issue via the introduction of new liquidity rules.

*   During the benign phase of the economic cycle preceding the crisis, financial institutions (especially in Europe) built up their assets quickly and substantially increased their financial leverage. This did not raise any concerns up to the point when the asset bubble burst, asset quality collapsed and the risk associated with various assets

skyrocketed. Banks with high financial leverage became hostages of their inflated assets. Hence, regulators decided to mandate the non-risk-adjusted financial leverage.

One can say that the above approach sounded perfectly reasonable. Regulators addressed key pressure points revealed during the global financial crisis. In addition, their direct and firm response on the crisis challenges helped to impress politicians and to demonstrate that they took steps proactively.

Nevertheless, I can see a substantial weakness in how regulators responded to the crisis and how they formulated the new regulatory changes. They were rushing with a solution and jumped to conclusions without a proper discussion and deep analysis of what actually caused the financial crisis. I am afraid that, as a result, regulators addressed the symptoms of the crisis rather than its causes.

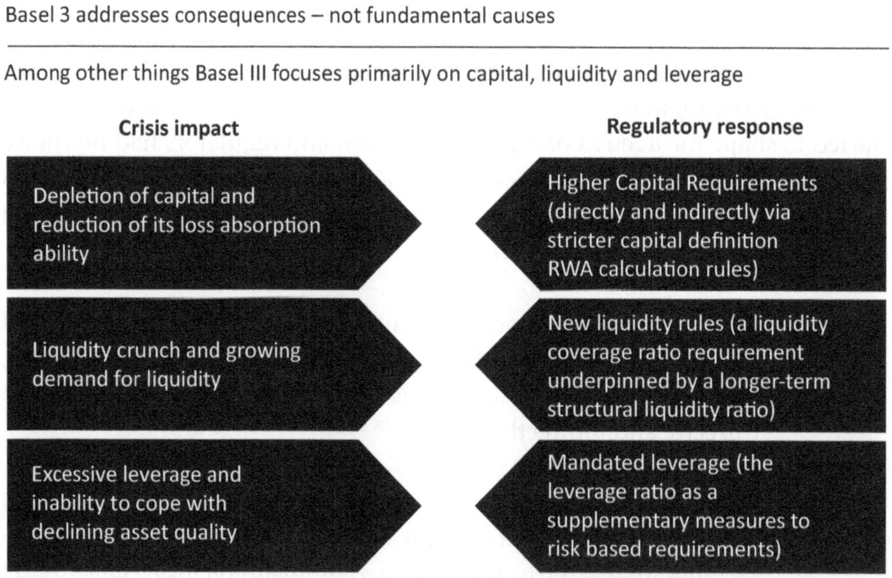

Basel 3 addresses consequences – not fundamental causes

Among other things Basel III focuses primarily on capital, liquidity and leverage

| Crisis impact | Regulatory response |
| --- | --- |
| Depletion of capital and reduction of its loss absorption ability | Higher Capital Requirements (directly and indirectly via stricter capital definition RWA calculation rules) |
| Liquidity crunch and growing demand for liquidity | New liquidity rules (a liquidity coverage ratio requirement underpinned by a longer-term structural liquidity ratio) |
| Excessive leverage and inability to cope with declining asset quality | Mandated leverage (the leverage ratio as a supplementary measures to risk based requirements) |

Figure 3.1    The global financial crisis impact and the regulatory response

## HOW MUCH CAPITAL IS ENOUGH?

One of the conclusions drawn by the regulators from the sub-prime financial crisis was that the financial industry needed to be better capitalised. Regulators have promptly addressed this in Basel III by changing the minimum capital requirements directly. There is no denying that an increase of the capital cushion adds more stability to the financial system. However, due to the high price that the financial system has to pay for keeping additional capital, it is necessary to consider what the optimal level of capitalisation should be. What is the capital level that provides enough loss absorption capacity to keep individual financial institutions sufficiently protected but at the same time does not elevate capital to the level when the business becomes unattractive due to low return on capital?

The Basel III measures do not address the question of the optimal level of capitalisation though. The financial crisis gave us some interesting information that can help us to understand to what extent capitalisation was important in coping with the systemic shock.

If we analyse the most spectacular banking failures when either a firm declared bankruptcy or was bailed out by a government or was acquired by a more successful rival, we can notice that failed banks were not necessarily weakly capitalised. Figure 3.2 illustrates the level of Tier 1 capital ratios of ten American and European failed banks. Figures of Tier 1 capital ratios that these banks reported in their last annual reports before their failure demonstrate that all banks comfortably met minimum capital adequacy requirements. Moreover, if we use the FDIC definition of well-capitalised banks, we can see that all of those failed banks would be classified as well-capitalised.

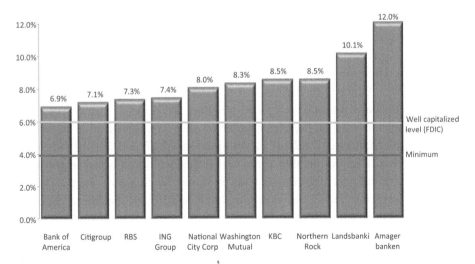

**Figure 3.2    Failed banks' capitalisation: Tier 1 capital ratios before the failure**

*Source*: Author's own figure using data from banks' annual reports.

By the way, an average Tier 1 capital ratio of 10 for these ten failed banks was 8.4 per cent – more than twice as high as Basel capital adequacy rules required!

Furthermore, two of the banks from the failed bank list – Icelandic Landsbanki and Danish Amagerbanken – were ranked among the highest by capitalisation level among European banks before their fiascos. Having remarkable Tier 1 capital ratios of 10.1 per cent and 12 per cent, respectively, these banks failed miserably when they faced the extreme risk shock. At the same time, there were many European and American banks that had much weaker capital ratios when the turmoil hit the financial sector, yet they managed to survive and some of them emerged as the new winners after the crisis.

One of the conclusions that we can draw from the above is that the relationship between the level of capitalisation and propensity to failure is not straightforward and is far from being linear. Moreover, some studies argue that there is no statistical relationship between Basel risk-weighted capital and probability of survival. Adrian Blundell-Wignall, Gert Wehinger and Patrick Slovik analysed the relationship between the Tier 1 capital adequacy ratios for the loss-making banks in different countries and their cumulative losses in the global financial crisis. They found that in countries where banks had higher levels of capitalisation (and were supposed to be more conservative from a Basel standpoint), the banks made higher losses. The authors concluded: 'It is of no comfort to supporters of the Basel risk-weighting approach (as it has been formulated to date) that this relationship is a positive correlation' (Blundell-Wignall et al. 2009: 18). In other words, they found that the better the Tier 1 ratios of banks of some jurisdictions prior to the crisis, the greater were the cumulative write-downs and losses during the 2008–9 crisis.

Andrew Haldane and Vasileios Madouros studied a sample of 100 large, complex global banks with diverse asset mixes and which were likely to have been using the Basel internal models prior to the crisis; at least, in principle, risks to these banks should be captured better by risk-weighted capital measures (Haldane and Madouros 2012). 37 banks in the sample failed during the global financial crisis. They found that there was little correlation between levels of regulatory capital and subsequent bank failure. The comparison of levels of risk-based capital in failed and surviving banks confirmed that these were not statistically significantly different.

I don't want to say that the level of capitalisation is entirely irrelevant. I think we are dealing with a two-dimensional problem. The first dimension relates to what I call the law of diminishing returns to capitalisation. The second dimension is the quality of risk measurement.

## THE LAW OF DIMINISHING RETURNS TO CAPITALISATION

The law of diminishing returns to capitalisation focuses on the optimal level of the capital: how much capital should be enough to ensure a reasonable sustainability of the financial business? It is undeniably clear that very low capitalisation should be considered as a factor of risk. However, it looks like after reaching a particular threshold for capitalisation (a critical level), the relationship between capitalisation and propensity to failure starts to become less obvious. Consider a comparison of two banks, one with a Tier 1 capital of 3 per cent and the other with 6 per cent; the second bank would naturally be in a much better position to sustain the extreme events. Then if both banks increase their Tier 1 capital by 5 percentage points (8 per cent and 11 per cent, respectively), it is likely that the gap in their level of sustainability would not be as much as before. Both banks are already sufficiently capitalised and have a material capital buffer to absorb the unexpected loss in case of an extreme event.

I called it the law of diminishing returns to capitalisation, when one or two additional percentage points of capitalisation (e.g. Tier 1 ratio) can be a strong reinforcement for low capitalised banks and, at the same time, insignificant for already well-capitalised banks. Therefore, the protective power of extra capital diminishes exponentially after a threshold capitalisation level has been reached. The ultimate survival of sufficiently capitalised banks would depend on other factors beyond just capital adequacy, such as the efficiency of risk management during the crisis.

## WHEN THE DENOMINATOR IS UNCERTAIN ...

In the midst of the global financial crisis, when the neatly constructed and built for years Basel capital adequacy framework suddenly cracked, Paul Tucker, Deputy Governor of the Bank of England, pronounced the sad truth: 'Almost no amount of capital is enough if things are bad enough' (Tucker 2009: 8). At first glance, this sounds very reasonable and the recent experience supports this view. We remember during the financial chaos of 2008–9, quarter by quarter the best-capitalised banks were losing money and their asset 'black holes' kept on consuming their capital, making government bail-out the only option for many of them to stay in business.

However, I do not fully agree with the statement that almost no amount of capital is enough. The problem with well-capitalised financial institutions, many of which failed miserably during the crisis nevertheless, resided in the underestimation of risk. Yes, before the crisis these banks had strong capital ratios on paper. But these ratios looked good just because the banks made terrible errors in their risk assessments. For example, during the pre-crisis period many banks warehoused in their balance sheets AAA-rated trenches of asset-backed security CDOs for billions of dollars and treated these assets as almost risk-free. When the crisis occurred, it became apparent that the risk was miscalculated. It triggered massive downgrades of CDOs, sometimes by more than ten notches. Had these banks calculated all risks correctly, their capital ratios would look much less impressive.

Here we come to the most important conclusion about the level of capitalisation. Financial institutions need capital to cover their losses. More precisely, tail losses. Banks do not need much capital to cover normal day-to-day losses. They do not lose much money under normal circumstances. What can kill them are extreme events like a systemic crisis or an idiosyncratic tail risk event. That is why banks need to keep substantial capital to cover these risks. However, do financial institutions have the ability to precisely estimate their tail risks? In the previous chapter, I argued that reliable tail risk quantification currently remains an unachievable task.

The Basel Accord has been conceptually correct: financial firms need to keep capital which is adequate to the risk that they are exposed to. Yet one thing had been forgotten: we cannot calculate risk precisely. The Basel capital ratio figures that the banks report and regulators prescribe and oversee are conditional on the ability to reliably measure risk that a bank is exposed to. The whole idea of capital adequacy is based on the assumption that dependable tools and models to measure risk exist. However, the experience of the last several years suggests that in many cases the risk has been severely miscalculated. Therefore, the whole Basel approach, which introduced risk-based capital measurements, appeared to be built on sand.

To calculate risk-based capital ratios we need to know the capital (the numerator) and risk-weighted assets at a high confidence level (the denominator). While we can be certain about the numerator (an amount of capital a firm holds), we are in the dark about what the right number in the denominator should be – the tail risk the firm is exposed to. Of course, financial institutions calculate some numbers using their internal models and regulatory risk-weighted asset formula, but they do not provide any assurance that what banks calculate is an accurate quantification of their risks. The recent crisis is clearly evidenced that the entire financial industry struggled to estimate its tail risk correctly. It is not surprising that many studies found no relationship between the level of risk-based capitalisation and propensity to failure. This is because the level of capitalisation that firms report is 'capitalisation on paper', calculated using internal models and regularity formulae.

This makes the whole capital ratio calculation meaningless. That is why until the problem of risk quantification remains unresolved I cannot take seriously any debates on how much risk-based capital should be enough. For example, I cannot take seriously debates on what should be the right figure of, say, the total capital ratio for banks. Is 8 per cent or 9 per cent or 10 per cent enough? If the number in the denominator is uncertain (and most probably wrong), does it really make sense to discuss one or two percentage points of the fraction?

I am convinced that while Basel risk-based approach has been conceptually correct, it has been put into implementation too early. The absence of reliable tools of the tail risk quantification makes the overall approach in the current situation meaningless: it sounds great, yet is currently impossible. In this sense, the Basel capital adequacy approach reminds me of a submarine sketched by Leonardo Da Vinci. He proposed the submarine concept, but sixteenth-century engineering was not able to build anything close to Leonardo's idea. It took about 400 years before this genius project became a reality.

At the current stage, the analytics can only deliver an acceptable accuracy of normal risk estimation (in the area close to an expected loss), but not for the tail of the loss distribution (with a confidence level of 99.5 per cent and higher). But the level of capital should be linked to the tail losses, which this capital supposes to cover. I think that regulators need to wait a little bit (maybe 25 years, maybe 50 years but hopefully not 400 years) before reliable tail risk quantification tools are introduced. At this point, regulators will have a chance to turn the capital-adequacy theoretical concept into the value-creating practical framework.

## 'NORTHERN WRECK' AND THE LIQUIDITY TRAP

The second 'silver bullet' that Basel III put in its magazine has been the new liquidity framework. Regulators introduced two liquidity ratios – liquidity coverage ratio and net stable funding ratio – that financial firms should report and comply with the binding minimum standards for funding liquidity. I am not going to provide the details of this framework, which can be found in the

Basel III full document as well as in other publications such as BIS (2010b) or Linklaters (2011). The introduction of new liquidity rules became a direct response to the liquidity crunch that the financial sector experienced during the global financial crisis. The Basel document clearly pointed out the reason:

> *During the early 'liquidity phase' of the financial crisis that began in 2007, many banks – despite adequate capital levels – still experienced difficulties because they did not manage their liquidity in a prudent manner. The crisis again drove home the importance of liquidity to the proper functioning of financial markets and the banking sector. Prior to the crisis, asset markets were buoyant and funding was readily available at low cost. The rapid reversal in market conditions illustrated how quickly liquidity can evaporate and that illiquidity can last for an extended period of time. The banking system came under severe stress, which necessitated central bank action to support both the functioning of money markets and, in some cases, individual institutions.*
>
> *(BIS 2010b: 1).*

While the aim of the framework is to ensure that financial firms will not become victims of the liquidity crisis, I doubt that the proposed measures will achieve the target. Moreover, I am going to say a very unpopular thing, especially today when after the liquidity crunch everybody is talking about the importance of liquidity for a firm's survival. My personal and possibly quite subjective opinion is that the importance of liquidity is highly exaggerated. Let me explain my view.

## Northern Rock and a recipe for disaster

I have spent a lot of time studying banking failures. Specifically, I wanted to find examples of when liquidity became the main factor that killed a bank. However, I did not find many cases. Yes, most of the failed financial firms experienced liquidity crises before their failure, but the liquidity crisis normally comes as a direct consequence of more fundamental problems that the firm was facing. In other words, the liquidity crisis usually plays the role of the 'final nail in the coffin' of a troubled financial firm. However, if we dig deeper into the situation, we can find that the fundamental cause of the failure was not insufficient liquidity per se, but other factors such as a flawed business model, reckless investment strategy, fatal mergers and acquisitions (M&A) error, etc.

You can argue that there were some classic cases when a liquidity crisis killed a bank. There were probably not so many in the last 20 years. One of the classic liquidity bank failures that people usually refer to is Northern Rock's failure. Let's have a closer look.

Northern Rock was a mid-sized British bank that specialised in the residential lending business. In the 2000s, the bank implemented a business model which used securitisation as its growth vehicle: the Rock borrowed funds in the UK and international money markets, investing in the UK mortgage market, and then securitised their mortgage assets and sold them on the capital markets.

In August 2007, conditions in the US sub-prime mortgage market deteriorated and Northern Rock faced difficulties with re-financing a large tranche of its mortgage securities as the market for new securitisation became, to a large extent, closed. On 9 August 2007, Northern Rock's board contacted the FSA and asked for liquidity support. When the news about the Rock's liquidity problem reached the market, it created a panic and the bank's customers rushed to the bank to withdraw their money. This turned into the first bank run on a British bank since 1866, when the Rock's customers queued in front of the bank's retail branches. After that, British journalists started to call the bank 'Northern Wreck'. The British government had to step in and provide financial support to the bank to prevent it from bankruptcy and in February 2008, the government took Northern Rock into a period of temporary public ownership.

At first glance, Northern Rock looks to be a victim of a liquidity crisis and market panic. However, if we step back several years before the crisis and look at the bank's financial strategy, the picture would be different. Figure 3.3 depicts Rock's asset trend for five years preceding the fiasco.

From the graph, one can see that Rock had been pursuing a very aggressive growth strategy. In the first half of 2007 (just before the collapse), Rock had grabbed about 20 per cent of the market share of new UK mortgage lending. Remember, judging by its size, Rock was a mid-sized bank in the UK market, but aggressively seized a huge portion of the market from its larger peers which it could not swallow. In the three and a half years since 2003, Rock had tripled its assets!

At the same time, Rock's risk-weighted assets grew marginally. In the period from 2001 until the first half of 2007, risk-weighted assets grew only by 28 per cent. In the period from 2003 until its collapse when Northern Rock tripled its assets, their risk-weighted assets decreased by 4 per cent! In other words, Rock's management believed that all assets that they acquired in the rush period of 2003–7 were risk-free!

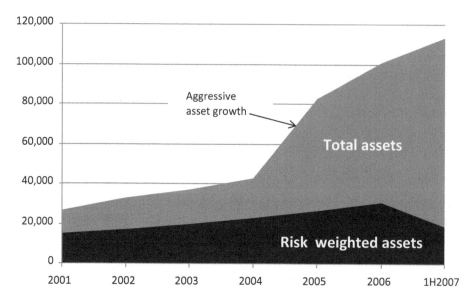

**Figure 3.3**     **Northern Rock's total assets and risk-weighted assets (£ m)**
*Source*: Author's own figure using data from the company's annual and interim
reports, Bloomberg.

One surprising thing: in the first half of 2007, the bank reported a substantial
decrease in their risk-weighted assets. Do you have any idea why Rock's risk
suddenly dropped just before the collapse? The reason was really unbelievable –
in the first half of 2007, the British regulators approved Northern Rock's
adaptation of Basel II and, according to Rock's internal models, actual risk
that the banks were exposed to appeared to be almost 50 per cent lower than
the bank previously reported! In their 1H2007 interim report Northern Rock
commented:

> *On 29 June 2007, we received notification of approval by the FSA of
> our Basel II waiver application. The implementation of Basel II results
> in our Pillar I risk-weighted assets at 30 June 2007 falling from around
> £33.9 billion under Basel I to £18.9 billion under Basel II, a reduction
> of some 44 per cent.*
>
> *(Northern Rock 2007: 14)*

Figure 3.4 displays the ratio of risk-weighted assets to total assets. It
demonstrates how Rock estimated its risk for each pound of assets. From
2004 to the moment when the bank collapsed, according to Rock's reports the
estimated riskiness of their assets reduced by 70 per cent! That was the period

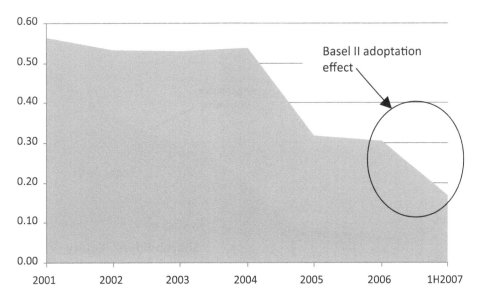

**Figure 3.4    Northern Rock's ratio of risk-weighted assets to total assets**
*Source*: Author's own figure using data from the company's annual and interim reports.

of Rock's most aggressive penetration into the UK mortgage market (at that period, Rock actively provided mortgages with 100 per cent loan-to-value and above), which ended in disaster.

Now let's look at the other side of Rock's balance sheet. In the five and a half years preceding the crash, Northern Rock increased its debt from £8.9 billion to £93 billion or 10.5 times! It sounds like madness: Rock piled up its debt at the pace of 50 per cent compound annual growth rate. At the same time, shareholders' equity grew modestly and increased from £1.1 billion to £1.6 billion (Figure 3.5).

If we calculate Rock's asset to shareholders equity ratio change for the period 2001–7 and compare it with those of British high street banks, we can see that Rock had been an aggressive outlier (Figure 3.6). While shareholders' equity as a fraction of total assets had reduced dramatically in three years before the crash, Northern Rock remained a 'well-capitalised' bank on paper.

On 25 July 2007, less than three months before the failure, Rock's management told their investors about a surplus of capital and planned to increase dividends:

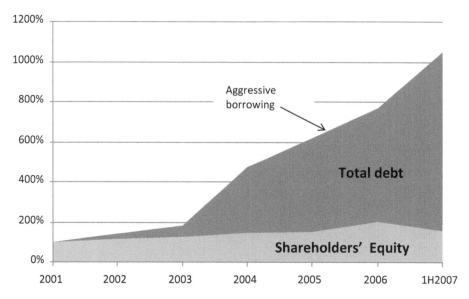

**Figure 3.5    Northern Rock's total debt and shareholders' equity growth (2001=100 per cent)**

*Source*: Author's own figure using data from Company's annual and interim reports.

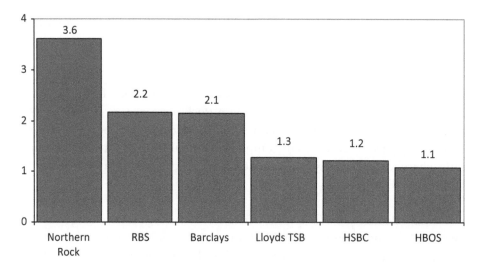

**Figure 3.6    Change in assets to shareholders' equity ratio (times) in the period 2001–7**

*Source*: Author's own figure using data from banks' annual reports.

*The introduction of Basel II, together with the planned disposal of
capital inefficient assets and continued capital management such
as the Whinstone programme results in an anticipated regulatory
capital surplus over the next 3 to 4 years. This surplus will enable the
reduction of previously planned subordinated debt issues and permit
capital repatriation of up to £300 to £400 million over this period ...
The introduction of Basel II, which requires less capital to support new
lending, also enables a review of the Company's dividend policy. It is
proposed that for 2007 and beyond, dividends will be maintained at a
payout ratio of around 50 per cent.*

Now when we look closely at how Northern Rock was running its business, we
can ask the question: 'Was it really the liquidity crisis that was responsible for
Northern Rock's fiasco?' Is it reasonable to blame liquidity in Rock's failure?
What Rock created in 2003–7 was a recipe for disaster. In the several years
preceding the crash, Northern Rock had continuously built the 'time bomb'
waiting for the right moment to explode.

## Liquidity crisis 'victims'

Would extra liquidity (e.g. 30-day liquidity coverage as Basel III requires) save
Rock? No, it would only prolong its agony for another 30 days! With its flawed
business model, the reckless financial strategy and terrible risk miscalculation,
Northern Rock was doomed to fail well before its liquidity crisis developed.
However, the liquidity crisis played the role of a final nail in the coffin of Rock's
flawed business. Therefore, the 'classic' liquidity-driven failure, after a close
examination, appears to be a business strategy failure. Other troublemakers
who also claimed to be victims of a liquidity crisis, such as AIG, Wachovia
and Landsbanki, did not fail because of the force of the liquidity crisis per se,
but because of their own reckless behaviour or strategic mistakes. Wachovia
experienced a silent bank run and lost $5 billion in deposits in just one day
(more than 1 per cent of the bank's $448 billion total deposits!) (Rothacker
2008). This is because depositors realised that the bank's mortgage business
model was flawed.

If liquidity rarely becomes the fundamental driver of banks' failure, then
why do we keep hearing so many 'horror stories' on how liquidity crises killed
many solid firms? I can see a psychological element here. It is much easier
for a top executive of a failed financial institution to explain the failure with
a liquidity problem. It is not so shameful to be a victim of a liquidity crisis.
A liquidity problem is normally associated with external hostility rather than

with internal stupidity. So it is an indirect way of blaming somebody else for a firm's failure. Indeed, the logic of 'a captain of sunk ship' here is straightforward and implicitly goes along the lines of something like this: 'While I continued to run the solvent firm, the market participants unexpectedly and unreasonably cut liquidity for us (or ran on the bank). They, not me, need to take full responsibility for ruining our solid business.'

### Greek sovereign bonds

One more comment about new liquidity rules. Regulators require banks to hold a stock of high-quality liquid assets to cover the total net cash outflows over a 30-day period under the regulatory prescribed stress scenario. We need to keep in mind that liquidity of assets is not a fixed characteristic and depends on market perceptions and market participants' behaviour. Liquidity is subject to huge variation during a crisis. At any point in time, liquid assets can become illiquid and 'sticky' deposits can be rendered 'non-sticky'.

Consider a recent example with the Euro crisis. How did the crisis affect the liquidity of the most liquid instruments such as sovereign bonds? For example, how did the liquidity of Greek sovereign bonds change? Greek sovereign bonds used to be an instrument that could comply with the regulatory definition of a 'high-quality liquid asset' for Greece. In the period of global financial crisis of 2008–9, while the trading volume reduced in 2008, sovereign bonds remained the most liquid financial instrument in the Greek market. By November 2009, the trading volume reached the pre-crisis level (approximately €50 billion in a month), which indicates that the market did not notice that the sovereign crisis was already knocking on the door.

When the Greek crisis began, the monthly trading volume of sovereign bonds reduced immediately and between March and May 2010 it dropped like a stone – from €34 billion to €1.3 billion or more than 25 times (Figure 3.7). In 2011, Greek sovereign bonds became fully illiquid, when the daily trading volume dropped to €1 million in September and zero in October!

The lesson of the Greek crisis is obvious. We don't know what the future liquidity of assets will be. Past and current high liquidity of a particular asset class may not hold in the future. I am afraid that even regulators cannot predict how liquidity can change in the future. When regulators mandate financial institutions to warehouse certain financial instruments for liquidity purposes, they can potentially create a new systemic risk. Consider a situation when one day the banking system becomes overloaded with certain assets,

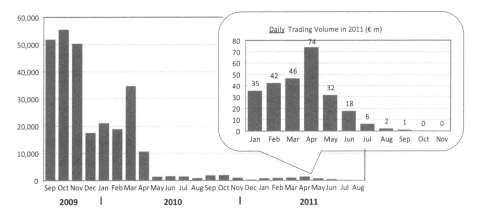

**Figure 3.7    2009–11 monthly trading volume of Greek sovereign bonds and the daily average trading volume for 2011 (€ m)**

*Source*: Author's own figure using data from Bank of Greece.

which suddenly become illiquid. It might be the perfect scenario for the next systemic crisis.

## LIQUIDITY AND THE 'WOLF PACK' SYNDROME

The new liquidity framework addresses the individual liquidity of financial firms prescribing how much liquidity they should maintain. While individual liquidity is important, as I described before, it rarely becomes the fundamental cause of banking failure. Usually, banks fail due to other reasons such as a reckless business strategy, while liquidity crisis plays the role of the final nail in the coffin of the failing financial firm.

While focusing on individual liquidity, the Basel III framework does not pay attention to another crucial aspect: the systemic liquidity crisis. A systemic liquidity crunch has a different nature from that of an individual liquidity crisis. It is driven not by financial but by behavioural factors. This phenomenon is well known and called the 'wolf pack' syndrome when individual banks become part of a system and follow the group physiology. Kenichi Ohmae describes the mechanism:

> *While the wolves are good at attacking the victim as a team, they have a tendency to attack the weakest of the cohort should extreme hunger prevail. The banking crisis is like this metaphor. If Lehman goes, people look at the 'next' and all of a sudden, the victim is the weakest of the*

*bunch. When Lehman goes, it is Washington Mutual, and the next is Wachovia. When Wachovia merges with Citicorp, then people look for another victim, and could point to National City. This is an endless process and continues until the last wolf no longer finds anybody to point its finger.*

*(Ohmae 2008)*

When panic prevails in the banking society, liquidity of individual banks does not really help to remedy the situation. A bank which becomes a target of the 'wolf pack' attack becomes isolated from the system, other banks cut their liquidity facilities and the bank will almost inevitably die. Once it fails, this accelerates the panic reaction of the rest of the banking society even more and the next bank becomes a new target.

The individual liquidity could not stop the process. So far, the financial system found only one effective medicine against the 'wolf pack' syndrome.

The Central Bank has to step in, provide necessary liquidity and guarantees and restore the order. During the last global financial crisis, this medicine helped to beat the 'wolf pack' syndrome and prevent the financial system from complete collapse. In the midst of global financial crisis, several lenders of last resort like the US Federal Reserve, the European Central Bank, the Bank of England and other central banks had to step in and inject liquidity of $2.5 trillion into the financial system in the last quarter of 2008 alone!

To conclude, while a firm's individual liquidity remains an essential factor of sustainability, it plays a secondary importance role as a fundamental factor of the bank's failure. Banks fail due to other fundamental reasons (mainly business- strategy-related) passing through the liquidity crisis in its dying agony. Therefore, the additional individual liquidity proposed by regulators cannot substantially change the survival ability of a firm. At the same time, individual liquidity cannot prevent a liquidity crisis of a systemic nature, which is driven by panic and total loss of confidence. This situation is unlikely to be solved without active intervention from Central Banks. Do regulators seriously like the idea of mandating financial institutions to sit on $2.5 trillion of liquidity just in case the 'wolf pack' syndrome hits the industry next time?

## ARMY TANK INSTEAD OF A CAR

When proposing the Basel III framework, regulators directly addressed the challenges which the financial industry faced during the global financial crisis when the banks' capital was depleted and liquidity dried up. Regulators formulated three 'postulates': the banking system needs higher risk-weighted capitalisation, more liquidity and lower financial leverage. I really doubt that the first two 'postulates' reflect the reality which I explained in the sections above. So far, due to the absence of reliable risk measurement tools, risk-weighted capitalisation remains subject to a larger calculation error. As a result, capitalisation numbers that banks report show no relationship with their propensity to survive a financial meltdown. Individual liquidity that regulators address in their second 'postulate' does not seem to be a fundamental factor of many banking failures.

Sorry for the brutal analogy, but people with AIDS often die from pneumonia, an infection that occurs due to very compromised immune systems. In the same way, financial firms, suffering from fundamental solvency problems, often face the 'deadly infection' of a liquidity crisis at some point, which leads to their collapse. Yet individual liquidity per se rarely (almost never) kills financial firms with sound business models and strong risk management cultures. At the same time, individual liquidity cannot prevent the systemic liquidity crunches which are often caused by group 'wolf pack' behaviour and are not strictly speaking the crisis of cash availability, but crisis of confidence.

### Landsbanki

The story of Landsbanki, the bank I have mentioned before, is particularly interesting in the light of two 'postulates'. Landsbanki was the largest Icelandic bank, and just eight months before its failure, the bank enjoyed a solid capital position: a total capital ratio of 11.7 per cent and a Tier 1 ratio of 10.1 per cent. This made Landsbanki the best-capitalised bank among its European peers! Moreover, Landsbanki had no exposure to the 'trouble-making' assets like US sub-prime mortgages, corporate synthetic CDOs, ABSs, SIVs, conduits, liquidity lines or monolines and any other complex, high-risk, structured vehicles. The bank also maintained a very prudent liquidity position. The bank's 2007 annual report sheds light on the bank's liquidity approach:

> *The bank's liquidity position should cover a situation where access to capital market funding is closed for up to 12 months and at the same time maintain a stable business volume. The bank comfortably meets*

*this target, as was recently confirmed by the stringent stress tests*
*applied by regulators and rating agencies.*

*(Landsbanki 2007: 10)*

If I can summarise Landsbanki's financial position before the crisis hit the industry, this bank could be the model for all European banks and would fully satisfy the Basel III capital and liquidity requirements. I was not surprised that Landsbanki's top management remained optimistic regarding the bank's future:

*With its strong liquidity and equity position and light repayment*
*profile of debt maturing in 2008, together with sound asset quality and*
*no exposure to US subprime, structured credit exposure or monolines,*
*Landsbanki is in an enviable financial position to navigate the uncharted*
*waters of world financial markets at present.*

*(Landsbanki 2007:11)*

Yet in spite of top management optimism and fully Basel-compliant conservative capital and liquidity positions, when the global financial crisis struck, Landsbanki became one of the first victims of the crisis. The bank failed due to its flawed business model. Landsbanki faced a bank run and was nationalised by the Icelandic Government in October 2008.

## 'White flag' of regulators

I cannot say so much about the third 'postulate' – the mandated financial leverage. By introducing the non-risk-adjusted leverage ratio, new regulations made a U-turn. It brings us back to the pre-Basel era, to the time when my finance professor criticised the non-risk-adjusted leverage for not differentiating asset risk. However, I fully understand why regulators took this step. It was the 'white flag' of surrender! By introducing the simple leverage ratio, regulators implicitly say to the financial community: 'We cannot trust your quantitative risk tools any more. Basel II risk quantification approach failed in the crisis and cannot be reliable going forward. Therefore, we have to introduce a simple safeguard against model risk.'

Regulators hope that the three 'silver bullets' of Basel III can effectively help to avoid a repetition of the financial disaster that happened in 2008–9. Unfortunately, these 'silver bullets' missed the target – they do not address the fundamental causes of the systemic crisis. The lack of capital and liquidity in the financial sector was a consequence of the crisis but not its cause. I believe that regulators failed to understand the main cause of the crisis, and therefore prescribed the wrong medicine.

## We do not need army tanks

The fundamental cause of the global financial crisis has not been the insufficiency of capital or liquidity per se but a combination of two reasons:

- accumulation of extreme systemic risk in the financial sector during the benign phase of the economic cycle;

- inability to mitigate its impact when this systemic risk event struck.

In other words, financial institutions kept on piling up extreme risk in the pre-crisis period, often without understanding how much risk they were exposed to. Many banks were sitting on a barrel of smoking gun powder and enjoyed the financial bonanza. But suddenly, the gun powder exploded and it appeared that most banks were ill-prepared to deal with this challenge and had no credible crisis-mitigating plans. Shock and panic resulted in the liquidity crunch and subsequent massive losses, which eroded the banks' capital. At this stage, many financial institutions found themselves in a terrible situation: suddenly, liquidity had gone and the capital was depleted.

The financial sector lost its capital because of huge losses and write-downs. IMF estimates crisis-related total bank write-downs and loan provisions for the 2007–10 period to be $2.2 trillion (IMF 2010b). Many financial institutions had no choice: either to default or to ask for the government bailout. The meltdown path of the financial sector is presented in Figure 3.8.

As you can see, the shortage of liquidity and capital was a consequence of the crisis, but not its cause. The global financial crisis was a crisis of risk management. Financial institutions need solutions to manage extreme risks efficiently and to prevent unexpected large and catastrophic losses rather than just building up capital and liquidity.

We need to clearly understand why banks need the capital. Capital is just a financial buffer, a loss absorption mechanism. It is like the airbag of a car. However, the airbag does not prevent the car from crashing.

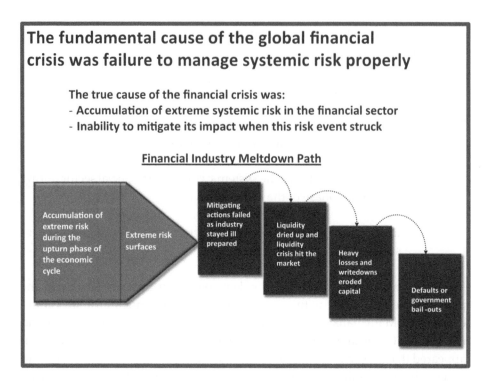

**Figure 3.8**   Global financial crisis causes and the financial industry
meltdown path

Capital per se does not influence the amount of losses and write-downs, which put the financial industry on its knees during the last financial crisis. Moreover, the perception that the firm is highly capitalised might incentivise managers to take more risk. The main question that regulators should ask: how did it become possible that the banking industry lost $2.2 trillion? Instead, regulators propose to keep more capital and liquidity.

It is clear to me that the regulators completely missed the point. Why did they do that? I understand that regulators had substantial political pressure and needed to make a decision quickly. I have my explanation as to why they missed the point. I will demonstrate this using an analogy.

Suppose you are the minister of transport, responsible for the creation of an effective transport system. Suddenly, you notice that there are many problems with the traffic, resulting in an unacceptably high level of severe accidents and casualties on the roads. You need to take particular actions to change the situation and you need a fast solution. What can you do? You call a meeting with various advisors and explain the situation to them: 'What we have is an unacceptable level of casualties on the roads. People are losing their lives. We need a solution.' One of the smartest advisors says: 'If there are too many accidents and many people have lost their lives on the roads, to change this trend we need safer vehicles.' And the discussion turns to the area of how safe should the vehicles be.

So what is the safest vehicle in the world? Yes, you guessed it. An army tank. That's the solution! As a minister of transport, you initiate a new law that from 2019, all car owners must upgrade their cars to army tanks. Car owners start screaming, but you reply to critics: 'Yes we know this is an expensive solution, possibly your driving experience would not be so enjoyable any more, but look on the bright side. We expect that with people driving army tanks there will be fewer casualties and you and your passengers will be safe'. That is exactly what the regulators proposed under Basel III – to upgrade the 'cars' to 'army tanks'.

This radical solution, however, ignores the deeper analysis of why roads have suddenly become so unsafe and begs the question whether it is actually the safety of the cars themselves that is the problem. The minister of transport should have asked his advisors the following question: 'Why do we have so many tragic road accidents?' Maybe the reason is actually that the drivers have poor driving skills, they have poor discipline, they have a drink-and-drive problem or they are not able to manage risk on the road properly. Probably, all of these cause massive levels of accidents. The solution should be, in parallel with the improvement of car safety, to restore road discipline, educate drivers and help them to manage their risk properly. Without fixing these fundamental causes, even driving army tanks would not guarantee safeness. Do you think that an unskilled and drunk driver can be less dangerous if he drives an army tank rather than a car?

Basel III proposes to drive 'army tanks' for the sake of safety in the form of mandating to massively increase capitalisation and liquidity of financial institutions.

Yet don't forget that banks' capital and liquidity represent nothing more than 'an airbag' and 'seat belts' for the banking industry's passengers. It is just an airbag which helps soften the impact. Banks' capitalisation answers the question of who is responsible for taking future losses: shareholders or the taxpayers and creditors but will not influence the ability to minimise business losses.

If regulators expect that the financial sector will lose $2.2 trillion again when the next crisis hits the industry, then they are possibly right to request a larger 'airbag'. But the large 'airbag' comes at substantial costs. It will result, among other downsides, in limiting banks' ability to provide funds to support economic growth and in the reduction of the banking sector's competitiveness on the global landscape.

At the same time, regulatory initiatives do not address the central problem of the financial industry – the efficiency of tail risk management, which directly influences the amount of write-downs and losses. The 2008–9 crisis demonstrated that the financial sector is not good at dealing with extreme risks that arise in a perfect financial storm. Without solving the problem of efficiency of risk management, the financial industry will certainly repeat the painful experience of the recent financial crisis over and over again.

We do not need army tanks! We need skilful and disciplined drivers who manage road risks properly and drive their cars responsibly and safely.

# PART II

# The Heads or Tails Principle and AAA Approach

# 4

# Heads or Tails: Building a 'Firewall' Against Extreme Risk

The global financial crisis of 2008–9 demonstrated that the majority of financial institutions were not able to proactively recognise and effectively manage extreme risks. The financial industry paid a very high price for its poor risk management skills: $2.2 trillion of direct losses and write-downs. Plus many banks and financial firms either defaulted or were bailed out by their governments. Yet new regulation does not address the issue directly, focusing on capital adequacy, liquidity and financial leverage. No constructive action plan to build the proper risk management framework for extreme risk events has been proposed, leaving the industry vulnerable to the next systemic crisis.

It is clear that an economic crisis is not something exceptional but rather a regular event. Carmen Reinhart and Kenneth Rogoff demonstrated in their publication *This Time Is Different: Eight Centuries of Financial Folly* that in the last eight centuries, crises hit economies regularly. The banking industry has always been prone to a crisis. Reinhart and Rogoff calculated that, for example, for Europe, the percentage of years of banking crisis since 1800 was 6.3 per cent, while for North America it was 11.2 per cent (Reinhart and Rogoff 2009: 154). The history of 800 years shows that the world economy is exposed to economic cycles which are half a decade long from peak to peak. There are no grounds to think that any regulation can eliminate cyclicality. Economic cycles with their downturns are unpleasant and often dramatic but they are natural and necessary for 'cleaning' market inefficiencies and misbalances. The conclusion from the research is apparent: the crises will not leave us alone and we need to learn how to live with this phenomenon and reduce the impact of systemic and idiosyncratic extreme events on the financial sector going forward.

The conventional risk management approach does not treat tail risk separately from normal risk. In the financial institutions, normally you will not find tail risk management desks or extreme risk event management committees, for instance. The generally accepted approach is that everything that constitutes the everyday risk management routine should be effective for tail risk as well. Practical experience, however, does not support this approach. The global financial crisis clearly demonstrated that the everyday risk management routine could be efficient for managing 'normal' risks, yet failed to provide an effective response when the extreme risk event struck. Teams of risk specialists, who worked very successfully in managing everyday risks in banks, suddenly lost control over the situation and appeared to be ill-prepared to deal with the challenges of the systemic crisis.

This was another painful lesson of the recent financial crisis: many elements of a contemporary risk management framework, including highly qualified teams of risk specialists with Masters and PhDs, failed the test on management of extreme risk events. Risk models looked reliable enough in estimating the risk parameters during normal times, but failed to provide the correct risk assessment for the crisis period. I have already explained in detail why risk models could not cope with the challenges of tail risk.

The same story happened to almost all key components of the risk management infrastructure. Risk engines and risk management information struggled to provide the necessary information for timely decision-making. There have already been classic cases of some banks spending days and weeks trying to figure out their exposure to Lehman Brothers and Madoff Investment Securities after their collapses. An array of standard mitigating actions successfully used to reduce risk in the everyday practice, suddenly became ineffective or unavailable during the financial stress. Overall, the decision-making process and corporate governance, which help to steer an organisation smoothly during good times, suddenly appeared too bureaucratic, too slow and too inflexible to cope with the tail risk challenges.

Why did it all happen? I am convinced that the problem resides in the special nature of extreme risks that I am going to discuss in the next section.

## Extreme Risk and the Modern Risk Management Framework

### THE FOUR TRAITS OF EXTREME RISK

The very first and superficial difference between extreme risk and normal risk comes from their definitions. Extreme risk events are low likelihood and very-high-severity events, while normal risk events show high probability and low or moderate severity. However, it is important to realise that extreme risk differs from normal risk not only quantitatively (e.g. the probabilities of default and market volatility greatly increase during the downturn period) but also qualitatively, which is even more important to consider.

Among other things, I would like to highlight four specific traits of extreme risk. They create a basis for extreme risk events (Figure 4.1).

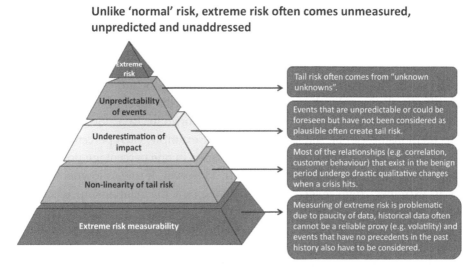

**Figure 4.1     Specific traits of extreme risk**

The fundamental trait of extreme risk is its problematic measurability. I have already described the modelling challenges for extreme risk in detail earlier in this book. The challenge stems from the paucity of data that can be used for modelling tail risk. This is not a technical issue, but a conceptual problem. By definition, we will never be able to collect enough historical data for events with very low probabilities. Available historical data often cannot be a reliable proxy (e.g. asset prices, volatility). Moreover, to measure extreme risk reliably, we need to take into account events that have no precedents in history. Obviously, there is no historic data existing for these events. Nevertheless, we cannot discard events without past historical precedents. Unlike normal risk events with their recurring nature, extreme risk is often driven by events that stand out of the recurring cycle.

This is true not just for unprecedented natural catastrophes (e.g. major earthquakes) or technogenic disasters (e.g. The Deepwater Horizon oil spill). Take interest rates. Who would have expected at the beginning of 2008 that in one year's time, the Bank of England would drop the interest rate to as low as 0.5 per cent? Between the formation of the Bank of England in 1694 and January 2009 (its entire 315-year history), the lowest interest rate has been 2 per cent (see Figure 4.2)!

The second trait of extreme risk reflects its non-linearity. The overall economic environment changes when the extreme risk events occur. Most of the relationships that exist in the benign period, and are successfully exploited in risk management practice, undergo many drastic changes when a crisis emerges (e.g. default correlation, liquidity of different financial instruments, customer behaviour). The changes under stress happen abruptly and often we can see a 'cliff effect'. Consider the relationship between the level of unemployment and the level of delinquency in a mortgage portfolio. In a normal situation this relationship can be stable and linear. For example, each percentage point increase/decrease of unemployment rate results in one percentage point of the respective change of the delinquency rate. However, if unemployment grows to an extremely high level, at a particular point the relationship reaches a 'cliff': the linearity suddenly disappears and an additional small increase of unemployment results in skyrocketing of the delinquency rate. Unfortunately, in most cases, we have no reliable ways to predict how exactly relationships will change and where there will be 'cliffs' when an extreme event unfolds.

Quite often the impact of extreme events is substantially underestimated. In this sense, many extreme events have been hand-made. Because people perceived the impact of the event as low, they stayed unprepared, and no risk management actions can prevent the risk event from unfolding in its full swing. This is the third trait of extreme risk.

Take UBS and the unprecedented losses from their CDO portfolio. As we now know from the UBS post-mortem investigation, the 2007 losses related to the US residential mortgage market amounted to $18.7 billion and further write-downs of approximately $19 billion on US real estate and related structured credit positions in the first quarter 2008 (UBS 2008: 7).

How was it possible that the bank lost such an astonishing amount? The answer: massive underestimation of the potential impact of adverse market movements. Most of UBS' losses were concentrated in their Super Seniors positions, which were supposed to be a very low risk exposure. UBS hedged

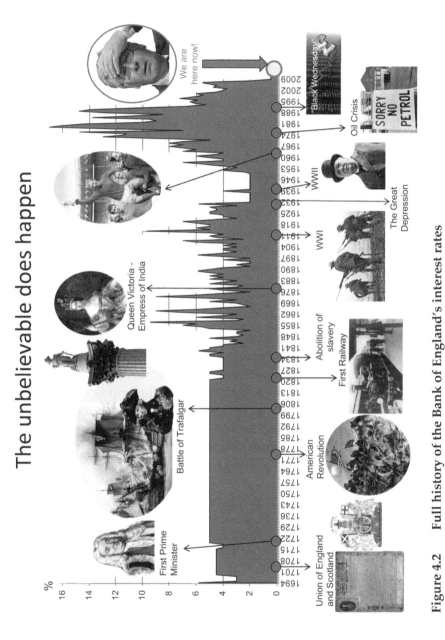

**Figure 4.2  Full history of the Bank of England's interest rates**

*Source:* Author's own figure using data from Bank of England

the largest portion of its Super Seniors through the purchase of protection on a proportion of the nominal position. Unfortunately, UBS severely underestimated the default risk of Super Seniors. As a result, the bank capped its hedging at 2–4 per cent of the first losses, leaving the rest of the exposure unhedged. The bank explains: 'This level of hedging was based on statistical analyses of historical price movements that indicated that such protection was sufficient to protect UBS from any losses on the position' (UBS 2008: 14).

Now we know that UBS severely underestimated the potential impact of price movements, but before the sub-prime mortgage crisis, the bank believed that their hedging strategy was conservative. Because the exposure to Super Senior tranches of CDOs was perceived as very safe, UBS did not take any risk-mitigating actions but, on the contrary, quickly built up its Super Senior portfolio, which grew from low levels in February 2006 to approximately $50 billion by September 2007. When the US market mortgage started to collapse in the last quarter of 2007, the thin protection that UBS had on its Super Senior tranches was easily exhausted and the bank faced huge write-downs in the portfolio that was supposed to be the most secure one. As a result, losses on the Super Senior positions contributed approximately three-quarters of the CDO desk's total losses (or 50 per cent of UBS's overall losses) as at 31 December 2007.

And finally, the fourth trait is that many extreme risk events stem from what is often called 'unknown unknowns'. The lesson that extreme events teach us is that there are some drivers and relationships that we do not know. Hence, we cannot predict many extreme events even with the help of sophisticated quantitative methods that we apply. Remember my story about the modelling of hands-free potato sorting when the law of gravity is missing from the model. The events stemmed from the 'unknown unknowns' are usually particularly devastating as they come out of the blue.

Numerous examples of extreme events which can be categorised as 'unknown unknowns' shaped the landscape of the business and affected not only separate companies and industries, but sometimes even entire economies of countries and regions.

Who expected that the volcanic eruption in Iceland would have such a devastating impact on European air travel? Literally, this event unfolded out of the blue sky in April 2010, when the ash cloud from the Icelandic volcano Eyjafjallajökull spread over Europe, leading to an unprecedented air space closure. According to the International Air Transport Association, the 'ash cloud crisis' hit almost a third of global flights and it was estimated that global airlines lost $1.7 billion in missed revenues (BBC 2010). European airlines such as Air France were severely affected in particular. Air France's shares lost 30 per cent of their value following the volcano eruption!

Who expected that a nuclear disaster would happen in Japan, a country which has been perceived as the perfect example of one capable of dealing with natural catastrophes? The combination of the earthquake and tsunami triggered the Fukushima nuclear accident, an extreme event with an unexpected level of severity, which nobody could predict.

Who could predict the Arab spring of 2011 when the protests and uprisings spread like wildfire across several countries in North Africa and resulted in changes of political regimes in these countries? For all gurus in geopolitics and even for Pan-Arabic experts and politicians, the phenomenon of the Arab spring was a complete surprise. This event, which surfaced unexpectedly, has had a huge political, social and economic impact (including a complete change of political regimes in countries like Egypt, Libya, Yemen and Tunisia). The Arab spring affected the lives of more than 150 million of people in the entire region.

## EXTREME RISK AND CONTEMPORARY RISK MANAGEMENT

The four traits of extreme risk, described above, must be taken into consideration when we build a framework for tail risk management. To what extent does the contemporary risk management framework implemented in the financial sector address these traits? Unfortunately, the current risk practice (including Basel III) does not really take into account the special nature of extreme risks (Figure 4.3). I have already described deficiencies of risk models used for risk assessment in the financial sector and why they fail to reliably measure tail risk.

The problem of non-linearity of extreme shocks and the 'cliff effect' detection does not currently have any plausible solution. The systematic underestimation of the impact of extreme events becomes one of the most serious drawbacks of current risk management practice. Risk managers try to stretch the quantitative methods, which perform satisfactorily for normal risk assessment, to the tail risk area. However, when for extreme risk events historical data is scarce, key risk factors are often unknown, and quantification is driven to a large extent by assumptions, the quantitative tools not only fail to calculate risk correctly, but normally all such calculations suffer from material underestimation of risk. The absence of a clear concept of how business and risk should deal with extreme events driven by 'unknown unknowns' complements the overall picture of weaknesses of the contemporary risk management framework.

The current risk management practice (Basel based) targets risks that are measurable, predictable and recurring, having known nature and drivers.

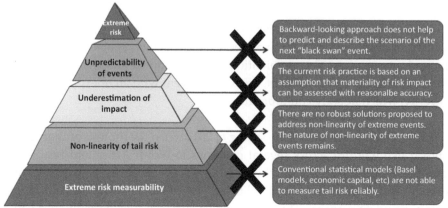

Figure 4.3     Specific traits of extreme risk vs. the current risk management practice

To conclude, I am afraid that I have bad news for you. The modern risk management approach, built around the Basel principles, does not really take into account the most important traits of extreme risk. The current risk management practice implicitly treats risk as a phenomenon which is measurable, predictable, recurring, and having a known nature and drivers. Yet extreme risk does not fit this description of risk. It has very different characteristics. At least at the current stage of development of risk management science and technique, extreme risk represents an 'unfamiliar creature' for us. It often comes unmeasured, unpredicted and unaddressed.

## The 'Heads or Tails' Dilemma

The Basel approach falls short of addressing the challenges of extreme risks. In the previous chapters, I shared my critical view on many aspects of the Basel framework and the way that this framework had been implemented. It is time to explain how I see the role of the Basel regulations going forward.

Since in this book I have focused on the weaknesses of the Basel regulation, you might get the impression that I view the Basel concept as absolutely useless or even harmful for the financial sector. This is not true. I have already mentioned that, from my perspective, the Basel approach in its capital adequacy idea is conceptually right. It makes a lot of sense to link the level of a bank's capital with the risk that the bank is exposed to. However, the absence of reliable methods of quantification of tail risk undermines the integrity of the framework when we put it into practical implementation. It still has a long way to go until we can create robust methods of extreme risk quantification and can see the real value of the capital adequacy concept.

On the other hand, in spite of all my scepticism I can also see the benefits of the Basel framework. Firstly, Basel opened up the risk quantification era and, as a result, financial institutions have a risk infrastructure and tools to assess their risk. It is true that we struggle to estimate and manage tail risk, but the industry has created an acceptable quality risk framework for managing 'normal' risk. In fact, today, most global and large financial institutions in Europe, North America and other countries which adopted and implemented the Basel accord, have decent solutions, tools and processes to measure and manage their day-to-day risks.

Secondly, the implementation of the Basel principles of capital adequacy makes me hopeful that in the future we will develop robust methods and tools to estimate and manage extreme risks. To achieve this goal, the financial industry needs substantial financial and intellectual resources and to create the effective risk analytics, risk infrastructure and reporting. The adaptation of the Basel rules has created a foundation for the future successful achievement of this goal. Before attempting to run, a baby needs to learn how to walk. Before solving the most complex risk problem – the effective management of extreme risks – we need to learn how to measure and manage normal risks. And in this sense, the Basel framework plays a positive role and becomes a necessary condition for successful tail risk management. Never before did the financial industry have such a concentration of brains, technical and material resources as it has in the Basel era.

Yet the problem with effective risk management of extreme risks remains unsolved. The special nature of the extreme risk dictates the inevitable next step towards the solution: extreme risk should be treated separately from the everyday 'normal' risks. Only if we separate extreme risk from normal risk and create a special framework to deal with tail risk can we expect a breakthrough in the overall efficiency in the extreme risk mitigation.

Today, the conventional risk management approach does not treat tail risk separately from everyday risks. The approach is based on the 'one size fits all' assumption. For some reason, the very different nature of extreme and normal risks has been ignored and no separation of risk has been applied. The global financial crisis clearly demonstrated that the conventional risk management routine (models, risk reporting and management information, governance) could be efficient for managing 'normal' risks, yet fail to provide an effective response when an extreme risk event unfolds. It would be nice to use a 'one size fits all' approach, but the special nature of extreme risks dictates the separation of the frameworks.

I am convinced that we need to introduce what I call the 'Heads or Tails' principle.

It articulates the two-step approach (Figure 4.4):

1.  Normal risk (everyday risk) should be managed via an array of traditional models, tools and methods including those that stemmed from the Basel approach (The Heads). Most financial institutions already have pretty good frameworks in place for dealing with 'Heads'.

2.  Tail risk requires the special risk architecture which should be created in addition to the traditional one (The Tails). This architecture should reflect special traits of extreme risk that I discussed above (unmeasured, unpredicted, often unaddressed and emerged from 'unknown unknowns').

The 'Heads or Tails' principle does not reject the risk management framework that banks have already created as a part of its Basel implementation. The approach is purely additive. The traditional framework should stay as it is and

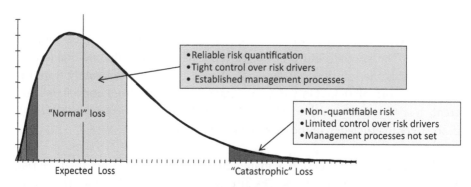

Figure 4.4    The 'heads' or 'tails' dilemma

continue addressing normal risk. One change, however, should be made to the traditional risk management framework (Heads): we should be honest and stop fooling ourselves that under this framework we can manage tail risk. The illusion that the Basel framework is able to deal with extreme risks effectively should disappear.

The bespoke architecture for 'Tails' should not be limited to 'hard' elements of risk management – development and implementation of analytical tools and risk reporting systems focusing on extreme risk measuring and reporting (e.g. tail risk modelling). This framework should include the hierarchy of 'soft' risk management elements – people, governance, management processes, information flows and communications which are built specifically to address challenges of extreme risks.

I can clarify the 'Heads or Tails' approach for managing risk using the analogy from different areas. This approach has already been implemented in some areas of our life and we use it often. Consider the healthcare service. In the UK (I assume that in many other countries the approach is pretty similar), the National Health Service (NHS) provides its service via a two-level framework. The first level includes general practitioners (GPs) and walk-in centres. They provide day-to-day primary healthcare to their patients and deal with most regular and non-serious illnesses such as colds, fevers, seasonal flu, stomach aches, minor infections, minor injuries, cuts, burns, strains, etc. The second level includes hospitals which provide specialist services for patients with more serious and life-threatening illnesses. Hospital service covers all accidents via the emergency department, intensive care, surgery department, etc. While both NHS levels work in parallel to each other, they clearly divide their responsibilities. The GP will immediately send a patient with a high risk of a heart attack to a hospital's cardiology department. At the same time, hospitals will not provide healthcare services to a patient with a common non life threatening cold.

Financial institutions have to deal with different types of risk in a similar way to the NHS, which deals with different illnesses. A vast majority of risks can be categorised as minor, regular and day-to-day. To address these risks, banks need (and most of them already build) a full scale 'GP level' risk management framework. On the other hand, there are some extreme risks, similar to life-threatening illnesses. To deal with them, financial institutions have to build an extreme-risk-management framework, like the NHS hospital service. This framework should include systems, tools, procedures, governance structure and all that is necessary to deal with extreme risk challenges efficiently and provide 'intensive care service' if needed. If we can build these two levels of risk management and organise their seamless work, it will resolve the 'heads or tails' dilemma. The full spectrum of risks will be embraced. In the following chapters, I will share my ideas on what principles the extreme-risk-management framework should be based and what the overall risk architecture should look like.

# 5

# Extreme Risk and the AAA Approach

*Failure to prepare is preparing to fail.*

*(Benjamin Franklin)*

Extreme risk often develops in areas where it comes unaddressed and unnoticed. In a typical case, the scenario of extreme risk events is like a forest fire: it unfolds very quickly and leaves no means of escape. However, there have been some interesting examples when extreme risk was identified early enough, properly communicated and mitigation deployed, which either led to a smaller-than-expected negative impact or resulted in the tail risk not surfacing at all as its drivers had been eliminated by pre-emptive actions. We need to study these cases in order to understand how to address the issues next time to ensure success.

## The War in Iraq

A good example of a well-managed extreme risk event is the US military operation in Iraq in 2003. Like any large-scale military operation in the modern world, the Iraq war campaign brought many extreme risks of various types. We will not cover here how neatly the military operation was planned and how good the strategy and tactics of the US troops and their allies were. We are more interested in the risks and potential crises outside the war zone and how these risks surrounding the 'hot war' were managed.

### RISK ASSESSMENT BEFORE THE INVASION

Before the US occupation, many analysts, politicians and journalists vividly described all these risks. Peter Vilbig in the *New York Times* wrote:

> *The war, America's second major military action since the September 11 attacks, took the nation into unknown territory, with risks and possibilities not only for the U.S. and Iraq, but for the rest of the Middle East and perhaps the world balance of power. At home, the war heightened fears of terrorist attacks and steep increases in oil prices that could further damage the nation's economy, and that of the world.*

Some publications and analytical papers depicted horrible scenarios of what could happen in the USA and Europe should the military operation start. The most obvious risk areas mentioned in these analyses were:

- oil prices;

- knock-on effect on the US economy;

- increase of terrorist activity in the USA and in countries supporting the US operation in Iraq.

Almost everyone agreed that if the ground operation went ahead, the global economy would face a severe oil price shock. A war in the very centre of the key oil-producing region could not leave the oil market unaffected. Iraq was a large oil producer with a daily oil production of over 2 million barrels in 2002. For an oil market with a very limited spare production capacity, a loss of 2.5 per cent of the global production (Iraq's share) would mean a substantial imbalance. The result is the price shock. In addition, the risk was that the contagion could spread outside Iraq. The stake was very high, with the Middle East accounting for 30 per cent of oil output. If the war led to disruption of shipping in the Gulf, this could be a disaster for the global oil market. Approximately 20 per cent of world oil supply is shipped via tankers through the Persian Gulf to major world economic centres. The real horror scenario for the global oil market was if the escalation of the war led to prolonged oil supply disruption in the Gulf area.

In addition to the devastating impact of the oil price shock, the US economy was exposed to very high costs of the military operation. While there were different opinions on how high costs could turn out to be, it was crystal clear that the war would be expensive. The combination of high energy prices and a growing US budget deficit created a high risk for the economic growth and could plunge the economy into a deep recession. Allan J. Lichtman, a historian at American University in Washington, DC, said 'His [George W. Bush] biggest danger is the economy. No incumbent President has ever been re-elected during an election-year recession, and that's one of the most potentially perilous effects of this war' (*New York Times*, 18 April 2003). And on top of these risks, everyone agreed that terrorist threats would grow after the first US soldier crossed the Iraqi border. The feelings about 11 September were very fresh at the time when the US started to plan its Iraqi campaign.

## NON-MATERIALISED RISKS

What happened after the US troops started their ground operation became a surprise for many people who expected that all bad scenarios would materialise. The first surprise came from the oil market. The long-awaited oil price shock appeared in the form of a deep dive of oil prices. From its pre-war peak of $37.8 per barrel on 12 March 2003, the price dropped to $28 per barrel by 8 April 2003, which was more than a 25 per cent decrease in less than a month. While the active phase of the military operation continued and until the day when Saddam was captured on 13 December 2003, the oil price stayed materially below the pre-war peak (Figure 5.1).

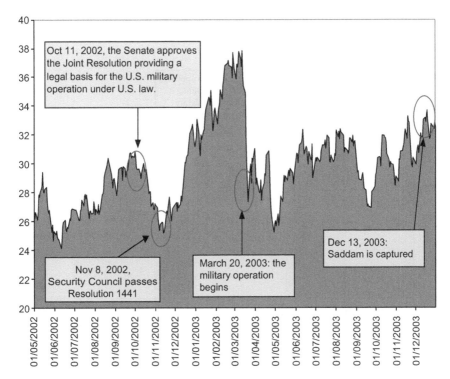

**Figure 5.1     Oil spot price ($ per barrel)**

*Source*: Author's own figure using data from Bloomberg.

All other 'big worries' that were described and expected prior to the US occupation have never materialised. Before the war, the stock markets were very nervous and declined materially, but after the 'hot' phase started they rebounded and continued with robust growth for the rest of 2003 and beyond (Figure 5.2). The US economy performed strongly as well, with a healthy annual GDP growth of 3.1 per cent (2002: 2.45 per cent).

When we look at the situation ex-post, we can ask three key questions: Why did bad scenarios not materialise? Why did all extreme risks intrinsically linked to the large military operation suddenly disappear? And did people look at the situation too pessimistically beforehand?

I don't believe that people overestimated the potential risks prior to the Iraq war. I think that there was a three-factor approach that played a key role in this story and enabled gloomy scenarios to be avoided. I call it the AAA approach (Alarm–Awareness–Action). The approach allows extreme risks to be successfully mitigated, even when the risk appears to be almost unmanageable:

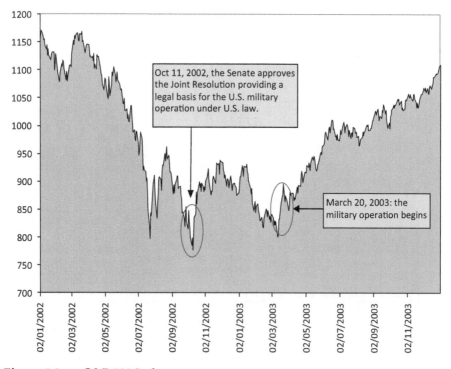

**Figure 5.2     S&P 500 Index**

*Source*: Author's own figure using data from Bloomberg.

1.  Alarm: an important factor of the successful risk mitigation is the timing. The alarm means early and honest recognition of the existence of the risk.

2.  Awareness: awareness of the risk issue, maintaining a constant sense of urgency and attracting the full attention of all stakeholders.

3.  Action: the key element of the success is the implementation of actions addressing the issue on all levels, from the very top to the ground level, and the determination to have things fixed. I cannot help but bring up the Noah rule here: 'Predicting rain doesn't count, building arks does'. Only if appropriate actions are taken can the extreme risk be mitigated.

**Alarm:**
Early identification and honest recognition of existence of the extreme risk

**Awareness:**
Awareness of the risk issue and maintain a constant sense of urgency among all stakeholders

**Actions:**
Addressing the risk drivers on all levels, from the very top to the "ground" level and determination to mitigate the impact

Figure 5.3    The AAA approach to address the tail risk challenge

## HOW THE AAA APPROACH WORKED

Let's look at how the AAA approach worked in the case of the Iraq war risks. The first factor was the 'alarm bell'. Unlike many other cases of tail risk events, the Iraq war risks were predicted well in advance. The situation around Iraq developed quite slowly. The tension between the USA and Iraq started to grow well before the spring of 2003 when US troops crossed the Iraqi border. Even at the beginning 2002, the escalation of the conflict was apparent. By October 2002, it became clear that it was highly unlikely that there was still any possibility left for a diplomatic solution. On 11 October, 2002, the US Senate voted on the Joint Resolution to authorise the use of US Armed Forces against Iraq and George W. Bush signed it off on 15 October 2002. This was a loud 'alarm bell'. For everyone, 11 October 2002 was a point of no return and a clear signal that the start of the US military operation was a matter of time. On 8 November 2002, the United Nations Security Council passed Resolution 1441, which called for Iraq to completely cooperate with UN weapons inspectors or face 'serious consequences'. This was another alarm bell of the upcoming war.

From this moment only one question remained unanswered: When? On 20 March, George W. Bush announced that he had ordered an 'attack of opportunity' against targets in Iraq. The military operation began. Therefore, the world had more than six months from the point of 'no return' on 11 October 2002 to the moment when special operations commandos from the CIA's Special Activities Division moved into the Iraqi territory.

The second factor was awareness. All important decision-makers and the public were well aware of potential risks that the USA would be exposed to in the case of the invasion. Americans knew well how significant the impact of the oil price shock on the US economy could be. Needless to say that the American people, who had just recovered after the 11 September tragedy, fully understood what the new wave of terrorist activity could mean for their lives. The seriousness of these risks was understood by the Presidential Administration, American politicians, the business community and the general public. It helped to mobilise the decision-makers to think about appropriate mitigation of potential risks. The same high awareness about the severity of risk was observed in all other countries that supported the USA in their Iraqi campaign.

And the third crucial factor was actions. In the case of the Iraq war, there were over six months to mitigate potential risks, and that people did not sit idle. As the risks were fully recognised, much effort was made on all levels to mitigate any potential impacts. In particular, there were a lot of pre-emptive mitigating actions to address potential oil supply disruption and shortage: from the measure to protect Iraqi oil production facilities during the military operation to the creation of additional oil reserves to cover the possible production shortfall.

The USA and other international businesses also implemented mitigating actions well before the war started. International companies which had operations in the conflict areas either evacuated their personnel or reduced it substantially. In addition, the potential impact of business was considered (e.g. disruption to the international trade in the conflict area) and, where possible, changes in the business model were adopted or the contingency plans were prepared.

Regarding the threat of an increase of terrorist activity, the USA, the UK and most of the allied countries that were directly involved in or supported the military operation shifted to the high level of security regime well before the invasion started. This included massive anti-terrorist actions implemented in different areas such as airport and transport security and the intensification of intelligence measures to uncover terrorist plots and any terrorist activity. As a result, the anticipated terrorist activity in the USA and Europe never became a reality when the 'hot' phase of the conflict started.

Therefore, the AAA approach – the early risk alarm, risk awareness and implementation of actions to mitigate risks – allowed the avoidance of worse case scenarios and minimised any negative consequences. Of course, these three crucial factors work well only if some degree of control over risk factors remains. It is clear that if risk drivers were absolutely beyond our control, then the early recognition of the problem and risk awareness would not help. On the other hand, without the proper alarm signal and risk awareness even the best array of risk-mitigating actions becomes ineffective and often completely useless.

When I researched the successful stories of extreme risk mitigation, I concluded that in most of the cases, we could talk not about 'lucky survivals' but about a systemic application of the AAA approach. How did a similar risk-mitigating approach work in other situations? Let's look at the millennium bug.

## The Millennium Bug

Today not so many people still remember the full story of the millennium bug (Y2K). The use of two digits to express the year in computer programs became problematic, with a possible serious logic error when the world was preparing to go into the year 2000. The risk of Y2K was identified well before 2000 and attracted global attention. There were many discussions and scenarios of how this computer logic error could lead to fatal outcomes if the most crucial services fail (e.g. computer programs that are used in aviation or in the energy sector). A lot of work was done under government or corporate programmes in most of countries to identify and rectify the logic errors related to Y2K. When finally the world turned to 1 January 2000, only minor problems were reported. Did the Y2K tail risk exist? The answer is still debatable. Some people believe that the Y2K risk was minor and the danger of not addressing it had been exaggerated. On the other hand, some system failures due to Y2K error did happen on 1 January 2000, luckily not in the areas that could lead to fatality.

If we agree that the millennium bug was a real danger, then it is important to learn from the Y2K risk-mitigation experience. In my view, it was another example of the practical implementation of the AAA approach. Indeed, all elements of the triple-A can easily be observed:

• Alarm: the early identification of the risk associated with Y2K.

• Awareness: a wide circle of international and government bodies, businesses, academia and IT specialists were involved in Y2K discussions, which led to full recognition of risk.

• Actions: implementation of a large array of measures to check software and identify Y2K bugs and re-write the programme codes. Some sources estimated that the global preparations for the millennium bug cost over $300 billion (BBC News 2000).

## What Risk Management Can Learn from the London Olympics Experience

The Modern Olympic Games have become more than just a sport event. They have become the greatest show on earth when every four years millions of people from all over the world gather in one city to celebrate the sport and cultural extravaganza. The organisation of such a global event requires an enormous effort from the host country. Dealing with extreme risks is a part of the host country's duty.

## 'MY GOD, WE WILL NOT MAKE IT'

When on 6 July 2005 the International Olympic Committee (IOC) awarded London the right to host the 2012 Olympic Games, two issues – the transport problem and the security threat – immediately overshadowed this great news for Londoners and all Britons. The initial euphoria and enthusiasm evaporated quickly. Just a day after the IOC announcement, suicide terrorists exploded four bombs on London Underground trains and on a double-decker bus. Fifty-two people were killed and more than 700 were injured. The immediate reaction of the UK was that London was not a safe place and that they could not provide security during the Olympics when millions of people would come to London. In August 2011, exactly one year before the Olympic kick-off, several London boroughs including Central and East London, the future home of the Olympic family, were plunged into street riots and looting. Five days of chaos, London enveloped in smoke and fire, broken showrooms, gangs of hooded youths on the streets – all these shocked the country. It again raised a serious concern about the ability of the British police and Special Forces not only to prevent possible terrorist attacks during the Games but even to keep ordinary street order and control of crime and hooliganism. The reaction was 'My God, we will not make it'.

The transport system was another major risk. The London Underground, railways and roads were also famous for their chronic problems. Periodic chaos on the London Tube and at railway stations, constant 'signal failures' and 'faulty trains' and huge traffic jams in Central London became a daily reality. How would this transportation system, which was already running at its maximum capacity, cope with an extra several million passengers and thousands of cars during the Olympics? It sounded like a mission impossible.

I was lucky. I moved to London soon after the IOC granted London the rights to host the Olympics. I witnessed the seven years of Olympic preparation and became a part of the million-strong crowd participating in the world's greatest sport show in August 2012. I had used my lucky chance not only to visit the main Olympic venues and see some unforgettable Olympic moments, but also to observe how London was dealing with the two greatest risks when the time came.

Several months before the Olympic kick-off, I had a discussion with my British friends about the two major London Olympics' risks – security and transport. They were sceptical and absolutely convinced that London would fail to solve the issues. I did not share their scepticism. I was sure that during the Games there would not be any major problems with either transportation or security, even though some facts supported the opposite view. Even when the fiasco with G4S, the main security firm for Olympics provider, suddenly surfaced, I did not lose my optimism. G4S was a security firm selected by LOCOG (the London Olympics Organising Committee) to provide security staff for the London Olympics. Just two weeks before the Olympics were due to start, G4S admitted that they would be unable to supply 10,400 guards agreed in the contract with LOCOG.

A few weeks before the Olympics, London bus drivers started to threaten strike action during the Games, but even then I remained an optimist. My belief was based not on any specific insider information. I did not rely on my intuition and I did not have a crystal ball to read the future. My optimism was simply based on knowledge of the AAA approach to deal with extreme risks. And I clearly saw that London was addressing the issues according to the approach.

## 'WHEN OUR TIME CAME – BRITAIN WE DID IT RIGHT'

This sounds pretty simple, but the experience suggests that it works. The London Olympics was just another success story of the AAA approach. In the seven years of preparation for the Games, two major risks were at the centre of government, media and public attention. There was no room for denial or underestimation of the problems. Seven years before the Olympics, the UK honestly admitted that the security level and the efficiency of the transport system were unacceptable. If we didn't want to fail, everyone needed to work hard to fix them. And they did.

I do not know details of how the terrorist threat was dealt with. Intelligence services do not talk much. We know the outcome. No terrorist attacks happened during the Games. When G4S failed to deliver security staff, plan B was implemented: the army were quickly deployed to take care of security and 1,500 extra police officers were called, which brought the total number of police to 10,500. Results surprised even optimists: the crime level fell across the board in London during the Olympic Games. The *Evening Standard* (Davenport 2012: 2) published the police statistics: only 253 arrests by officers on Olympics duty in the two weeks of the Games! Most of the arrests were for ticket touting. There were only 21 arrests for drugs, 16 for assault, only 11 for theft, one for a bomb hoax and one for swimming in the Thames. For comparison, during the two-day Notting Hill Carnival in London in August 2011 the police made 245 arrests and called the event 'peaceful' (BBC News 2011).

The police explained this unexpectedly low number of crimes, most of which were not serious, by the 'feel-good factor of the Games'. Commander Bob Broadhurst commented: 'We have not had huge numbers of tourists attacked, robbed or fleeced, nothing like that. The mood out there has been friendly and happy' (Davenport 2012: 2). Sceptics could say: all that noise about the security problems was just an overreaction and mania. There would have been the same result, even if the police and intelligence service had done nothing. Maybe. I cannot prove or disprove it. But how about the transport problem?

Everybody who interacts with the London transport system on a regular basis can say with 100 per cent confidence: if nothing had been done, the London transport system would have collapsed during the Olympics. But it did not. How this could be? The AAA approach proved its effectiveness. The problem was addressed at all levels to mitigate the risk of the transport collapse:

- The UK Government, the Mayor of London and the London Olympic Committee level: Not only was there direct investment into the London transport infrastructure (£6.5 billion was spent to enhance the Tube and rail services), but also there was the full commitment from the top level to support all measures necessary to ensure transport efficiency.

- Transport for London (TfL) and the Train Operating Companies level: the transport service providers made a huge effort to ensure an effective service. This included extra capacity for trains and buses; optimisation of bus/train schedules; hiring thousands of extra staff (including Travel Ambassadors); changes on London roads (e.g. adjustments of traffic signals, Games lanes, road works ban, removing pedestrian crossings, temporary restriction of parking); communication to business, drivers and passengers (e.g. various route optimiser apps, text messaging, warning email service); and rapid response teams to resolve problems fast (e.g. extra spare part supply). TfL created a transport coordination centre where all transport operators were represented. Operating 24 hours a day, the centre was responsible for the coordination of problem-solving and communication across all transport systems. In addition, the readiness of the transport system had been tested.

The Queen's Diamond Jubilee celebrations in 2012, when millions of people were gathering in London, was used by the transport service providers as the main pre-Olympic test.

- Business level: major business areas of London (including the City and Canary Wharf) were expected to be affected by transport stress during the Olympics. London businesses had no illusions and took serious action to mitigate the impact. Companies encouraged employees to take holidays during the Olympics and, where possible, to work from home to reduce travelling. Private businesses invested money in remote working solutions and implemented special Olympics working schedules (to avoid busiest times). And it worked well. During the Olympics, many offices were quiet, with empty floors, empty desks with only a few people on duty. Freight operators and delivery companies used special freight journey planners and out-of-hours deliveries. Where possible, businesses stocked up before the Games.

- General public level: A national public campaign was launched to alert people about the stress on transport systems during the Olympics and how to cope with the unusual situation. Londoners followed the advice and did a lot to reduce their travels, avoid travelling during rush hours and re-routing from busy roads and stations in Central London. Motorists substantially reduced using cars.

The result of mitigating actions was impressive. There was no major public transport disruption in spite of the record number of passengers. Andrew Neather wrote; 'It was an Olympic win more jaw-dropping to Londoners than any gold medal: our transport system managed just fine during the Games' (Neather 2012). During the Games, the Tube carried over 60 million passengers, an increase of 30 per cent compared to a year before, which was more passengers than at any time in its 149-year history. On 9 August 2012, the Tube hit an all-time daily record – 4.52 million passengers. The DLR carried over 6 million passengers (an increase of over 100 per cent), while London Overground carried almost 6 million passengers (an increase of 47 per cent) (Everitt 2012).

Yet no major problems were reported. Traffic on the roads kept moving and buses coped well. My personal experience was that during the two Olympics weeks London transport worked much better that it normally does. I experienced no delays or queues when travelling to and from busy Olympic venues, even in the peak periods. During the Olympics, I was amazed to see empty roads in many central areas of London like Sloane Square and New Kings Road, which are famous for their dreadful traffic.

What a surprise!

At the London 2012 closing ceremony the chairman of LOCOG, Sebastian Coe, said to millions of Britons, who still could not believe that they managed to organise possibly the best Games ever: 'When our time came – Britain we did it right.' He did not reveal the secret though: 'we did it right because of the AAA approach'.

## The Eurozone Crisis and the AAA Approach

Since the Eurozone (EZ) crisis was recognised and attracted global attention, becoming the main headache not only for Europe but for the global economy, much effort has been made to mitigate the situation. While the process of finding a political solution (EU, IMF, European governments) was not straightforward and often disappointing, some powerful mitigating actions were implemented. In addition, private business did a lot to mitigate the Eurozone impact on their business. For example, many banks either exited the problem EZ countries or substantially downsized their exposure to those countries. All these efforts keep me optimistic about the possibility of avoiding the tail risk event in the EZ. Of course, the EZ problem was recognised quite late. European policy-makers, politicians and government bodies started to address the issue when 'the army moved to within shooting distance of the border', if we can build a parallel to the Iraq war. This late recognition and reaction, no doubt, make the mitigation less effective. Nevertheless, the firewalls that were already built to prevent the EZ crisis becoming a forest fire for the whole of Europe meant that there was a good chance to avoid the true tail risk event.

The key success factors of addressing the tail risk remain visible here: the alarm bell (although quite late), increasing risk awareness and the sense of urgency, and actions of all stakeholders. When even a London taxi driver can tell you how much sovereign default risk for Spain and Italy is and how this can affect the French banking system, it is a good sign that the AAA approach is underway. When the whole world talks about a particular tail risk, the chance of it unfolding in its ugly form diminishes.

# 6

# When All Hell Breaks Loose

*If you are going through hell, keep going.*

*(Winston Churchill)*

The experience of managing risk during the Iraq war or London Olympics demonstrates that under particular conditions (when the AAA approach is implemented), we can be quite successful in managing extreme risks. On the other hand, the Iraq war risk mitigation experience contrasts with the experience of some other extreme risk events when the worst case scenarios materialised. Two relatively recent crises illustrate this.

## The 9/11 Crisis

The 9/11 event and its consequences had a deep and long lasting devastating impact on US society, certain industries and on the US economy as a whole. This single day in US history had a serious knock-on effect.

The reaction of the markets to 9/11 was panic. Trading on the New York Stock Exchange and New York Mercantile Exchange was suspended for several days. NASDAQ cancelled trading and the London Stock Exchange was evacuated. After the trading resumed, all leading stock markets fell sharply. The oil price went up straight after the event but as soon as the world realised what really happened, the price fell sharply from $30 per barrel peak to $18 per barrel, a drop of 40 per cent in just two months – one of the most dramatic price reductions in recent history (see Figures 6.1 and 6.2).

The 9/11 impact stretched beyond the market reaction and had an impact on the real economy. At the time of the event, the US economy was already on a downward trend. The quarter that followed the 9/11 event became the worst since 1991. The GDP growth was only 0.2 per cent (see Figure 6.3). The next

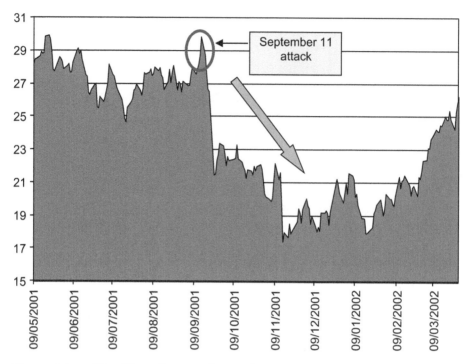

**Figure 6.1    West Texas Intermediate oil spot price ($ per barrel)**

*Source*: Author's own figure using data from Bloomberg.

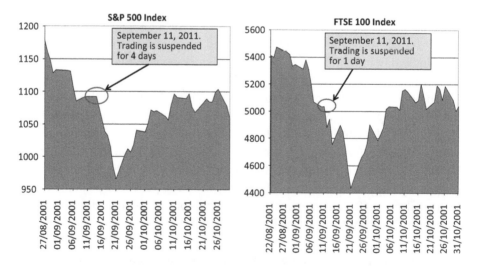

**Figure 6.2    S&P 500 Index and FTSE 100 Index**

*Source*: Author's own figure using data from Bloomberg.

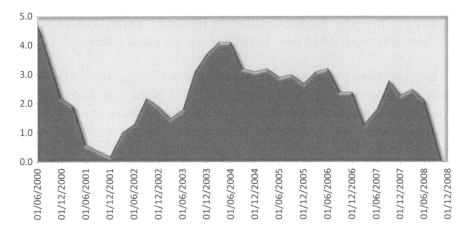

**Figure 6.3    US GDP growth rate (per cent)**
*Source*: Author's own figure using data from Bloomberg.

time that the US quarterly GDP growth fell below this level was only in the last quarter of 2008 after the Lehman Brothers event.

The airline industry, together with the insurance industry, was possibly affected more than other sectors. Airlines faced an unexpected and heavy impact. After the 11 September tragedy, the industry had to cope with a sharp drop in customer demand due to fear of further terrorist attacks. The impact was aggravated by the economic situation when leisure travelling was already under pressure. As a result, after several tough months of fighting for their survival, several large industry players like US Airways and United Airlines defaulted. Moody's wrote in their report: 'The transportation sector also saw heightened default rates in 2002 as several airlines, including UAL, parent of United Airlines, defaulted or filed for bankruptcy as a result of industry overcapacity and the aftershocks of the September 11th attacks' (Moody's Investors Service 2003: 7).

Why was the impact on society and the economy so dramatic? An element of surprise is likely to have played a key role. Not all measures that the USA took after the event were effective. George Bush placed the US military on high-alert worldwide and for the first time in US history, SCATANA (Security Control of Air Traffic and Air Navigation Aids) was invoked. The US Federal Aviation Administration landed all aircraft and closed the US airspace. The national ground stop continued for three days, but it was already too late and unnecessary. While this measure was fully logical in the context of the 9/11 attack, it had only a negative impact on airlines and other businesses which suffered due to US airspace closure. All security measures would have been effective had they been implemented at the right time. The SCATANA would have been effective if it had been invoked before the attack rather than after.

Two key factors necessary for successful crisis mitigation – Alarm and Awareness – were missing in the wake of the 9/11 event. The absence of any strong alarm signal of possible terrorist attacks did not leave any time for an effective response. Society remained unaware of the aeroplane attack scenario, the ways in which this scenario could unfold and the gravity of its consequences. The absence of sufficient time to prevent or mitigate the impact appeared to be crucial. The simultaneous hijack of four aeroplanes left no time for an effective anti-terrorist response.

## September 2008

Interestingly, the same two factors were missing during the global financial crisis of 2008–9. While many people claimed that they predicted the crisis correctly, I do not believe that a deep awareness of the financial disaster was present prior the point when all hell suddenly broke loose in September 2008. What possibly reflects the overall mood of the business and financial elite at the beginning of 2008 was that the financial bonanza was possibly coming to an end and the economy was slowing down and going for a soft landing. Therefore, the famous approach described by the former Citigroup CEO Charles Prince ('keep on dancing as long as the music is playing') looked not so stupid at that time and was adopted by the majority of financial institutions. Financial businesses were in a hurry to accumulate 'fat' before the difficult times arrived. I suspect that not so many people among decision-makers (politicians, regulators, financiers, etc.) really expected the financial disaster.

The retrospective view reveals that before the crisis the alarm bell was not properly heard and the risk awareness was very low. It is enough to look at what the key decision-makers were busy with in the wake of crisis. *The Telegraph* published an article by Andrew Pierce: 'Financial crisis: Our masters' summer of denial', where he revealed what the key persons in the UK government did days before the financial system collapsed (Pierce 2008). There was no sign of UK national leaders having a clear understanding that the UK economy was on the brink of a financial disaster. Pierce wrote about M. King, Governor of the Bank of England at that time:

> As Mervyn King took his seat in the Royal Box at Wimbledon for the
> men's singles final in July, he could never have known that he was about

*to witness one of the greatest matches in the history of the All England Club. The Bank of England governor presumably did not realise either that the Stock Market was about to be pitched into the most tumultuous period the world has experienced since the Wall Street Crash.*

*(Pierce 2008)*

The Prime Minister Gordon Brown spent his holidays in his cottage in Suffolk. The media reported that

*the Prime Minister being hard at work not, as you might expect, on a response to the financial upheaval, but on his physique. Downing Street, supposed to be a spin-free zone in the aftermath of Tony Blair, leaked to the tabloids the revelation that Mr Brown had hired a personal trainer to teach him Pilates.*

*(Pierce 2008).*

The Shadow Chancellor George Osborne flew to Corfu as a guest of his schoolmate and friend Nat Rothschild, the billionaire hedge-fund owner, who was holding a 40th birthday party for Elisabeth Murdoch, just a few days before the Lehman collapse. David Cameron also was on holiday. He spent his time off the Greek island of Santorini with Rupert Murdoch on his yacht, *Roseharty*.

The gold market – a good indicator of market participants' sentiment – was calm before the storm began. The gold price reached its peak of $1,006 per ounce in March 2008 during the Bear Stern crisis. But then markets cooled down. The most tranquil time started in mid-July and lasted until the first week of September, when Fannie and Freddie and Lehman Brothers shook the world. During the 'summer of denial', gold lost 25 per cent of its value, dropping from $986 to $740 (Figure 6.4).

Also surprisingly good signals kept on coming from other sources while the world enjoyed the 2008 'summer of denial'. The IMF published its research on the financial stability of Iceland. In the executive summary, it was highlighted that while the environment was deteriorating and vulnerabilities increasing, 'the banking system's reported financial indicators are above minimum regulatory requirements and stress tests suggest that the system is resilient' (IMF 2008b: 5). The assessment was approved on 19 August 2008 by Jaime Caruana, IMF Counsellor and Director (former Chairman of the Basel Committee on Banking Supervision)! In only one month the entire Icelandic financial system collapsed, including three major Icelandic banks.

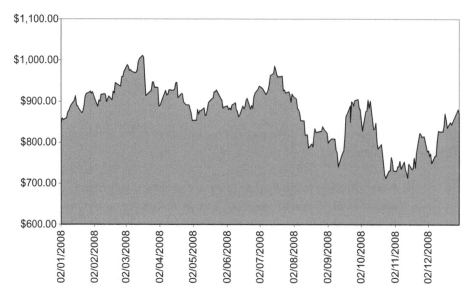

**Figure 6.4    Gold price ($ per ounce)**
*Source*: Author's own figure using data from Bloomberg.


The time factor played against the economy during 2008 crisis. The events unfolded with the speed of a forest fire on a dry and windy day. If we start counting the time of the crisis from the day when the US Government bailed out Fannie Mae and Freddie Mac, after this event each week brought new events. This created the situation where mitigating actions once agreed were either too late to be sufficiently effective or often did not make sense at the moment of their implementation as the situation had already moved on too much. The *New York Times* called this period '10 weeks of financial turmoil'. Indeed, during the period of only 10 weeks the economic landscape of the USA and Europe changed beyond recognition. The most dramatic period was September 2008. The market news during this month sounded like a wartime bulletin from the front line:

## 7 SEPTEMBER

- US Government bails out Fannie Mae and Freddie Mac.

## 14 SEPTEMBER

- Lehman files for bankruptcy.

- Merrill Lynch agrees to be taken over by Bank of America.

## 16 SEPTEMBER

- US Government bails out troubled insurance giant AIG.

## 17 SEPTEMBER

- Lloyds TSB announces its takeover of HBOS after an unprecedented run on HBOS shares.

## 21 SEPTEMBER

- The Fed announces that Goldman Sachs and Morgan Stanley would transform themselves into banks.

## 25 SEPTEMBER

- Washington Mutual fails and JP Morgan agrees to buy it.

## 28 SEPTEMBER

- The credit crunch hits Europe.

- Dutch–Belgian bank and insurance giant Fortis is given a lifeline as part of a bailout plan agreed to by Belgium, the Netherlands and Luxembourg.

## 29 SEPTEMBER

- UK mortgage lender Bradford & Bingley is nationalised.

- The Icelandic bank Glitnir struggles and the Icelandic government has to take control of the bank.

- The US stock market collapses, the Dow Jones index drops 7 per cent, a record one-day point fall.

- Finance Minister of Germany announces a €35 billion lifeline for troubled Hypo Real Estate from the government and a consortium of German banks.

## 30 SEPTEMBER

- Dexia is bailed out by French, Belgian and Luxembourg states.

- The Irish government announces a guarantee on all deposits to stop a run on Irish banks.

Again two key allies of success – Alarm and Awareness – were absent from the scene. But without these allies the financial industry had little chance to win the battle against the extreme risk crisis.

## Who Needs Pro-Active Risk Management?

Extreme risk recognition and pre-emptive measures to disable the risk driver are key. The situation can be dubious: if the risk is recognised early enough and effective pre-emptive measures allow killing the risk driver, the risk will never surface. This is good news. The bad news is that ex-post people who were actually heroes, who raised concerns at an early stage of the tail risk event development and implemented effective mitigation and eventually demonstrated that they are masters of managing extreme risk could be accused of being panic prone and ineffective managers. Nassim Taleb, in his book *The Black Swan* (Taleb, 2007) described a 'thought experiment' – a hypothetical case of a person who initiated bullet-proof doors in every airplane cockpit. Taleb concluded that while this person would have prevented 9/11, he would have been criticised for this 'superfluous' measure and would have retired with a great sense of failure and died with the impression of having done nothing useful.

This hypothetical case is quite realistic. From real life, we know many stories when risk managers who identified the exposure to extreme risk in their organisations were fired just because they became a stumbling block for the top bosses to keep running their risky businesses. Normally these stories become public after the organisation faces fiasco.

The millennium bug story followed the same pattern. When after 1 January 2000 arrived and the global software meltdown did not happen, press and the general public immediately started to suggest that the Y2K problem was either a scam or a paranoid idea created by software companies and IT consultants, which cost society a huge amount of money.

People who have been fired for ringing the alarm bell cannot apply for the perfect risk manager certificate. Yes, they did their job well by identifying the threat for the organisation. But for different reasons, they were not able to prevent a fiasco. And the fiasco helped them to become heroes in the eyes of the public and get the recognition. It is unlikely that the perfect risk manager can get this. He often becomes an unrecognisable hero or sometimes even a disgraceful person. The pre-emptive tail risk measures require a lot of effort and resources. The person who takes pre-emptive measures effectively steers the organisation through extreme threats uneventfully. For most people who cannot see the extreme risk at its early stage (the vast majority of us belongs to this category), the effective risk manager can be seen as a time- and money-waster. The logic is simple: we implement a number of projects addressing threats – but these threats never materialise. Therefore, the person who identified these threats made a mistake.

This is in sharp contract with the risk manager who addresses normal risks like day-to-day credit losses on credit cards. This manager can easily demonstrate his results. He just needs to show the loss trend and compare the cost of the risk-mitigating actions taken with the loss reduction.

The lesson: if you deal with extreme risk, be smart. Recognise the tail risk earlier (of course, if you can) and develop an effective mitigating plan. Propose it but don't push too hard and don't expect an easy buy-in from the top bosses. Only a small number of intelligent people can recognise tail risk at its early stage. Normally bosses are too busy to think of something which sits outside the next quarterly report. When the fire starts burning and bosses start to see that their business report is in trouble, it's your chance to push your proposal. If your contingency plan works well, bosses will reward your efforts.

Yes, it is not an ideal moment for implementing pre-emptive measures – time has gone – but hopefully at the moment when bosses are ready to give their buy-in, there is still a good chance of fixing the situation and reducing the impact to an acceptable level. On the positive side, you eliminate your personal risk to become a pain in the neck for your bosses. In addition, you obtain a chance to be recognised as a best risk manager for your organisation. From common sense, this strategy might sound strange, but our lives are often very strange and, as the French philosopher Voltaire said, common sense is not so common.

# PART III

# Survival Strategy in the Extreme Risk Wilderness

# 7

# First Line of Defence: Business and Risk Strategy

## Minefield or My Field: Comfort Zone Concept

The business strategy and the strategy of risk-taking seem to be the crucial 'ingredients' for overall success or failure for any organisation, including financial institutions. So many times in the past we have witnessed how flawed business models or strategic mistakes led organisations to large-scale disasters. The issue with the business strategy is the time lag required to understand whether the strategy is effective or not. This is normally a slow-moving world because the strategy is always about the long term. Not so often can the destructive nature of a particular business strategy be immediately spotted. It takes time, and sometimes many years, before people can reasonably judge the effectiveness of the strategy.

Very often, a flawed business model or erroneous strategic decision can look very robust at the moment of its initial implementation. There are always enough people (including, of course, those who made the decision) who eagerly applaud and explain why this business model or decision is efficient, wise and not risky. Moreover, the intrinsically flawed strategy could show a decent return for some time (and normally does) that can fool people even more. At the same time, the firm keeps on warehousing extreme risk, not even spotting that they are sitting on a barrel of smoking gunpowder. Then the moment comes when the extreme risk explodes and the recklessness of the strategy becomes clear to everyone. But it is too late to change the situation and de-risking is not possible. It can happen suddenly, turning the world around. What we see quite often is that the path 'from hero to zero' can take just a few days. Most of the crashes that we saw in the last several years followed this pattern: LTCM, Enron, Northern Rock, Lehman Brothers, AIG, RBS, Hypo Real Estate, Dexia and many, many more.

Of course, after the disaster happens, there is no shortage of smart people who immediately come up with plausible explanations why the strategy was 'foolish', too risky and ultimately led to failure. An obvious question exists: if the strategy flaws were so obvious, why did nobody (or almost nobody) raise the concern at the moment when this strategy was at its early implementation stage?

The answer is also quite obvious: we are all wise after the event, but the early recognition of recklessness of a business model or a deadly flaw of strategic decision requires extraordinary analytical and business thinking. Not everyone has this ability. If so, does it mean that the situation is so hopeless that we cannot recognise strategic mistakes early enough to prevent accumulation of unbearable risks?

There is a light at the end of the tunnel. One of the possible methods is an analysis of business comfort zones. The concept of the comfort zone stems from understanding that each firm (providing it has been in business for a relatively long time) has a business area or areas that can be called its 'comfort zones'. The comfort zone can be defined as an area of business, product or service where the firm has its core competencies, competitive advantages, deep knowledge of risks and decent control over key risk factors, and all of the above are proven by long, successful business experience in both benign and downturn periods.

The clear demarcation of a comfort zone has not only theoretical significance, but also paramount practical sense. The extensive business experience suggests that a comfort zone is the area where a firm is less exposed to risks including extreme risks. It could be a particular traditional customer group that the firm provides its service to and has an in-depth expertise, products in relation to which the firm has its 'know how', knowledge and infrastructure, key geographical areas etc. The longer the history of its successful business within the comfort zone that the firm has, the stronger is its ability to moderate its business in different circumstances. On the other hand, numerous historical precedents demonstrate that tail risk is especially distractive outside the firm's comfort zone when the firm does not have thorough knowledge of its business or ability to exercise effective control over key risk factors. And firms are killed by their risk exposure to the outside comfort zone business over and over again. Therefore, the firm can say: 'My comfort zone is my field, but what is outside it remains a minefield'.

Even if risks in the normal situation look pretty much identical inside and outside the comfort zone, when an extreme risk event strikes, the organisation is normally much more effective in dealing with it in its core business area because the efficacy of soothing risk depends on the knowledge, skills and ability needed to control the situation. On the other hand, outside the comfort zone due to limited experience and incomplete knowledge the firm can manufacture extreme risk situations by their actions. Sometimes the firm can accumulate extreme risk for many years and has a sense of a full control. But this time bomb is just waiting for an external trigger like the economic downturn. And then this risk entails a disaster as the firm has no or restricted control over the situation.

As an illustration of this rule I can mention here the cases of AIG and UBS. Both firms are exceptionally good in running business in their comfort zone. AIG is one of the best if not the best insurance firm for its core traditional insurance products. UBS is a brilliant wealth management company. However, at a particular point both firms decided to jump outside their traditional comfort zones. AIG started to aggressively build up their exposure to fancy insurance products like CDS via its AIG Financial Product division. USB aggressively penetrated into traditional investment banking business without being especially strong in understanding this business and the risk of some innovative derivatives. Its Dillon Read Capital Management division built up exposure to sub-prime mortgage derivatives. For some time, both firms enjoyed their new businesses, which looked very profitable and quite safe. However, the extreme risk that both firms had been warehousing for several years was not obvious to them until the risk surfaced during the financial crisis. Both firms suffered a devastating impact. Since the beginning of the crisis in 2007, UBS has written off more than $50 billion from sub-prime mortgage investments, while AIG reported a $99 billion loss (most of it was attributed to the 'innovative' insurance products) for 2008. AIG and UBS were not the only two firms from the financial service industry that were brought to their knees by businesses outside the comfort zone. Most spectacular financial failures replicate the following pattern:

- a jump from my field to the minefield (a fast aggressive penetration outside the comfort zone);

- euphoria about the new business;

- a trigger event (e.g. liquidity crunch, economic downturn, systemic crisis);

- heavy losses and the business meltdown.

## LEARNING FROM WARREN BUFFET

The view that extreme risk is mostly to be found outside a firm's comfort zones is not something new. While a lot of books have been published to explain why Warren Buffet was so successful and what his key principles of investing were, for me the most important message from Buffet is his phrase 'Risk comes from not knowing what you're doing.' Buffet invests in businesses that he understands. His determination to avoid investing in the business that he does not fully understand is well known. He refrained from buying the 'attractive' and 'extremely promising' technological companies because he believed that his knowledge of the business was not sufficient. He formulated Berkshire Hathaway's approach as follows:

> *If we have a strength, it is in recognizing when we are operating well within our circle of competence and when we are approaching the perimeter. Predicting the long-term economics of companies that operate in fast-changing industries is simply far beyond our perimeter. If others claim predictive skill in those industries … we neither envy nor emulate them. Instead, we just stick with what we understand. Fortunately, it's almost certain there will be opportunities from time to time for Berkshire to do well within the circle we've staked out.*
> *(Berkshire Hathaway 1999: 16)*

In other words, Warren Buffet always runs his business within his comfort zone – the circle of competence. It sounds very conservative, maybe even too conservative. But this 'orthodox' dedication to the comfort zone business, undoubtedly, helped him a lot in avoiding major crashes in his long investment career.

## KNOW YOUR BUSINESS 'GENOME'

How does a firm distinguish which businesses are within its comfort zone and which are outside? Length of experience here is an important factor. By definition, for start-ups and relatively young financial firms there is no comfort zone. A young firm needs to 'graduate' and to prove sustainability of its business. Acting with no comfort zones, the new financial firm is intrinsically risky and prone to failure. In order to survive, the firm needs to establish its comfort zone. It takes time, but as time passes and once it is done, the firm might think about new business areas and expand its business to uncharted geographic territories or add new financial products and services, which can lead to establishing new comfort zones after years of successful experience.

The first step in building the map of business 'genome' is to break down the firm's business into homogeneous areas. This task could be quite challenging for large and diverse organisations like global banks. The large international banks could run its business in several dozens of countries, selling many different financial products and providing a very wide array of services. To arrive at an acceptable level of granularity, we need to cut through the existing organisation structure and the existing way of how different businesses and products are managed in the organisation. It is quite often that different financial products have similar names and are sold through the same channels. Moreover, the same people in the organisation are responsible for managing these products. However, these products can be intrinsically different and should be considered separately when we build the map of a business 'genome'.

A good example is mortgages. While the product range includes all mortgages, there are numerous different products inside this broad category. Thus, buy-to-let mortgages should be treated as a separate product because its risk drivers and target customers differ from those of traditional home-occupier mortgages. For normal market conditions this difference might not be material or even invisible. But when the situation in the market deteriorates and the worst comes to the worst, with all other things being equal, buy-to-let mortgage holders are much more likely to default and walk away from their property. The traditional home-occupier mortgages show stronger resilience under extreme circumstances because home occupiers normally keep on fighting for their 'home sweet home' dream to the end. This difference in behaviour is crucial for the purpose of extreme risk assessment.

Even if we analyse a narrow category like home-occupier mortgages, we still need to ensure that this product is homogenous enough, first of all from a risk perspective. For example, mortgages with the loan-to-value (LTV) of 75 per cent and below are intrinsically different from mortgages with LTV of 100 per cent and above. Not only do these two sub-products differ in their quite obvious security levels (no or even negative equity for the latter sub-product), but also they are different in their target customer group. The low LTV mortgage proposition targets people with substantial savings who are able to make the down-payment of a significant part of their property value and, therefore, expect to obtain a better interest rate for their mortgages. In most of the cases, this customer group comprises people with a disposable income large enough to make regular savings, people who prefer long-term and financial planning and conservative financial decisions. Conversely, people who have no large savings (and therefore have to accept high interest rates for their high LTV mortgages), and possibly no regular income in the past, often rely on future income or expect that in the future their disposable income will grow; these people form the customer group of the high LTV mortgages.

Separation of products and sub-products that sound alike but are intrinsically different results in making the right decision about what business falls in or out of the comfort zone. If a firm has a long history of managing traditional low LTV mortgages (and reasonably defines these mortgages as a core business) but a relatively short history of offering 'innovative' high LTV mortgages, then the clear separation of these sub-products helps the firm identify that a certain part of their mortgages cannot be included in their comfort zone.

Each broad product category can be broken down into narrow categories and analysed from different angles. While there is no one standard approach that exists, the firm should decide on what is the appropriate way of product segmentation and granularity in order to achieve the homogeneity needed for further analysis. One of the possible segmentation approaches for products under the 'mortgage umbrella' is presented in Figure 7.1.

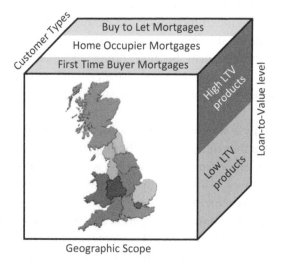

**Figure 7.1**    **Example of the multi-dimensional product segmentation approach**

The creation of a firm's business 'genome' requires slicing and dicing of the business for the purpose of further analysis in several dimensions, which can most likely be:

- geographical scope

- product/service scope

- customer scope.

## COMFORT ZONE: IN OR OUT?

When a firm's business is broken up into relatively homogeneous areas, then the next important question is to set up the right criteria in order to distinguish between the business inside and outside of a comfort zone. The following questions can help determine if a particular business can be called a comfort zone business.

### How long is the firm's experience of running this business?

Any business area with less than 20 years' experience is unlikely to qualify as a comfort zone business. Indeed, time is an essential examiner, especially if the experience includes periods of market turmoil. Twenty years can sound too conservative and one can ask: why are 10 years not enough?

Even for human beings, less than 20 years' practical experience might look too short a time to become a top-notch expert. Would you consider someone with 10 or 15 years of practical experience to be a real top-level expert? Take, for example, medicine, engineering or risk management. In general, if we are demanding enough, 10 years of experience would be rather too short and not sufficient for most professions. Organisations have more inertia and less dynamism compared to human beings. Accumulation of a firm's knowledge and experience and the learning processes take more time. Therefore, the criterion of a minimum of 20 years' experience does not sound like an overly conservative estimate.

In addition, this takes into account not only the number of years that the business has existed, but also the nature of these years. If the experience covers only or mostly a benign phase, then it would be difficult to conclude whether this experience is sufficient to support any conclusion about the comfort zone business. The crucial real-life test has always been to run the business through the downturn of the economic cycle. If this test is missing, then the business should be treated as outside its comfort zone.

### Is the size of the business significant?

If a particular business is a very small part of the firm's activity, it means that this business is auxiliary to the firm. Hence, it is unreasonable to treat this business as 'my field'. As soon as the business reaches the 'optimal level', the chances of including the business in the comfort zone increase.

### Does the firm have competitive advantages in this business, including the effective control over major risk drivers?

In particular, the important indicator is a track record of steering the business through the crisis. Is there strong evidence that the risk management has done a good job to mitigate the adverse impact?

When a firm starts an assessment of its business areas and portfolios in order to consider which area is 'in' and which is 'out' of its comfort zone, there will definitely be some disagreements. The question is indeed very sensitive as it can affect the future strategy of the firm and shift the power within the organisation. You do not need a PhD in psychology to understand that many managers will claim that the business for which they are responsible falls into the comfort zone of the firm. Especially when the criteria for 'my field' or 'minefield' are not always quantifiable and some degree of judgement is necessary, there is always a room for argument. In this case, one quantitative filter can be very helpful to reduce the chance that the whole process becomes derailed due to endless debates: the length of experience that the firm has in running each business, service or product. This filter can be very effective and substantially reduces room for different interpretations. The firm needs to set up the firm benchmark for being qualified as a comfort zone: for example, a minimum of 20 years of experience in the business area.

How should this work? For example, you need to decide whether a credit card business in Romania, which the bank started 16 years ago, should be treated as 'in' or 'out' of the firm's comfort zone. If the bank set the benchmark at a minimum experience of 15 years, this business can be included in the comfort zone providing that it will also pass other criteria like the size of the business. On the other hand, if the benchmark is 20 years, then this business should be treated as outside the comfort zone. This strict filter can help dismiss potential claims of managers who run the credit card business in Romania that their business should be in the comfort zone because 'we know this market very well', 'we have only the best customers', 'our card business has demonstrated superb results in the last 10 years', 'our Romanian business is similar to those in Hungary, where we have 25 years of experience'.

I think that it is worthwhile learning from other industries. I like the airline sector because it is much more advanced in managing extreme risk than, for example, the financial sector. How many years of practical experience are needed to qualify as a captain of a passenger jet of a major US airline?

While there is no specific age requirement (they have to comply with the equal opportunity law), the whole system has been designed to ensure that only highly experienced people aged in their mid-40s or older can be promoted to the role of Captain. The time to reach the required ratings, pass all compulsory trainings, accumulate flight time, etc., make the path to the Captain seat long, with no short cuts. Usually, a pilot needs to work 5–7 years flying a small aeroplane of a regional airline. Then there is an opportunity to be hired by a major airline as a First Officer. And then it takes on average 10–20 years of successful flying practice to be upgraded to the Captain position. It is virtually impossible to jump to the Captain seat of a passenger Boeing 747 for any person younger than 40. Possibly the youngest full captain for a passenger Boeing 747 of major US airlines was Stan Barfield. He qualified for a full captain licence at the age of 43.

This example demonstrates that it requires 20 years for a human being to acquire experience to qualify for a professional 'comfort zone' in modern aviation. Therefore, when building the map of the 'business genome', a financial institution also needs to establish its own strict non-compromised minimum time required for a business to qualify for 'comfort zone' status. This filter can make the process more transparent, less emotional and less 'political'.

## MAPPING THE GENOME

After going one by one through all the business areas, we can finally draw a map of the business genome. It can come as a surprise that the business genome can look quite different from what one expects to see. In many cases, the firm's management has an optimistic picture about their business and what could be their comfort zones. People normally expect that most of the businesses they currently run fall in their comfort zone. The reality, however, is quite different, especially for diversified and fast-growing financial institutions. For many areas of business and products, financial institutions do not have a strong experience and deep knowledge of risks. Starting from 2000, the financial sector has been experiencing a period of rapid proliferation of new products and services.

In addition, in 10 years or so preceding the global financial crisis, the financial sector demonstrated the unprecedented growth of M&A deals, aggressive 'diversification' and expansion to the new area (e.g. geographic expansion). As a result, the traditional business that can be qualified as a comfort zone business became proportionally smaller and all acquired new businesses are still too young to be included in the comfort zone.

The final outcome of the business 'genome' analysis should be the 'genome map' (see Figure 7.2). This map depicts how a firm's businesses are positioned with regards to its comfort zones. In addition, this map allows us to identify areas where the probability of large and catastrophic losses is the highest – all business areas which are sitting outside the traditional comfort zones represent the hidden danger.

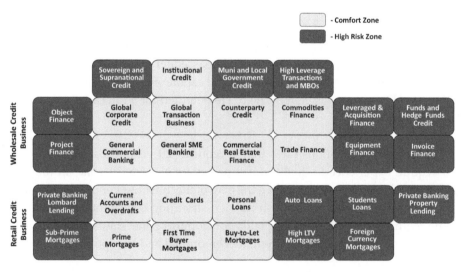

**Figure 7.2    Illustration of the 'genome map' for credit businesses**

## Going Outside the Comfort Zone

The next step in trimming the business strategy is to determine the appetite to run the businesses which are considered not to fall within the firm's comfort zone. In other words, it requires an answer to the question: to what extent is the firm going to stretch its business outside its comfort zone? The question is not a simple one. The move outside the traditional comfort zone means the firm takes an excessive risk, quite often an extreme risk, that is neither easily visible nor controllable. On the other hand, always keeping the business within the comfort zone could also be risky from a strategic point of view: the stand-still approach can reduce the upside potential for the business and can limit its ability to remain competitive in the future. The task really is to strike the right balance between businesses that the firm is going to run inside and outside its comfort zone.

There are some important aspects that need to be considered:

- Maturity of the firm. For start-ups and young firms, comfort zones do not exist. All their businesses are immature and intrinsically exposed to extreme risk. They are struggling to find their place and the chances of success are not very high. Those who survive their infancy after being in the business for 20–30 years can establish secure comfort zones. The longer the firm stays in the business, the more its business is expected to be in the comfort zone.

- The nature of the business. Different businesses have different dynamics and these dynamics should be considered when making the decision about the desirable balance of inside/outside the comfort zone split. For example, for hi-tech businesses, where technologies change beyond recognition every 10–15 years, the desirable share of the business within the comfort zone should be much less than that in mature industries. Sticking to the traditional business becomes a very risky strategy as the business success can be achieved via innovation and swiftly adopting the business to the new technological reality. The financial sector is a mature industry and financial innovations do not play such a crucial role as in, let's say, the media sector. The lion's share of the business belongs to more traditional financial products and services. Therefore, for mature financial firms a substantial part of the business should be run within the comfort zone.

- Size of the firm. The natural advantage of small companies is their good adaptability to new business conditions. Conversely, large firms are not normally able to make quick adaptations to the changing environment. They are more rigid, more bureaucratic and need substantial time to make a strategic decision and to implement it. Therefore, all other things being equal, a small company can afford to maintain a higher proportion of the business outside the traditional comfort zone than a large firm.

- Social responsibility. I know that in the brutal world of capitalism, there is not much space for social responsibility. On paper, everybody declares that they run their business according to 'good citizen' standards. The reality, of course, is quite different. Numerous scandals on unethical and irresponsible behaviour of bankers just prove the truth that we live in an imperfect world where words and actions do not always match. Nevertheless, a decision regarding the right balance between the comfort zone business vs. the business in the less traditional area ideally should include consideration about what extent the firm could put its employees and customers at risk. It is clear that for a large organisation such as a systemically important financial institution it is not morally permissible or acceptable to jump outside its comfort zone and put at risk the savings of millions of its customers and the jobs of thousands of its employees. There have been many sad examples in recent years: aggressive strategic decisions of RBS, AIG, HBOS, Northern Rock and many other large financial firms put the finances of millions of taxpayers at stake. On the other hand, smaller organisations can accept the risk of stretching outside the comfort zone. Their social responsibility is much smaller. Their strategic mistakes can be costly for some of their stakeholders (e.g. shareholders) but will not affect thousands or millions of people.

The result of the analytical work should be a strategic decision on the right balance of the business within and outside the comfort zone. The related question is how to reach this balance. It could be that the firm's business already sits close to its optimal level and not many changes are needed. Conversely, if the optimal strategic balance represents a substantially different equilibrium point, therefore the firm needs to come up with a plan how to reach the optimal business mix and what should be a reasonable timescale. At this stage, it is necessary to revisit the 'genome map' and set the quantitative growth targets for each portfolio (e.g. exit the business, downsize the portfolio, expand the business) so that the overall right balance of the business within and outside the comfort zone could be achieved. These growth targets should be further translated to quantitative and qualitative metrics that will form the strategic risk appetite of the firm.

## Ghosts, Commandments and Risk Appetite

We have arrived at a discussion about risk appetite and how to link business strategy and risk appetite. But before we go into detail, I need to clarify the whole concept of risk appetite.

Today, the concept of risk appetite has become very trendy. All large, medium and even many small financial institutions developed their risk appetite statements and proudly informed their investors, regulators, equity analysts and general public how 'comprehensive', 'holistic' and 'conservative' their risk appetite statement is. Regulators give a lot of attention to risk appetite as well, and encourage firms to produce their risk appetite statements and include them in their regulatory reporting (e.g. Internal Capital Adequacy Assessment (ICAAP) document).

For people who do not know much about risk appetite and only discovered its existence from annual reports, all noise around risk appetite can create two illusions:

1.    The concept of risk appetite emerged after the global financial crisis. Had banks developed their risk appetite approach before the crisis, many of them would have escaped the financial disaster.

2.    A firm which implements its risk appetite framework automatically enhances its risk management and becomes less risky.

These are just illusions. The risk appetite concept (in the form that we see it now) started to spread before the global crisis hit the industry. A number of banks reported on the implementation of full-scale risk appetite statements in the mid-2000s. Strangely enough, some banks which pioneered the risk-appetite concept and set the industry best practice in mid-2000s failed when the financial crisis started. For example, in their 2006 annual reports, HBOS, RBS and Northern Rock described in detail how robust their risk appetite framework was and how it enhanced their risk management practice. How come risk appetite did not stop these banks from making stupid mistakes and reckless risk taking? That is, what risk appetite was designed to prevent. Was their risk appetite real or just a window-dressing trick for regulators and investors?

I was very curious. I read the Risk Appetite section of the RBS 2006 Annual Report:

> The Board delegates the articulation of risk appetite to GEMC and ensures that this is in line with the strategy and the desired risk reward trade off for the Group. Risk appetite is an expression of the maximum level of residual risk that the Group is prepared to accept in order to deliver its business objectives and is assessed against regular (often daily) controls and stress testing to ensure that the limits are not compromised in abnormal circumstances. Risk appetite is usually defined in both quantitative and qualitative terms. Whilst different techniques are used to ensure that the Group's risk appetite is achieved, generically they can be classified as follows:
>
> - Quantitative: encompassing stress testing, risk concentration, value at risk and credit related metrics, including the probability of default, loss given default and exposure at default.
> - Qualitative: focusing on ensuring that the Group applies the correct principles, policies and procedures.
>
> (RBS Group 2006: 80)

Then I started to read Northern Rock's annual report and, suddenly, I felt as if I was a lunatic suffering from hallucinations. The report described:

> The Board delegates the articulation of risk appetite to Management Board Asset and Liability Committee ('Management Board') and ensures that this is in line with the strategy and the desired risk reward trade off for the Group. Risk appetite is assessed against regular (often daily) controls and stress testing to ensure that the limits are not compromised in abnormal circumstances. Risk appetite is usually defined in both quantitative and qualitative terms. Whilst different techniques are used to ensure that the Group's risk appetite is achieved, they can be classified as follows:
>
> - Quantitative: encompassing stress testing, risk concentration, credit related metrics, including the probability of default, loss given default and exposure at default.
> - Qualitative: focuses on ensuring that the Group applies the correct principles, policies and procedures.
>
> (Northern Rock 2006: 49)

Wait a minute! I have seen the same text in RBS's annual report! Who copied from whom? The fact that banks copied each other's risk appetite sections just supports my suspicions that their risk appetite framework was no more than just a ghost. They only looked real on paper, but did not exist in reality and had no impact on the real business whatsoever. It is not a surprise that such risk appetite frameworks did not protect these banks from their failure. If robust risk appetite existed in reality rather than just 'ghosts', it would have prevented Northern Rock and RBS from making 'stupid' mistakes that cost their shareholders and UK taxpayers billions of pounds.

The situation with the 'risk appetite ghost' is quite typical. The herd behaviour pushes financial institutions to create these trendy ghosts called 'risk appetite statements' to please regulators, rating agencies, creditors and investors. This paper factory produces nice reports and presentations. But how can this influence the real business from a risk perspective?

What is called 'the risk appetite statement', in most cases, appears to be just a collection of financial metrics and, sometimes, useless catchy phrases like 'We will not take risk that could lead to breaching regulatory requirements' or 'We have a zero tolerance to reputation risk.' Most of these metrics are not unique and normally borrowed from numerous reports that already existed before (e.g. financial reports, regulatory reports, annual plans). Usually the list of metrics is long and many metrics have very little or no direct relationship with risk (e.g. cost-to-income ratio, EVA (economic value added), dividend pay-out ratio). In the best case, this is just set of parameters of the annual business plan, but with the new fancy name 'risk appetite statement'.

When I see such a statement with 30–50 financial metrics, I ask the question: by looking at this collection of numbers do you really understand what the business strategy and the approach to risk are? What is the message from a risk perspective that this bunch of financial metrics is providing to people in the organisation? Assume that I tell you that our risk appetite for this year is to achieve 10 per cent revenue growth, 5 per cent asset growth, return on investment (RoE) of 12 per cent, cost-to-income ratio below 50 per cent and to have no significant instances of regulatory breach. What can this statement tell you about the risk strategy? Is it acceptable under this statement, for example, to build a portfolio of high risk bonds or to make a major acquisition in the emerging market or to enter in a large currency swap agreement with tenor of 30 years? There is no clear answer. The standard risk appetite statement includes long lists of financial metrics and quantitative targets (often not even risk related) but does not provide answers to questions that have major importance for the firm's survival:

- How can the firm's comfort zone be defined?

- Which businesses outside the comfort zone can be deemed acceptable and what sort of risks taken in these areas can be considered tolerable?

- What types of business should be treated as unacceptable from a risk appetite perspective?

- What speed of the organisational transformation and other related organisational change risks are considered adequate (e.g. an acceptable M&A policy)?

Most firms either have no clear answers to these questions above or never even try to address them. If the risk appetite statement confuses risks inside with the ones outside the comfort zone, from the tail risk perspective it would be the same as 'comparing apples with oranges' due to the fundamentally different nature of tail risk as described earlier.

The lack of a clear risk strategy message is the main weakness of the modern risk appetite approach: we give you a bunch of numbers, but we are silent on what the cornerstones of our risk strategy should be. While being very prescriptive in terms of metrics, these risk appetite statements are absolutely unclear on what strategic steps are acceptable or intolerable. This approach fully dilutes the strategic power of the risk appetite statement and relegates the important role of risk appetite as a tail risk killer. It adds zero value to risk and business. Why do many firms develop such risk appetite statements? Let's be honest: to create a nice window dressing for regulators and investors.

The idea of formulating a risk appetite statement is relatively new for business, but the concept per se is rather old and has a thousand-year-long history of practical use in human society. Role-wise, risk appetite statements can be compared to the ten religious commandments. The Bible tells us that Moses came down Mount Sinai carrying two stone tablets with commandments for his people. These religious imperatives provide a clear and simple way of explaining the key rules of living correctly to the people. Rather than telling people what they have to do, commandments point out what people should not do ('You shall not murder', 'You shall not commit adultery', 'You shall not steal'). Therefore, they trace out the boundaries for acceptable behaviour within human society.

Risk appetite statements should play a very similar role to commandments within commercial organisations. By formulating the risk appetite statement, top executives and the Board should clearly convey the sort of business they should not practice (the business which lies outside the acceptable level of risk appetite). At the same time, it allows freedom to choose and run businesses that are positioned within the firm's level of risk appetite. In addition, a set of financial metrics should provide a necessary quantitative description of risk appetite boundaries.

This approach is very different from what most financial institutions do when they prepare risk appetite statements. Starting with financial metrics, they put the cart before the horse. We need to establish the right order: from defining the business and risk strategy to detailed quantitative metrics.

The analysis of the 'business genome' and the decision on the optimal balance between businesses within and outside the comfort zone should precede the process of setting financial metrics. And the final risk appetite statement should provide key strategic messages ('commandments') and quantitative targets for its implementation.

## Five Steps to Optimise the Strategy

We can now summarise what is needed to provide the diagnosis of the business strategy and make necessary changes in order to reduce the potential exposure to the tail risk (Figure 7.3):

1.    Draw a map of the business 'genome' using 'filters' to distinguish between portfolios and businesses inside and outside of the comfort zone, as has been described earlier (see pp. 187–90).

2.    Make a decision on the firm's optimal level of tolerance for running the business outside the comfort zone.

3.    Based on the level of tolerance, choose the strategic actions on how to achieve the desirable balance between inside and outside comfort zone business (e.g. increase the exposure to businesses outside the comfort zone; exit some businesses outside the comfort zone in order to achieve the targeted balance) and set the timeline for these changes.

4.    Based on the agreed balance between inside/outside comfort zone business and the strategic action, review each portfolio/business line and make a decision on its future growth and speed of change.

5.    Set the risk budget (maximum risk that can be currently accepted overall and for each area) and risk appetite metrics for each portfolio /business. This is a way of translating the strategic decisions made during the first four steps to the language understandable to the people who run the business at the ground level. This provides a direct and effective connection between firm's strategic decisions and its practical implementation.

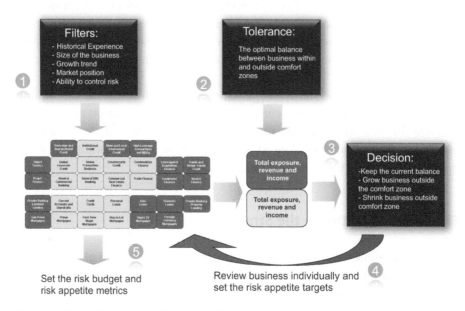

**Figure 7.3    Steps to optimise business strategy**

This approach ensures that the risk appetite statement remains a powerful strategic tool. It undoubtedly adds value to business and risk processes because it prescribes the 'rules of the game' and makes the decision-making process clear and better structured. More importantly, if risk appetite is formulated properly with a clear focus on comfort zones and potential tail risks, it becomes an effective tool to control a firm's exposure to extreme risks and prevents reckless strategic decisions that jeopardise the sustainability of the business.

One final remark regarding 'my field' vs. 'minefield'. I highlighted that the analysis of past failures strongly suggests that in most cases financial institutions are hit by large and catastrophic losses emerging from the business which they run outside their comfort zones. But it does not mean that the business within the comfort zone should be treated as a risk-free zone. Under particular circumstances, a firm can struggle with the core business which they reasonably called 'my field'. Usually it happens when the economic and business environment changes abruptly and the old good business model suddenly starts slipping.

The so-called savings and loan crisis in the USA in the 1980s provides an example of how some banks lost a fortune in their comfort zone. The main driver of the crisis was the sharp increase of interest rates. At that time many savings and loans companies used the business model when they attracted short-term deposits and provided fixed rate mortgages. When interest rates jumped to an unprecedented level, this business model, which had been successful for many years, became unviable, which led to massive defaults. In fairness, most crisis victims were companies for which savings and loans business had not been in their comfort zone (e.g. those who moved to this business not long before the crisis). Yet some old traditional savings and loans firms have been filed for Chapter 11.

Therefore, a firm needs to constantly monitor the risk in its comfort zones: the world is changing and the firm needs to question whether their business in the comfort zone remains sound. If the environment changes and new risk drivers emerge, this can create tail risk situations. But a firm which operates within 'my field' always has a much better chance to weather such difficulties than a firm for whom this business is a 'minefield'. Being within its comfort zone, the firm has all necessary skills and business knowledge for an effective response, should adverse changes in the business environment happen suddenly and abruptly.

## Diversification from Hell

When we talk about business within the comfort zone vs. the business outside the comfort zone, one other important topic springs to mind – diversification. It is a commonly accepted statement that diversification is a good thing. The theory explains well why asset diversification can be a powerful risk management strategy. The textbooks describe how diversification helps to reduce the reliance on few revenue sources, avoid business cyclicality and ensure higher and more stable growth.

While agreeing that diversification is an effective risk management strategy, I need to clarify that not all business diversification can be treated as positive. Moreover, quite often (more often that one can expect) the diversification which technically sounds right leads to a substantial increase of the firm's risk. The simple test question regarding the asset correlation is not enough. Even if the new business does not correlate with the existing ones, it will not necessarily mean that after diversification the new business mix has less risk than that before the diversification.

The questions which help to distinguish between the real (risk-reducing) diversification and the foolish diversification are as follows: Does the new business we are going to add in order to diversify our current portfolio lie within or outside the firm's comfort zone? What will our post-diversification business mix look like in terms of exposure to extreme risks? Will our post-diversification portfolio be stretched far outside the comfort zone?

If the diversification strategy is no more than diving into a new area where a firm has no proper experience, competitive advantages, knowledge and control over risk drivers, then this diversification can add only more exposure to extreme risks. Remember that most extreme risks are always sitting outside the comfort zone business. Even if the new business is not correlated with the existing ones, on paper, adding it to the existing ones would lead to 'diversification' towards less volatile and more predictable revenue. But instead, the jump outside the comfort zone will eventually make the position more vulnerable.

What we often observe is that the concept of diversification is used as a legitimate reason to do stupid things. A good example of such diversification of business is MF Global ('MF'), also known previously as Man Financial, which collapsed and filed for bankruptcy in October 2011. MF Global was a major global financial derivatives broker and commodities brokerage firm. When the new CEO Jon Corzine arrived in March 2010, he decided that the firm was a niche player and the diversification of the company would be a good thing.

Jon Corzine was a former Chairman and CEO of Goldman Sachs. Perhaps he wanted to turn MF Global into a new Goldman Sachs. In January 2011, in his interview on CNBC he said about MF Global's strategy: 'We are transforming from sort of an old-like brokerage firm into an investment bank ... We have a great position in the globalised world. I think MF Global will be a very very strong participant over the next 3–5 years' (CNBC 2011).

Perhaps he believed that his ample investment banker's experience could offset the lack of investment capabilities of MF Global. But he started a fast and aggressive 'diversification' of the traditional broker dealer by adding traditional investment banking businesses where MF's experience and knowledge fell short. In particular, MF started to make large aggressive bets on its own behalf. According to Reuters, MF made an enormous $6.2 billion on Eurozone repo bets, exposing to the problematic peripheral sovereigns like Italy, Spain, Portugal and Ireland (Elias 2011). This business was not only miles away from MF's broker business comfort zone but also MF's exposure to Eurozone grew quickly to a size that they could not swallow. This eventually killed the firm, when it appeared that its bets went wrong. When MF Global collapsed, leaving a $1.6 billion shortfall in customer funds, it became one of the top 10 bankruptcies in US history.

At first glance, MF's 'diversification' looked reasonable. I deliberately use quotation marks here when I mention the word diversification. Before, the firm focused on its narrow broker dealer business, which created a high concentration. The investment activity (in particular, Eurozone repos) was not correlated with MF's core business. Therefore, on paper, this diversification led an overall risk reduction. Yet the diversification strategy was foolish, aggressive and irresponsible. The price that MF paid for this diversification was the large amount of extreme risk that they onboarded. This extreme risk stemmed from MF's incapability to understand and effectively control risk drivers associated with their new investment activity. Instead of building their business slow and expand it carefully in the pace consistent with growing knowledge and ability of risk control, MF jumped in Eurozone repos and made bets of enormous size. It ruined the company in just 1.5 years.

MF Global is just one example of diversification from hell. Many other firms in the financial sector and beyond became victims of the wrongly understood diversification concept.

Diversification almost always leads to a stretch outside the comfort zone with rare ideal cases when a firm rebalances its exposure within several core businesses. Therefore, it is important to understand that:

- diversification is not always good, even if this diversification includes non-correlated businesses;

- beware the diversification that stretches the existing business outside comfort zones;

- size and speed of the diversification should be considered cautiously.

## Why So Many Mergers Fail

The success and failure of large merger and acquisition (M&A) deals represent a fascinating topic for equity analysts, business strategists, journalists and the general public. Each large acquisition generates a lot of attention, inspiring questions about whether this multi-billion dollar deal is a waste of money or a future success. But most of the time it is a waste of money.

The consultancy firm VSC Growth undertook a comprehensive review of M&A deals analysed in more than 70 technical research papers and considered hundreds of M&A deals from North and South America, Europe, the UK and Australia over a 30-year period (Coote 2011). The conclusion is that 70 per cent of mergers and acquisitions fail to achieve expectations and more than half destroy value. Usually, people who analyse M&A deals mention that the main causes that lead to M&A failure are poor integration process, cultural differences of the acquisition target company and underestimation of costs associated with combined business. However, one aspect does not attract the attention it deserves – the extent to which M&A deals push the business outside the comfort zone.

### HSBC: JUMPING OUTSIDE THE COMFORT ZONE

Indeed, in many cases an acquisition leads to adding new business to the existing comfort zone, but quite often M&A represents an aggressive leap outside of the comfort zone. The organic growth of the new business normally takes a substantial amount of time while the new business starts to be significant at the company's scale. It can take many years until the new business reaches the 'optimal size'. But during these years the firm accumulates substantial experience and knowledge and the new business integrates naturally to the business model. The slow movement of the organically grown business reduces the chance of taking unbearable, extreme risks in the new area. Conversely, a large M&A deal, if the acquiring business sits outside the traditional comfort zone (geographically, product-wise or customer-group-wise), means that overnight the firm starts running a sizable business which still needs to be integrated into their current business model and an effective control over risk drivers needs to be organised. Some people call it a challenge of integration. I prefer to call it a challenge of running the business outside the traditional comfort zone.

Interestingly, most of the disastrous M&A deals possess the following two characteristics:

1.    the acquired business is very different from the core business of the acquirer (in our terminology, 'outside the comfort zone');

2.    the acquired business is sizeable compared to the core business, which leads to a substantial shift of the balance (it stretches the firm too far and too much from 'my field' to the 'minefield').

Let's look at one of the largest M&A deals in the US financial sector. In 2003, HSBC bought Household Finance Corporation, one of the largest US consumer lending companies. The deal looked almost perfect. HSBC published a presentation such that everyone could understand that this deal had no disadvantages, only advantages. In particular, the strategic rational for the deal included (HSBC 2002):

•    bringing together one of the world's top asset generators (Household Finance Corp.) with one of the world's top deposit gatherers (HSBC);

•    significant geographic and business line diversification;

•    international roll-out of Household's business model.

It sounded like a very good deal: Household would receive cheap funding from cash-rich HSBC. HSBC would add a substantial piece of retail business in the USA, aggressively penetrating a relatively new market for HSBC. Household's business model can be replicated in other countries where HSBC had retail operations. However, there were at least two aspects of the deal that should have made HSBC think twice.

Firstly, Household had a very different business model, product mix and customer base. HSBC only saw the positives in this diversification, fully forgetting that some diversification comes from hell. 'Household's consumer lending business is one of the largest sub-prime home equity originators in the US, marketed under the HFC and Beneficial brand names' (HSBC 2003: 12). Even the fact that this acquisition would make HSBC one of the leading players in the sub-prime and near prime US lending market (37 per cent of Household's customers) had been interpreted as a positive diversification. In fact, this was a case when the bank completely mixed up 'my fields' with 'minefields'.

Secondly, the size of the acquired business was very material, which increased the risk of potential consolidation problems. By the time of the merger, in the USA, HSBC had 423 branches and managed total assets of $90 billion. Household owned total assets of $101 billion and had 1,300 branches in 45 states and more than 53 million customers across the entire USA, most of whom belonged to customer groups largely unfamiliar to HSBC. In other words, by acquiring Household, HSBC USA more than doubled its assets and became one of the largest sub-prime home equity originators in the USA.

From this perspective, for HSBC the deal represented an aggressive gamble and a huge leap outside its traditional comfort zone to the 'minefields'. HSBC was buying a very large firm which was running a substantially different business model, focusing on largely unfamiliar and more risky business products for HSBC, dealing with customer groups mostly new to HSBC USA. I don't want to say that this deal had no chance of success at all from its very beginning, but the acquirer should not have overlooked and should have seriously considered the obvious high risk factors that the deal had. And the *Financial Times* later wrote: 'Eyebrows were raised immediately the Household deal was announced in 2002.' At the time, Simon Samuels, banks analyst at Citigroup, described the acquisition as 'the riskiest move in HSBC's modern history' (Croft 2009). Yet HSBC's decision-makers focused on the bright side and painted a rosy picture of a future large success, which in reality became a huge failure.

When the US real estate market started to sink in 2007, HSBC finally realised that Household's business model was not as successful as they believed and described in the pre-merger communications. Household's 'best practices' in consumer finance that HSBC referred to and wanted to roll-out internationally appeared to be a reckless short-sighted lending business. The legacy Household portfolio started shrinking in value very quickly. HSBC stopped taking any new business and had to raise massive provisions against losses and write-downs. In 2008, the loan impairment charges and other provisions in HSBC Finance (Household's new name) reached $16.3 billion.

In March 2009, HSBC Chairman Stephen Green finally officially expressed regrets that HSBC acquired Household: 'With the benefit of hindsight, this is an acquisition we wish we had not undertaken' (Croft 2009).

Four years after the crisis started, HSBC Finance's portfolio shrunk to $44.2 billion at the end of September 2012 from $101 billion in November 2002, when HSBC announced its acquisition of Household. 55 per cent of the 'dream portfolio' had been written-down or sold at a loss. But the story has not ended yet. It will likely take several more years to sell and run off completely.

## A MERGER IS AN EYE-OPENER

Someone once said that love is blind, but marriage is an eye-opener. One of the lessons that we need to learn from M&A stories is that an M&A deal is like the marriage of a very passionate couple: before the marriage the lovers are blind or wear rose-tinted glasses and see their future married life only in rosy hues. There is no point in telling such lovers about a possible mistake (sometimes quite obvious to an outsider) in his or her choice of future spouse. The lovers will stay blind during their romantic period. But when the honeymoon finishes and the naïve passion evaporates, the young wife suddenly can see that her 'perfect man' has a lot of shortfalls and bad habits that poison their life together. The young husband suddenly realises that his 'perfect woman' has a nasty attitude and a not-so-attractive figure. But it is too late.

In a merger deal, when the acquirer evaluates the future pros and cons, it would be highly important to avoid the 'honeymoon' trap. Regardless of how perfect the fit can look and how much synergy there might be, the decision-makers need to understand the following:

- If you do not see any high risks of the deal, it does not necessarily mean that they do not exist. Sometimes it is very difficult to clearly see future risks, especially through rose-tinted glasses.

- The simple acid test for an M&A deal should include questions on to what extent the target business differs from the core business of the acquirer and how sizeable the new business is compared to the core business.

We know that it is always very difficult to correctly identify extreme risks ex-ante and quite easy to connect all dots of a failure ex-post. In order to escape from the 'honeymoon' trap, before diving into the merger, the acquirer needs to look at least at two risk factors – the deal size and the fit of new business to acquirer comfort zone. By doing this, the acquirer can get an idea of how much extreme risk might be hidden in the Pandora's box of the proposed deal.

Perhaps the most well known spectacular failure in the history of M&A deals was the merger of AOL and Time Warner, which is a perfect illustration of how the two risk factors described above can create a recipe for disaster.

In 2000, during the wave of the dot-com bubble, AOL merged with Time Warner, whose business was 'miles apart' from AOL's core business. In addition, Time Warner was too large for AOL to swallow. In December 2009, after almost 10 years of struggle to make the new business model work properly, the largest merger in media history came to an end. AOL and Time Warner finally separated.

In the list of largest 'M&A deals from hell', one can find many other cases when the targeted business was outside the comfort zone of the acquirer and, in addition, was large enough to shift the balance too much outside the core business and, as a result, led to business and operational problems and destroyed shareholders' value. Quaker Oats and Snapple Beverage Company, Sprint and Nextel Communications, HSBC and Household, Wachovia and Golden West – all these deals tell a similar story.

Conversely, often success comes when the acquirer buys a business which sits within its comfort zone. The Exxon and Mobil deal in 1999 represents a success story of business integration within the comfort zone. Actually, the track record of M&A in commodity and utility sectors looks much better than that in diversified product and service industries just because the commodity and utility sectors are much more homogeneous in their product and services range, which naturally prevents significant movements outside the comfort zones.

The eBay and PayPal deal also demonstrates the importance of buying a business that the acquirer understands. Although this could sound like eBay and PayPal businesses are very different, in reality eBay had a good grip on online payment business. When eBay bought PayPal in 2002, eBay already ran its own online payment system, BillPoint, which tried to compete with PayPal. Therefore, in its business model eBay had an integrated online payment component though not as powerful as the one that PayPal offered. In addition, prior to the takeover eBay and PayPal operated in the same market space and served the same customers. According to some sources, 70 per cent of eBay's customers had already been PayPal clients at the moment of the merger (Awoga 2012).

We can expect one typical argument against the view that if the target company's business is outside the comfort zone of the acquirer, it does not automatically lead to the 'jump outside the comfort zone'. If the target company has a long history, all competitive advantages and operates well within its comfort zone, the formal change of ownership after the takeover does not mean that business has moved outside the comfort zone. That's true if the change of the ownership is no more than a formality. I call it the Berkshire Hathaway style of acquisition. Warren Buffett explained his approach in a letter to Berkshire Hathaway's shareholders:

> Berkshire is another kind of buyer – a rather unusual one. We buy to keep, but we don't have, and don't expect to have, operating people in our parent organization. All of the businesses we own are run autonomously to an extraordinary degree. In most cases, the managers of important businesses we have owned for many years have not been to Omaha or even met each other. When we buy a business, the sellers go on running it just as they did before the sale; we adapt to their methods rather than vice versa.
>
> (Buffett 1990)

It is, indeed, an unusual approach. And if we mean 'Berkshire Hathaway' type of acquisition, then there is no risk of a leap too far outside the comfort zone for both the acquirer and the target.

However, nowadays Berkshire-Hathaway-style acquisitions are pretty unique. Usually, after the acquisition, the target company's business undergoes significant changes. The spectrum of changes can include the 'soft' transformation like alignment of the strategy and removal of duplication functions. But in most cases, the acquisition leads to a situation when the acquirer 'swallows' and 'digests' the target company completely. The target business undergoes a change of top management (partly or completely); the departure of some other key specialists and an injection of 'fresh blood'; business re-branding; changes in operating strategy and plans; a revision of products and services; alignments of IT systems and technological 'upgrades'; transitions of internal policies, the governance structure, HR services and other support functions, etc. But in any case, after the consolidation the target company will never be the same. Its business culture will change. This means that areas that have traditionally been in the comfort zones for the target company will likely be high-risk zones for the consolidated one.

To summarise, I do not want to say that each time we see the acquisition of the targeted business which is outside the comfort zone and sizeable enough, the deal is destined to fail. Not really. But each time it happens, the deal faces a substantial challenge to control new and often unknown risk factors. It requires extraordinary management skills and, to some extent, luck to succeed under these adverse circumstances.

To conclude my story about the first line of defense, we cannot calculate extreme risk that a firm is exposed to with any acceptable precision. Yet we know where the most of extreme risk is likely sitting. These risks reside outside the firm's comfort zone. Therefore, it is paramount to understand where the comfort zone starts and ends and to have a 'business genome' map in place. We need to be clear about an optimal balance between a business' mix of 'in' and 'outside' the comfort zone and strike the right balance via the holistic risk appetite approach.

# 8

# Second Line of Defence: Day-to-Day Extreme Risk Management

*One thing that makes it possible to be an optimist is if you have a*
*contingency plan for when all hell breaks loose.*
*(Randy Pausch, American professor of computer science)*

The first line of defence creates a protection from extreme risk exposure at the strategic level. At the same time, the first line of defence also helps to detect the areas where the extreme risk is likely to be sitting. These areas are where the business and risk knowledge is shallower and control over the risk drivers is weaker. On a map of the business 'genome', these areas are located outside the comfort zone. In fact, in the absence of reliable models for extreme risk assessment, the analysis of the 'genome' helps to create awareness about the areas and products that require a constant monitoring for extreme risk events. This is a first step to having the proper AAA approach in place.

However, to successfully deal with extreme risk, the optimisation of business strategy is necessary but not sufficient. We need to build the second line of defence, focusing on the day-to-day management of extreme risks and addressing the first two As in the AAA approach: Alarm and Awareness.

## Extreme Risk Identification and Stress-Testing

Considering that quantitative tail risk models are still in their infancy, we need to turn our attention to other approaches that can help to identify and estimate the tail risk. One of the principal ways of doing it is to implement a stress-testing framework for extreme risks and supplement it with the emerging and top tail risk tools (Figure 8.1). There is no novelty in including scenario- and

## Day-to-Day Extreme Risk Management focuses on analysis of extreme risk areas and developing contingency plans.

The task is to create a 'flight simulator' for training people to manage extreme risks and keep a sense of urgency within the organisation.

Figure 8.1     Key elements of the day-to-day extreme risk management

stress-testing in risk management practice. Moreover, regulators mandated banks to perform different stress tests on a regular basis. What is necessary to clarify here is the stress-testing priority: what is important and what is not when it comes to stress-testing of tail risk events and how to use stress-testing techniques to maximise the added value for a firm.

Broadly speaking, stress-testing is essential because it helps to enrich our experience in dealing with extreme risks. By definition, extreme risk events happen rarely and hit very hard. Lessons in dealing with tail risk in real life are painful and costly. Luckily, the stress-testing technique gives an opportunity to acquire virtual experience of dealing with different tail risk events without paying a very high price. Stress-testing, in a way, can be likened to a flight simulator for pilots. This technique helps a firm train its staff to deal with various risk challenges. From a risk management perspective, the experience and skills needed to mitigate the devastating impact of tail risks represent the main benefit of stress-testing.

Stress-testing for extreme events differs substantially from testing for mild and even severe events. In the following sections, I will discuss these differences and describe how to avoid typical mistakes at the stage of stress scenario creation, selection and implementation.

## Stress Scenarios and the Probability Trap

I believe that one of the most exciting tasks in stress-testing is the scenario writing. The team that is responsible for the scenario creation normally either uses a historical approach, adopting one of the past real stresses (e.g. the Asian financial crisis of 1997) to the current situation, or writes a hypothetical 'what if' scenario which does not replicate any particular past stress but rather describes possible changes in some risk drivers (e.g. what if the oil price increases by 20 per cent?).

One of the typical traps is to assess a probability to potential extreme stress scenarios. While a selection of stress scenarios requires substantial analytical and consultation work with various stakeholders, I would discourage the use of quantitative methods at the scenario selection stage. In particular, one typical trap is to attach a probability of occurrence to potential extreme stress scenarios and choose the one based on these probability numbers.

It is important to understand the difference between an extreme stress scenario and a close-to-'normal' risk scenario for which a probability assessment can be accepted. The probability is a statistical property; therefore we need to ensure that the probability makes sense from a statistical point of view. When assessing moderate stress scenarios (e.g. decline of the housing market by 3 per cent from the current level or increase of inflation from 2 per cent to 4 per cent), we can infer the probability of its occurrence from historical experience. As the scenario describes a situation which is not far from normal, we can expect enough historical precedents and hence this historical experience can provide a reliable base for the probability assessment (yet a judgemental overlay is required).

If we try to attach a probability to an extreme scenario, we are in the territory where historical experience either is not helpful (e.g. if the event never took place in real life) or can be even misleading (e.g. if a similar event happened just, let's say, once or twice in the last 100 years and we try to use this statistically insignificant number to infer the probability of its future occurrence). The danger is that in playing with probability numbers that don't have much sense, risk managers could discard some decent extreme scenarios at an early stage due to its 'improbability' (e.g. think about the 'ash cloud' scenario, unrest in

Egypt, a nuclear power station incident in Japan). Past experience is not a good guide for future extreme events. When constructing extreme scenarios, we need also to consider events that have never happened before. Therefore, the probability of occurrence (either calculated on historical data or implied via 'expert' judgement), like a broken GPS, can route decision-makers in the wrong direction.

I am an advocate of removing the probability attachment approach from the stress-testing practice with the exception of cases of 'normal' variation around a base case when probability can be explicitly derived from the statistically significant sample.

In all other cases, the probability attachment is not only confusing (being more gambling than analytics) but can also lead to the biased scenario selection. We know that many plausible stress-testing scenarios were discarded at early stages just because experts attached low probability to their occurrence.

During the scenario discussion and selection, we need to ask people one key question: Are we going to implement a 'regular' stress scenario or an 'extreme' stress scenario? If the answer is a 'regular' scenario, then we can talk about probabilities of different events. However, if the answer is an 'extreme' scenario, by definition the likelihood of extreme stress should be a very low number and we would like to run this scenario not because it looks very likely to happen, but because we need to understand what to expect if this highly unlikely scenario suddenly unfolds.

I even think that we need to pay more attention to scenarios that look 'implausible' based on past experience but potentially can be very severe (the tail risk events). As experience suggests, these scenarios, if they crystallise, lead to a devastating impact because nobody expects them to happen (e.g. Arabic revolutions, the nuclear disaster in Japan).

The practical approach for extreme scenario selection should not be based on perceived probability, which is very small anyway, and can hardly be justified; the decision should be based on consideration whether the analysis of the event and the contingency plan (mitigating actions) can add value to business and current risk management practice. Adapting the famous phrase of John Kennedy, we can say: Ask not what the probability of the scenario can be, ask what this scenario can do for your organisation.

If the simulation of the scenario can help to acquire important knowledge and skills in the mitigation of risk, then we need this scenario. Could an analysis of this scenario help us to spot 'fault lines' that we don't know? If yes, then we need this scenario.

Have we looked at similar scenarios before? Do some current contingency plans already address key threats of the scenario? If the answers to the last two questions are 'no', then it makes sense to seriously consider these scenarios for inclusion in the stress-testing programme.

## 'Illogical' and 'Implausible' Scenarios

The use of models for the extreme stress scenarios is questionable due to the non-linearity of relationships between risk drivers and depended variables and paucity of data that can help to adjust the modelling results. Suppose you have been tasked to create the extreme oil price shock scenario. In this case, in your scenario you need to specify how key macroeconomic variables will move in the case of extreme movement of the oil price. Based on the large number of observations, we have a pretty good understanding about the sensitivity of the main macroeconomic parameters to the oil price change. But most of these observations are concentrated in the area of minor deviations. Therefore, we can easily model the slight oil price shock (e.g. an increase of the price by 10 per cent will lead to decrease of the annual GDP growth by 0.3 per cent) and write a robust scenario. However, we have a very vague understanding about the impact of extreme shocks: for example, if the current oil price of $120 per barrel doubles and remains in the area of $240 per barrel for a period of 12 months. The answer is a difficult one. Firstly, we have no historical precedents for such a shock. Secondly, due to non-linearity of relationships the extrapolation of normal price sensitivity becomes unreliable: it is likely that such an extreme oil price shock triggers the cliff effect, when at a particular point of stress all observed relationships suddenly brake and start to move unpredictably.

Therefore, unlike the creation of 'normal' stress scenarios, extreme scenario writing requires more than just utilisation of past experience and pure statistical modelling. The out-of-the-box thinking becomes an important condition for creating a robust extreme scenario.

In addition, this work becomes more art than science. If we study real-life extreme events and how they unfold, we can spot the element of irrationality almost in each scenario. This is very strange 'ex ante irrationality': before the event occurred, it looked improbable, something unthinkable and it was even difficult to imagine that such a scenario could ever materialise. But after the event, the picture looks purely rational and people ask, 'Why didn't we think about it before?'

Past experience suggests that these 'illogical' and 'unthinkable' stress events, when they unfold, lead to the most devastating impact because nobody expected this to happen and thus nobody planned any actions to prevent or mitigate the event. For example, after the nuclear disaster happened at Fukushima Daiichi Nuclear Power Plant in March 2011, Chief Cabinet Secretary Yukio Edano said: 'The unprecedented scale of the earthquake and tsunami that struck Japan, frankly speaking, were among many things that happened that had not been anticipated under our disaster management contingency plans'.

Therefore, in order to develop a good extreme stress scenario, the scenario writer should always think about the unthinkable and sometimes needs to be 'illogical', meaning to include in the scenario events or risk drivers that may sound implausible at first glance. Quite often the tail risk arises from several little-appreciated events (errors, failures) with very low individual probability, which could trigger a drastic event if they happen at the same time. In this sense, the extreme risk can be literally manufactured by sequences of several non-critical rare events.

## How to Create a Disaster from Nothing: The Gimli Glider Case

The aviation incident, which happened with an Air Canada airplane and known as the Gimli Glider case, should be recognised as a classic case of how an extreme event emerged out of the blue and crashed the normal logic. I am not going to restate the Gimli Glider story, which, undoubtedly, many readers have heard before. Here I am going to analyse this extraordinary incident from a new angle – from the tail risk perspectives. The Gimli Glider case demonstrates two things:

- even in a highly regulated industry, where safety is a top priority, extreme risk is always nearby;

- the extreme risk event can develop from almost nothing but a few human errors and misunderstandings.

The incident happened on 23 July 1983, when Air Canada's Boeing 767 with 61 passengers and eight crew members on board ran out of fuel at an altitude of 41,000 feet during its flight from Montreal to Edmonton. How on earth could this event happen in the era of modern aviation with one of the most sophisticated aircraft in the world equipped with all necessary instruments to prevent such a horrible situation? How come the aircraft took off from the runway in Montreal with less than half the amount of fuel required to reach the destination?

There were several triggers of this extreme event:

- At the moment of incident, Boeing 767 was still a new model and some documentation (e.g. minimum equipment list) was incomplete, with some pages blank pending development of procedures.

- At the time of the incident, Canada was converting to the metric system from the imperial system.

- The 767 was the first of a new generation of aircraft that made the flight engineer position redundant and the responsibility for checking the fuel load moved to the captain.

- One of the two channels of the fuel indicator failed (but the other channel operated correctly, which allowed the flight to continue).

None of these triggers in isolation and even jointly could cause an extreme event, but they created the situation when a few human errors and misunderstandings manufactured the extreme risk event, which almost resulted in a disaster. The first human error happened a day before the incident when the aircraft arrived in Edmonton. The engineer who was servicing the plane found the malfunction of the fuel indicator. He restored the function of the indicator by disabling the failed channel, but he did not make clear in the servicing log that he fixed the problem.

When the plane arrived at Montreal, the crew changed and the new captain was informed about the fuel indicator problem but understood that it remained unserviceable. A ground engineer tried to solve the problem. He enabled the failed channel but, distracted with other tasks, he forgot to restore the single channel function – another small error. As a result, the one correctly-operating channel indicator became unserviceable. The captain looked at the minimum equipment list to check if the plane could fly without the fuel indicator, but he found the list incomplete. So he made a decision to fly because he knew that the day before, the plane flew to Montreal with, as he believed, the non-functioning indicator (in reality, the indicator operated correctly on the single channel). Another small misunderstanding!

The new Boeing 767 was the first aircraft type calibrated for the metric system while all other Air Canada aircraft used the imperial system. The member of the ground crew responsible for fuelling calculated the required quantity of fuel for the flight to Edmonton but used the wrong conversion factor. The captain checked the fuel requirement calculation but arrived at the same results as he used the same wrong conversion factor given to him by the ground crew. One more error! As a result, instead of the required 22,300 kg of fuel, the jet was loaded with 22,300 pounds or less than 10,000 kg.

The Boeing 767 had an on-board computer controlling the fuel consumption. As the fuel indicator was perceived unserviceable (actually, it was not), the captain manually entered the fuel quantity into the system. This completed the chain of errors. Now the computer erroneously indicated that the aircraft had 22,300 kg of fuel to fly to Edmonton. The tail risk event had been manufactured and the aircraft was doomed!

This story should have ended with a crash. But a miracle happened. Flying from an altitude of 41,000 feet with all engines out, the crew managed to land the aircraft on the former Royal Canadian Air Force base Gimli by using an exceptional gliding technique. This was the only safe landing of a commercial aircraft from this altitude without engines. The pilots were awarded the first ever Diploma of Outstanding Airmanship and the aircraft was repaired and remained in service with Air Canada until 2008.

Now, suppose that you have been asked to write a stress scenario for an airline company. Assuming that the Gimli Glider scenario never happened in reality, you write the similar scenario and submit it for the approval to the airline governance body (e.g. the stress-testing committee). What reaction would you expect to this scenario? It is almost certain that smart and experienced people, who sit on this governance committee, would immediately spot that this scenario is simply 'implausible', 'unrealistic' and 'silly'. In addition, these people would, possibly, say that the person who wrote the scenario, had little or no understanding of technical aspects and procedures in modern commercial aviation. But this 'unrealistic' scenario did materialise in reality when several risk drivers suddenly coincided (Figure 8.2).

All crucial systems of the modern airplane have double and triple protection. The service processes and procedures also include a lot of checks and cross-checks to eliminate the very possibility of a critical human error. The verdict: the scenario would be rejected with the recommendation to prepare the more plausible and 'logical' scenario.

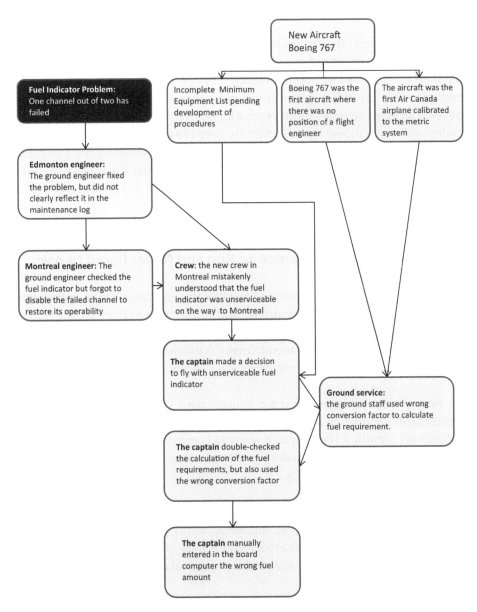

Figure 8.2    Gimli glider: drivers of the accident

This is another difficulty of extreme stress-test scenarios. Not only the scenario should be, to same extent, 'illogical' and 'out of the box', but the approval process for such a scenario becomes a challenge. 'Illogical' scenarios have a small chance of being accepted. Usually, these scenarios become easy victims of the governance and approval process. I call it the 'massacre of the innocents'. It is so easy to rubbish an extreme stress scenario using logic. It is so easy to label such scenarios 'implausible'.

People do not always understand that the risk management already eliminated the possibility for 'logical' ex-ante extreme events. In many highly regulated sectors like aviation, financial services and health care, all 'logical' and 'plausible' tail risk events were eliminated many years ago. If we want to develop an extreme stress-testing scenario, we need to think out of the box and go beyond conventional logic. Somebody needs to explain to key stakeholders the key principles of extreme scenarios. And key stakeholders need to fully recognise the difference between the normal and extreme stress-test scenarios and accept the unusual logic as a necessary ingredient of any good extreme risk scenario.

## Scenarios You Always Wanted to Run and Never Dared to Ask

Some interesting extreme scenarios have literally no chance of going through the governance filters to be approved and implemented. I am talking about scenarios where the top management of a firm represents the main risk driver. For example, this can be a scenario of a major fraud done by the top management of a firm. Do you think that these types of scenarios can be so implausible?

Recent history suggests that top management's fraudulent behaviour can represent the source of extreme risk. The scenario where top executive (or executives) commit a fraud, which leads to corporate disaster, is not so rare. Enron, Worldcom, Bernard Madoff Investment Securities – all these companies were ruined by their own CEOs.

While these cases represent the most spectacular corporate failures, there are many others, maybe not so infamous, which were caused by the top management's involvement in accounting frauds or controversial behaviour. This has led to enormous financial and reputational damage.

## EXECUTIVE TROUBLEMAKERS

### Daewoo Group

Kim Woo Choong, the founder and chairman of Daewoo Group, was sentenced to ten years in jail after being found guilty of charges including embezzlement and accounting fraud. Daewoo Group survived this scandal but suffered substantial financial and reputational losses.

### Parmalat

In 2003, Parmalat, a multinational Italian dairy and food corporation, suddenly defaulted on a €150 million bond payment while the company was reporting that it had been sitting on €3.95 billion of cash. The company officially went bankrupt and thousands of investors lost their money. The investigation revealed a major accounting scam created by Parmalat's top management, which resulted in a huge, multi-billion 'black hole' in Parmalat's accounts. Parmalat's CEO, Calisto Tanzi, who was perceived as one of the most successful Italian business figures, was arrested. Tanzi was sentenced to ten years in prison for fraud relating to the collapse of the company. Parmalat's bankruptcy was the largest in European history, representing 1.5 per cent of Italian GDP (proportionally larger than the combined ratio of the Enron and WorldCom bankruptcies to the US GDP).

### Ahold

On 24 February 2003, Ahold, the largest Dutch retail group and one of world's largest food retailers, announced that significant accounting irregularities had been discovered at its US food service operations. As a result, 2001 and 2002 net earnings became significantly lower than the management previously reported. Ahold also announced that it has been investigating, through forensic accountants, the legality of certain transactions. Ahold's share price dropped from €11 to €3. Ahold's CEO and CFO both resigned. In May 2006, the Dutch federal court found both of them guilty of false authentication of documents and they received suspended prison sentences and unconditional fines. The former CFO of Ahold's US food service was charged with conspiracy, securities fraud and making a false filing with the Securities and Exchange Commission. He was sentenced to six months of home detention and three years of probation. In January 2006, Ahold reached a settlement of US $1.1 billion in a lawsuit filed against the company in the USA by shareholders.

The former chief marketing officer was sentenced to 46 months in prison. The former CFO was sentenced to six months of home detention and three years of probation.

## Refco

On 10 October 2005, Refco, a large US financial services company and the largest broker on the Chicago Mercantile Exchange, announced that its CEO and Chairman, Phillip Bennett, had been involved in an accounting fraud. He had hidden $430 million of bad debts from the company's auditors and investors. After the news reached the market, Refco's share price fell off a cliff. The company filed for Chapter 11. On 19 October, trading of Refco's shares was stopped on the New York Stock Exchange. The former CEO, Phillip Bennett, was arrested. The court found him guilty of 20 charges and sentenced him to 16 years in prison.

## 'ROGUE BOSS' VS. 'ROGUE TRADER'

There is a long list of other cases when fraudulent actions or controversial behaviour of top executives either completely destroyed their companies or severely damaged their corporate reputation and financial position. Therefore, a fraud at the top executive level is not something which is impossible. I would even go as far as saying that the large scandals with top management happen on a regular basis. For example, CNN Money provides a list of the ten largest bankruptcies in US corporate history based on the value of each company's assets before its bankruptcy filing (CNN Money 2009). Among the top ten we can find two companies in this 'league table', which have been ruined by 'rogue bosses' (WorldCom #3 and Enron #6). It means that about 20 per cent of the most sizable corporate disasters can be attributed to cases of top management fraud. By the way, if we expand the list to the Top 15 corporate bankruptcies, another victim of the executive's fraud – Refco, with its $33 billion of assets – will occupy 14th place. Again, 20 per cent. This is an alarmingly high number which does not allow us to ignore the 'Rogue boss' scenarios.

Interestingly, many banks have now included scenarios associated with rogue trading in their stress-testing. The UBS fiasco with their trader Kweku Adoboli, who lost $2.3 billion in 2011 and which resulted in the UBS CEO's resignation, encouraged banks to develop this stress scenario. At the same time, I have never heard of any bank which looked into the scenario of a fraud at the executive level. It is interesting because if 'rogue boss' scenarios materialise, the consequences normally are more severe for a firm than in case of the 'rogue trader' event. During recent times, only one large financial institution failed due to a rogue trader (Barings Bank in 1995). At the same time, there were many cases when large or even global organisations have been demolished by top executives' fraudulent actions.

In short, if we compare these two types of fraud, we can summarise as follows: 'With a rogue trader, you can lose a fortune. With a rogue executive, you can lose a bank...' It gives me strong grounds to think that a 'rogue boss' stress scenario deserves close attention in the stress-testing programme.

## WHO SHOULD CARE?

However, how many people do you know who have the guts to stand up and say: 'Dear Mr CEO and Mr CFO, I propose to run a stress test for the "rogue boss" scenario. We need to assess what would happen to our organisation if you were involved in a major fraud or controversial behaviour.' I have never heard of such brave people.

Nobody wants to put his or her career progression at risk. But even if a brave person were ready to risk his or her career for the sake of the firm's interest, the chance of this scenario going successfully through the corporate governance filters and getting the approval would be zero. For success, we need more than one brave person. We need a governance committee (or committees) dominated by brave people. Even if a miracle happened and the governance body recommended the scenario, the last word from the CEO or CFO would most likely be 'No'.

I fully appreciate why top executives are not interested in running a 'rogue boss' scenario. If such a scenario was to happen in reality, they would no longer be responsible for the firm's business. Yet there are a lot of other stakeholders who should be interested in running this scenario. I am sure that the board and shareholders, in general, should be interested to know the magnitude of the possible impact and how the firm could mitigate it. Regulators, lenders of the last resort and government bodies should be interested as well: if this scenario suddenly crystallises in real life, they will need to step in and clean up the mess. Employees are also an interested party: if this scenario occurs, many of them will possibly lose their jobs.

I feel that it is important to educate people in the organisation: everyone should clearly understand that if the 'rogue boss' stress scenario is proposed, it does not mean that somebody has serious reasons (or any reasons) to believe that the CEO or some other top executives are about to commit a crime. The stress scenario is not a forecast. It is not the 'base case'. Moreover, the extreme stress scenario is always about the event that is highly unlikely to happen at all. When an airline company trains their pilots by simulating the failure of some critical systems during the flight (e.g. landing gear failure) using the flight simulator, it does not mean that the company expects that this failure will necessarily happen. But everyone understands that if this highly unlikely event occurs, it could result in a catastrophe, for which the airline company has zero tolerance. Hence, pilots need to be ready and able to prevent the worst. The same logic should be applied for a 'rogue boss' scenario. It is just training for a highly unlikely event. No offence.

When I shared my view with some bankers and risk people, they agreed in principle that the 'rogue boss' scenario is interesting and plausible but often ask the practical question: 'How could this scenario, if tested in an organisation, help to improve the risk management practice? This scenario is about our top bosses who are beyond our control.' It is a reasonable question. However, an earthquake or a tsunami is also beyond our control. Nevertheless, nobody questions the usefulness of stress-testing on a natural catastrophe scenario. In the case of the 'rogue boss' scenario, the added value of this stress test for the firm would be similar to that of any other extreme operational risk stress tests. The 'rogue boss' stress test can do at least two things:

1.    Identify any weaknesses or loopholes in the existing governance structure and control practice that could allow a major top executive fraud to occur. If such weaknesses are identified, actions that can help to fix the problem area and effectively prevent the firm from this scenario need to be proposed.

2.    Develop a detailed contingency plan which will help to mitigate the impact in the case of a major fraud or controversial behaviour of top executives.

I have no doubts that a 'rogue boss' stress scenario is not only useful but also necessary for the majority of large financial firms (especially for global, systematically important ones). I doubt that people who are responsible for stress-test implementation and approval of its result can be impartial in this case. Can this extremely sensitive scenario be evaluated objectively and sincerely without a hidden agenda to please big bosses? It is difficult to imagine how this challenging task can be achieved. This can only happen with either a bunch of courageous folk who drive the stress-testing process or the establishment of a framework which ensures full impartiality of people involved in the stress-testing. Is that realistic? The first alternative is rather unrealistic, while the second one looks quite achievable within the stress-testing approach; I will discuss this below in the section 'Stress-Testing and Conflict of Interest'.

## Stress-Testing Methodology

Unfortunately, stress-testing is often treated as a predominantly quantitative exercise. Regulators focus on the quantitative side of stress-testing because they often see stress-testing as a tool to check if a firm has sufficient capital buffer to withstand a particular adverse event. The use of quantitative methods and historical data has become the central element of this approach. Once I talked to a risk specialist of the US Federal Reserve who had been involved in the supervision process of US banks. He confessed that regulators preferred and asked banks to run stress-testing as a quantitative exercise because in this case regulators were in a better position to challenge banks' results: models, data and assumptions used during the stress test can be scrutinised by regulators.

The internal stress-testing stakeholders, such as top management, and external bodies (regulators), firstly worry about the stress-testing results. These results signify numbers of stressed balance sheet and profit-and-loss statements, estimated stressed losses, impairments, figures of risk weighted assets under stress, stressed capital ratios, etc. The desire to obtain a set of numbers dictates the currently prevailing approach: the lion's share of time and effort during stress-testing is spent on number crunching and discussing how these numbers were derived and why. People who have been involved in stress-testing can tell stories of long battles around stress-testing numbers: which number is wrong and which is right.

This number crunching exercise can be justified and accepted for scenarios emulating a mild stress when the aim is to test slight variations around the base case. Say, for example, we were to analyse what would happen to the credit portfolio if the macroeconomic climate deteriorates marginally. In this case, we can rely on historical data, as similar slight deteriorations happened in the past many times and we have quite a sound understanding of the sensitivity of the business with respect to the macroeconomic situation.

However, stress-testing of extreme event scenarios is fundamentally different. If an extreme scenario is considered, the stress-testing team ends up dealing with historical data that is scarce, if not unavailable. Quantitative models that can be effectively used for assessing the impact of mild stress scenarios appear useless for extreme ones. These models are built on large samples of data, which reflect the 'normal' or close-to-normal relationships between risk drivers and dependent variables. Extreme scenarios describe abnormal changes in risk drivers (e.g. the large negative GDP growth or a hyperinflation situation). This pushes the system to its new state and normal relationships no longer hold due to non-linearity and cliff effects. In addition, when we talk about the extreme scenarios we can expect that the new state of the system can trigger new risk drivers, which are not visible in the normal situation (e.g. customer behaviour in the stress situation can be unpredictable and very different from what we normally observe). So we need to include 'unknown unknowns' in our assessment. In this situation, the number crunching technique is rendered unreliable due to high uncertainty regarding the potential outcomes.

The rule of thumb is: the more severe the stress scenario is, the less reliable calculations are. The exercise moves from the predominantly analytical type for mild stress scenarios to the assumption-driven one for tail risk scenarios when numbers reflect opinions, expectations and the level of optimism/pessimism of experts. The power of analytics diminishes rapidly when we move to the territory of extreme events. Let's be honest: what we can achieve in reality when we try to assess the impact of the tail risk scenario is no more than the 'best guess'. Therefore, for extreme scenarios, results per se (a set of numbers) are subject to significant error margin.

At the same time, business and risk should be interested in testing for severe adverse scenarios. The whole idea of stress-testing is to virtually simulate an event that does not occur often in real life but can be potentially devastating. Regulators are also deeply interested in severe scenarios. CEBS Guidelines on Stress-testing clearly specifies that: 'Stress testing should be based on exceptional but plausible events' (CEBS 2010: 18).

How can this controversy – motivation to use exceptional scenarios and inability to derive reliable results – be resolved? In my view, results (a set of numbers that experts derive) are not a top priority for extreme stress-testing. The process itself should be a top priority and the process, if carried out correctly, creates the main added value for the organisation.

Instead of the main outcome of the process being a set of numbers, it should be:

- an action plan for immediate implementation that addresses the business weaknesses that have been identified during the discussions of the stress scenario;

- a contingency plan for implementation if the stress scenario unfolds.

Ironically, action plans, the most important part of stress-testing for extreme scenarios, are often ignored or relegated to a box-ticking exercise. In fact, developing a credible, effective and detailed action plan for mitigating tail risks is the most difficult task of stress-testing. Instead of crunching numbers, which might sometimes be exciting but adds a questionable amount of value to the tail risk stress-testing, stress-testing participants should spend their time thinking of what can be done practically in order to prevent/mitigate the extreme risk. Top managers who review and approve the results of stress-testing should also worry much more about credibility and efficiency of the contingency plan rather than a set of numbers produced under particular assumptions.

The devil is in the detail. A good contingency plan contains all of the details and this can guarantee its flawless implementation and ultimate efficiency. What we need is the WWWH plan: What, When, Who and How. It contains not only what is required to be done, but also assigns personal responsibility for carrying out each action point, and includes estimates of timing, costs, resources, dependencies and necessary implementation steps. It should not only cover the business actions, but also clarify who should make and approve various decisions and how actions should be communicated, internally as well as externally.

Therefore, if we run stress tests for extreme scenarios, we need to worry less about number crunching, trying to figure out precisely the amount of potential loss or additional capital due to stress. Instead, we need to shift our focus to the process of developing a robust contingency plan and ensure that all stakeholders know well the mitigating actions and their responsibilities.

This approach reinforces another important function of stress-testing, which I mentioned at the beginning of this section and which is often ignored or forgotten by stress-testing participants. Stress-testing can be and should be used as a 'flight simulator' for people in the organisation. The stress test emulates a stress environment and gives an opportunity to train staff on how to mitigate the impact of the adverse events. If participants of stress-testing spend most of their time crunching the numbers and arguing about final figures of impact, they miss the educational value of stress-testing. If we focus on the development of a WWWH contingency plan and engage all stakeholders to participate in this process, we therefore put these people in the 'flight simulator'. Via this activity people can obtain the 'virtual' experience of dealing with stress events.

## WWWH Contingency Plan: Why We Need It

When I talked to some managers about WWWH Contingency planning, many of them did not sincerely understand why they need to spend their precious time writing a detailed plan which can be used for an event with almost zero probability of occurrence. Their arguments were two-fold:

- We need to be practical and not allocate our scarce resources for writing something that is unlikely to be in demand. They often repeat: 'If we see that something really nasty is moving in our direction, we will sit down and prepare the proper plan on the spot.'

- In real life, the actual scenario will not be exactly the same as in the hypothetical stress scenario. It is not possible to anticipate exactly all nuances of the real life stress scenario. Therefore, the contingency plan, prepared based on a hypothetical scenario, will be useless once the real extreme scenario crystallises.

I don't buy these arguments. For the first one, the idea of drafting the contingency plan during the crisis does not sound great to me. Past experience teaches that if an organisation does not have a robust contingency plan, it will likely not be able to escape the vicious spiral of the crisis behaviour when the crisis hits (I will discuss this in the following chapter). Conversely, firms which have proper contingency action plans in place tend to have a better survival chance in extreme situations.

For the second argument, I do agree that real life is always the most creative scenario writer. The real tail event is unlikely to mirror exactly the hypothetical stress scenario written well before the event. I also agree that not all action points from the contingency plan can be implemented and some new actions should be considered as the extreme event unfolds. However, the robust WWWH contingency plan can be a decent starting point when the extreme event suddenly crystallises. It will help to start mitigating actions in the first, often the crucial, stage of the crisis.

## Flight Simulator for Bankers

It is also important to complement the detailed contingency plan with a proper 'dry run' of the action plan because it culminates in the transformation of stress-testing from a hypothetical and academic exercise into the practical 'flight simulator for bankers'.

In my office, every six months we undergo an evacuation drill. Not so many people challenge this practice. We all agree that while a fire in a modern and well-managed office building is highly unlikely, nevertheless we see a reason to have not only an evacuation plan but also a periodic full scale drill. Why do some people question the necessity to develop robust contingency plans for cases when business faces a turmoil?

The importance of detailed WWWH contingency plans for extreme events and full dry runs can be seen from experience gained of other areas. In particular, it can be helpful to look at the training programme for Russian cosmonauts. Each cosmonaut goes through the Gagarin State Scientific Research-and-Testing Cosmonaut Training Centre (GCTC), where he or she has to complete the long and very intense training programme. The programme includes training for about 1,000 (!) emergency situations that might happen during the flight. All 1,000 situations are simulated and the cosmonaut is required to implement the contingency plan for each situation.

Once, one of the future cosmonauts asked the Chief of the GCTC whether it was feasible to include 1,000 different emergency situations in the training programme as it is still not possible to anticipate all possible emergencies anyway. The Chief answered: 'Yes, it is highly possible that when you are in space, you will face 1,001st emergency situation, which is not part of our training programme. But if you complete our training and know how to resolve 1,000 different emergency situations, I am sure that you will successfully resolve the 1,001st.' I think that this is a great achievement of the GCTC and its emergency situation training that Russians have managed to escape fatal incidents in space since 1971.

It is unlikely that a financial institution needs to create 1,000 contingency plans as a response for 1,000 different extreme events. My experience suggests that, unlike cosmonauts, bankers do not need to look at so many extreme scenarios and prepare the individual WWWH plan. The array of responses to the tail risk situation that bankers have is not so wide. We can talk about, possibly, 10–20 different contingency plans that exhaust possible crisis-mitigating options. The point is not in numbers of WWWH plans per se but in the quality of these plans: five robust and detailed plans can help in the crisis situation much better than 25 superficial ones.

## Stress-Testing and Conflict of Interest

The credible WWWH plan is a result of an effective stress-testing process. When we say 'process', we mean how a firm organises information flows, discussions and decision-making in each step of the stress-testing, starting from the scenario selection and ending with the approval of the contingency action plan. The 'process' can be as effective as the firm is successful in eliminating a potential conflict of interest that often arises in the stress-testing process. As demonstrated earlier, tail risk stress-testing is more of an opinion-driven procedure than a precise science. Therefore, it is important to avoid any conflict of interest and exclude any biased opinions in the process of stress-testing.

If we start to build a big picture of stress-testing practice in the financial sector, we inevitably see that, in general, firms prefer to run mild scenarios rather than extreme ones. In addition, firms tend to be optimistic rather than pessimistic about their ability to sustain the stress under different stress scenarios. These trends were spotted by regulators who pointed out: 'Stress-testing should include challenging scenarios and should be designed so that the likelihood of severe events is not consistently underestimated and the bank's ability to manage crises in an effective and timely manner is not overestimated' (FSA 2008: 20). The trend of systematic over-optimism in stress-testing requires our special analysis.

Business is normally actively involved in the stress-testing process, as it should be. However, the conflict of interest is apparent: business managers are responsible for ensuring that the business they run is sound. The very nature of extreme risk stress-testing requires the searching and uncovering of potential business weaknesses. These two tasks do not match up smoothly. In many cases, business managers tend to prefer mild stress scenarios because they can demonstrate that their business remains solid under stress. However, if they have to run extreme scenarios, the 'overly rosy' assumptions prevail.

The business managers are optimists by the very nature of their job. They are used to looking at the 'bright side' rather than the 'dark side'. This inclination becomes especially visible during extreme stress-testing when predominantly subjective opinions, not analytics and data, drive the process. Business is not only too optimistic regarding potential impact under extreme stresses but also tends to be bullish regarding its ability to mitigate and sustain the stress.

Strangely enough, this over-optimism can be contagious and even risk managers often find themselves advocating optimistic points of view during stress-testing. There is a rational explanation of this behaviour. Ultimately, risk managers are responsible for creating a 'bullet-proof' defence for the business. Hence, it sometimes requires courage to step in and admit that the defence can be flawed under particular circumstances, especially when this verdict needs to be shared with top bosses. Nobody wants to be the messenger bringing the bad news, especially when magically transforming it into good news is a simple procedure of changing a few assumptions during the stress-testing process.

This human nature should be taken into account when the stress-testing process is conceived. When we talk about mild stress-testing, this factor is not highly visible because the process is to a large extent analytically driven. But when we start to test for extreme scenarios and people's subjective opinions become the major driver, we can no longer ignore this conflict of interest.

The best way to resolve this potential conflict is to assign responsibilities for selecting stress scenarios and making key assumptions regarding the possible impact on the business to a special team of experts who are not directly responsible for the execution of the company's activities (e.g. risk taking or risk managing). This team should report to the Board of Directors. Consulting with business and risk managers, but maintaining independence in the decision-making process, this team selects and shapes stress scenarios, assessing any potential threat and impact on the business (a gross stress test). Like the internal audit, this independent team has no incentives to make the picture 'overly rosy'. Moreover, they are rewarded for providing an unbiased opinion about the ability of the business to bear the tail risk pressure.

Does it mean that the business will be excluded from the stress-testing process? Does this approach make stress-testing an academic exercise without the business playing a role in the process? Not at all: business should be involved in the stress-testing and be directly responsible for constructing a contingency plan to address the challenges (but not for selecting scenarios and assessing potential threats and stress impact). After the independent expert team selects a stress scenario and assesses the gross stress-test results, the business managers should take over the process. The task of the business and risk managers is to come up with a credible contingency plan using their knowledge of the business.

To overcome a potential conflict of interest at the stage of developing a contingency plan, an additional set of checks and balances should be used. After the business side prepares the plan, it should be sent to the independent team of experts for review. Their task is to challenge the credibility of the mitigating actions proposed by the business. The independent validation of the plan creates a healthy competition process at the most important stage of stress-testing. Knowing that the contingency plan will be scrutinised and challenged by the independent experts, the business managers will be more rigorous and less bullish in their mitigating action proposals. Finally, the stress-testing documents, including the contingency plan and its independent review, should be dispatched to the stress-testing governance body for final approval, chaired by a Non-Executive Board Director (Figure 8.3).

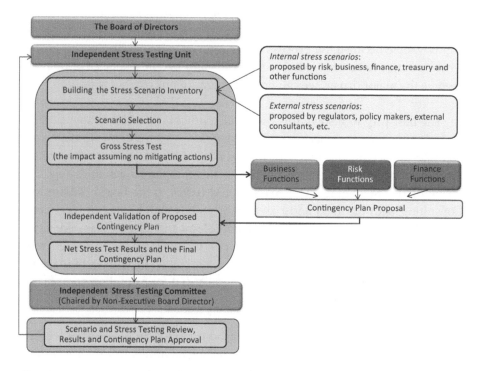

**Figure 8.3    Stress-testing government framework**

The proposed stress-testing process is not unrealistic. Actually, it mirrors the approach that is already used by financial institutions in certain areas where a potential conflict of interest would otherwise be apparent and derail the process. Internal audit is an example of such areas. The proposed stress-testing process, which I think is absolutely necessary, ensures a healthy competition of opinions and makes the process largely free from a conflict of interest. Simultaneously, it also guarantees the involvement of the business in the process and utilisation of the business and risk management expertise.

Stress-testing should be a tool used continuously and the outcomes that it produces must be employed on a regular basis for adjusting a firm's risk appetite and business strategy as well as enhancing the firm's crisis mitigation framework.

# 9

# Last Line of Defence:
# When the Perfect Storm Begins

*A bad sultan is not one who did not foresee a drought, but one who did not prepare for it.*

*(Arab proverb)*

Regardless of how good a firm is at setting its business strategy and risk appetite profile, as well as identifying any potential extreme risk exposures, no firm can guarantee that its business is immune to a tail risk impact. Especially, when a large systemic crisis develops and a contagion spreads across all businesses, each firm (even the most risk-averse) is subject to the effects of financial turmoil in one way or another. Those who failed to build the first line of defence and adopted reckless business strategies are as good as doomed. They will soon find themselves right in the epicentre of the 'perfect storm'.

Those who were successful in positioning their business predominantly within their comfort zones have a chance not only of survival but also of triumph. The ones who can survive and emerge after the crisis as winners are determined by how good the firms are in managing risks at the last line of defence – when an extreme risk event strikes.

## Vicious Spiral of Crisis Reaction

As with any other technical operation, crisis management requires special tools, methods and skills. An organisation which does not have an effective crisis management framework in place is almost destined to go through the classic stages of the crisis reaction. If a human is unprepared and a crisis situation emerges abruptly, the natural responses are often not just inadequate, but also destructive. The spontaneous crisis reaction aggravates the situation and sometimes even amplifies the damage relative to the crisis per se. These natural responses during a crisis situation create a vicious downward spiral. We can tease out four typical and distinct stages:

- overlooking the moment when a crisis is looming or beginning;

- sense of denial when the existence of the crisis is actively denied;

- shock when the existence of the crisis becomes undeniable;

- panic when an urgent response is required to remedy the situation but there is an absence of an apparent action plan.

These reactions are typical not only of human beings, but also of human societies and organisations. In order to demonstrate how this works in practice, I would like to analyse the starting phase of the Greek sovereign crisis. Now most people have already forgotten the very first stage of the Eurozone saga, which represented a 'classical' case of the vicious downward spiral of crisis behaviour.

## Trapped by Crisis Reaction: The Greek Saga and Beyond

### PHASE 1: MISSING THE MOMENT WHEN FIRE STARTS

The Eurozone problem surfaced as Greece's national issue in 2009. The Greek government admitted that they substantially underestimated its budget deficit and the revised number for 2008 appeared to be 7.75 per cent of GDP, i.e. up by four percentage points compared to the previously estimated number. In addition, the European Commission updated its forecast for Greece for 2009 and uncovered an unpleasant surprise: 'With both rapidly falling revenue-to-GDP and rising expenditure-to-GDP ratios contributing to the fiscal deterioration in 2009, the October 2009 EDP (an excessive deficit procedure) notification estimate the government deficit in 2009 at 12½ per cent of GDP' (European Commission 2009: 5).

The 12.5 per cent budget deficit was more than twice as high as the previously announced figure. This sounded like a loud warning signal for the Greek government and it is clear that the problem emerged not just yesterday, but several years ago. But the Greek government overlooked the moment when the fire started, and then they found themselves in the epicentre of the uncontrollable budget deficit crisis. The question is: why did the Greek government overlook the problem? Why did nobody sound the alarm in 2007 or 2008? Would it have been easier to resolve the issue had they started taking remedying actions immediately? Do not try to overcomplicate the answers. This is just a 'normal' path of the vicious spiral of the crisis reaction – a typical behaviour for a human being or an organisation which is unprepared.

## PHASE 2: CRISIS? WHAT CRISIS?

Did the government, which faced a severe budgetary crisis, take immediate mitigating action, especially when this news shook the markets (Greek credit default swap (CDS) prices grew from 125 basis points (bps) in October 2009 to 200 bps by year end), state organisations such as the European Commission, rating agencies and the general public? No way. Instead, the government preferred not to see the ugly problem and buried its head in the sand. The crisis behaviour exhibited a lot of irrationality. The 'ostrich effect' is a part of this reaction.

People who find themselves in a crisis situation often shift to denial mode. The way of thinking is: it should not be so serious because we are not stupid enough to be caught out by the nasty situation and we are smart enough to sort out this minor inconvenience quickly.

As for the Greek government, their response to the budget crisis arrived at the beginning of 2010. Greeks unveiled the Stability Programme, which aimed to cut the deficit from 12.5 per cent to 2.8 per cent by 2012. It sounded like a joke to many. Who could take seriously the plan to slash the country's deficit by more than 75 per cent in just three years?

The denial continued at the World Economic Forum in Davos, where the Greek Prime Minister Georgios Papandreou attracted massive attention. But he seemed pretty relaxed and did not show any signs of distress. His message can be summarised in two points:

1.  Greek economic problems have been exaggerated and Greece can fix this problem without external support.

2.  Greece does not need loans from other states and is only looking for funds in the capital markets.

In particular, Papandreou said: 'The problem we have is home-made. We Greeks are responsible for putting our own house in order' (Elliott 2010).

Jean-Claude Trichet, the president of the European Central Bank (ECB), backed Papandreou's denial position and ruled out help for Greece. He said: 'Each country has its own problems. It [the Greek budgetary crisis] is a problem that has to be solved at home. It is your own responsibility' (Elliott 2010). In March 2010, Angela Merkel joined the 'Eurozone Denial Club'. 'There's no looming insolvency,' Merkel said. 'I don't believe that Greece has any acute financial needs from the European community and that's what the Greek prime minister keeps telling me' (Wray 2010).

A reader could respond that the Greek problem did not look so ugly in March 2010, and European leaders did not realise the threat of Greece's insolvency. It is difficult for me to imagine that leaders suffered collective blindness. At least the market reaction showed that Greece was in deep trouble. For market participants, the denial position of European leaders provided an impression that they were unwilling to interfere and sort out the mess. This adds even more uncertainty and nervousness. The turmoil hit the markets and Greek sovereign CDS prices jumped to 400 bps.

## PHASE 3: SHOCK

Any denial phase should sooner or later come to an end. The Eurozone states discussed the situation with Greece at their summit at the end of March 2010. Finally, they realised that the Greek crisis was not a slight inconvenience and Greece alone could not resolve it. But what was the solution? European leaders needed to come up with remedying actions. Without a contingency plan in place, they proposed the most straightforward way out, which appeared to be wrong – a rescue package involving bilateral loans of €30 billion, with Germany demanding an above-market rate on the loans. But the Greek government was still in denial mode and refused to ask for a lifeline. The market situation continued its deterioration while European leaders were still in a state of shock.

## PHASE 4: WELCOME TO HELL

The final phase of the crisis reaction, also known as panic, follows shock. People who have been hit by a crisis finally understand that they are facing a serious problem which will not disappear on its own. They needed to implement mitigating actions quickly, decisively and properly. But there was no contingency plan and they quickly ran out of time. And here comes the panic.

In April–May 2010 panic was revealed in the European house. On 23 April 2010, Greek Prime Minister Papandreou finally changed his mind and asked for activation of the Eurozone/IMF loan. At the same time, Angela Merkel made it clear that Germany would not provide funds until Greece showed a credible plan to reduce its budget deficit. German government lawmaker Frank Schaeffler went even further, saying that Greece should be prepared to leave the Eurozone if it couldn't implement the deep austerity measures: 'If Greece can't push through these savings measures, it must voluntarily leave the Eurozone' (Thesing 2010).

The markets reacted immediately and the Greek CDS jumped to 750 bps.

Finally, on 2 May 2010 the Eurozone states agreed on a €110 billion rescue package for Greece. In order to calm down the markets, on 3 May 2010, the ECB announced an unprecedented decision. It agreed to accept as collateral all outstanding and new debt bonds guaranteed by the Greek government, regardless of the nation's credit rating.

As a response to the Eurozone rescue plan, thousands of people congregated in the centre of Athens, protesting against the austerity measures. The demonstration turned into clashes with the police, escalation of violence, vandalism and street riots. Three people were killed.

This fully undermined the market participants' confidence in Greek politicians and their European peers to manage the crisis. The Greek CDS prices exceeded the psychological barrier of 1,000 bps (Figure 9.1). It became clear that the rescue measures did not achieve the goal and the European leaders finally admitted that they were dealing with a widescale Eurozone crisis, rather than an isolated Greek problem. The bilateral loan strategy failed.

At the emergency meeting, Ecofin adopted a €750 billion European financial stabilisation mechanism and the ECB announced a new liquidity package to purchase distressed Eurozone sovereign debt. And straight after these steps, Merkel's government announced a sudden and unilateral ban on 'naked' credit default swaps, which came as a surprise to their peers in other Eurozone countries. What else could you possibly do to confuse the markets and undermine their confidence? The *Washington Post* commented on this decision: 'It was so transparently political and, in policy terms, so irrational that it raised doubts about Berlin's leadership in the euro crisis. Whatever short-term domestic political benefits it had were offset by the damage it caused, and may yet cause, on financial markets across the world' (*Washington Post* Editorials 2010).

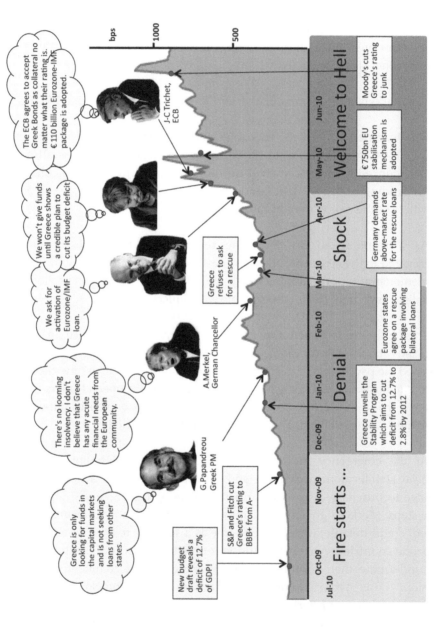

Figure 9.1   Greece sovereign five-year CDS price (bps) and the crisis 'reaction' trap

This decision to impose the unilateral ban on 'naked' CDS had a long-term impact. It destroyed the belief (if there were any left after a year-long agony of the crisis behaviour) in the Eurozone leaders to unite their efforts and come up with a robust solution of the Eurozone crisis. From this moment, the markets started to believe that the 'fire' of the Eurozone crisis could not be stopped in Greece due to the inability of decision-makers to implement coherent anti-crisis actions. Thus, the contagion would inevitably spread to Spain, Portugal, Ireland and even Italy. At this point, Pandora's box had been opened and the Eurozone countries faced a full-blown Eurozone disaster.

Therefore, when the crisis started the Greek government together with their Eurozone peers were caught by the crisis reaction trap and went through all four stages. They wasted several months when they had a chance, at least, to mitigate the impact and prevent contagion spreading across the Eurozone. The damage that was done by the crisis reaction of Eurozone politicians and policy-makers was enormous. The task of regaining trust became unachievable.

Why has it happened? Were Eurozone leaders so incapable of dealing with crises? Were there major economic or political obstacles that prevented them from being effective in the crisis situation? Not really. They were just not prepared. It is obvious that Eurozone politicians and policy-makers had no coherent crisis management framework in place to deal with a multi-country extreme financial risk event. I guess they did not even have a contingency plan for Eurozone space. In particular:

- They had no view on who should drive the process of the emergency action development and implementation. At different stages, different people tried to lead the process (the Greek government, the President of the European Commission, the German Chancellor, ECB, IMF) without a clearly defined responsibility and strategy.

- The Eurozone had no guidance on how emergency actions should be agreed to ensure the effective decision-making process. Endless EU summits stretching to the overnight debates, Eurozone Finance Ministers' talks, the Troika meetings and bilateral consultations demonstrated that the Eurozone did not have proper governance for the extreme risk situations and tried to establish one during their crisis journey.

- The Eurozone lacked a clear view on what point the national budget problem should be treated as the single currency block issue.

The long debates about who was responsible for cleaning up the mess impeded the decision-making process in 2009 and in the first half of 2010.

- The Eurozone had no any early warning signals in place that could help to identify the problem at its early stage. The Eurozone crisis alarm sounded too late.

The Eurozone crisis demonstrated once again that without a robust crisis management framework an organisation almost certainly falls in the crisis reaction trap. To avoid this, an organisation must develop and implement a crisis management framework before the storm starts. In this case, it not only helps restrict typical crisis reactions, but also deals with challenges faster and mitigates the crisis impact significantly.

So what should the crisis management framework consist of? There are five elements that I believe are absolutely necessary for the robust crisis mitigation (Figure 9.2).

Figure 9.2    Extreme risk crisis management framework

## Crisis Identification Mechanism

As I have already mentioned, the moment when a crisis emerges is often overlooked. As a result, time is lost and the situation deteriorates. The crisis identification mechanism allows an organisation to save precious time at the early stage when an extreme risk strikes. This mechanism should have two essential elements:

- warning signal tools;

- an established process of triggering the 'red alert'.

## WARNING SIGNAL TOOLS

I have never overestimated the ability of different early warning signal tools to predict the next extreme event. Let's be honest: even the most sophisticated modern automated systems and analytical tools do not give any guarantees that they can provide the right signal well in advance, even in the case of macroeconomic, credit and market risk events, where availability of data and its quality are normally very good and the analytical methods are well developed. For extreme operational risk events, warning signal tools remain in their embryonic stage. Reasons why analytical tools cannot give us reliable predictions of tail risk events have been already given in previous chapters. So I am not going to repeat myself. Yet I believe that warning signal tools are necessary.

While the ability to predict tail risk events well in advance is still questionable, warning signals can help to identify the tail risk event at the early stage of a crisis. It means that we are unlikely to be able to identify with a high degree of confidence an extreme event two years ahead or one year or even several months. It is probable that warning tools will not leave much time to react before the storm starts, but in the crisis environment even several days can be the difference between a business surviving and failing.

If we focus on credit risk and market risk events, it is unlikely that only one indicator can reliably predict a tail risk strike. The popular macro-economic factors and industry data, often used in different warning signal tools, have two drawbacks:

- they are too generic, too broad to identify the exact threat;

- normally, they represent lagging indicators (some of them like GDP are published quarterly only and with a significant delay).

Nevertheless, they can be useful to some extent as a general background story. These high level indicators, together with market data, can be considered as a first level of warning signals.

The second level should include the signals derived from the firm's portfolio analytics. These signals are no longer generic and reflect the unique structure and specific features of the firm's portfolio and its business. While these signals can be very useful for detecting the major risk drivers, they are unlikely to be sufficient. The problem is that only specific economic and business information can be structured and quantified. The substantial volume of valuable information is purely unstructured. The warning signal tools should utilise both structured (e.g. market data, portfolio performance data) and unstructured information (e.g. views of experts), which should then be converted to an alarm system. Therefore, the third level of the warning signal tool should include unstructured information.

The value of unstructured information as a warning signal sometimes outstrips the value of structured data and advanced analytics. This can be illustrated by the real situation that happened some time ago, around 2005. During networking drinks at a business forum, two people were sipping champagne and having the traditional chat that often happens between two strangers at different business network drinks. As usual, the conversation started with weather and sport. Then one man asked another: 'What business are you in?'. He replied: 'I am selling loans to people who will never be able to pay them back'. This man worked as a sub-prime mortgage broker! This piece of unstructured information arrived during happy days – a period of 'sub-prime mortgage honeymoon', when everyone liked sub-prime for their high profitability and nobody particularly worried about 'sub-prime doomsday'.

Structured indicators based on the general economic and mortgage data in 2005 looked very strong from the height of Manhattan's ivory towers. But some people in the 'boiler rooms', who dealt with sub-prime mortgage clients on a regular basis, already felt the smoke of the big future fire.

Therefore, the three-level warning signal tool can utilise and distil information from the macro level, the micro level and the expert level. If the red flag approach (or the traffic light approach) is implemented, then the total number of red flags/signals on different levels, and the sequence in which these flags pop up, can provide an objective picture of the risk evolution.

## TRIGGERING THE 'RED ALERT'

Yet the efficiency of the warning signal tool does not guarantee the success of crisis identification. This tool alone is not sufficient for introducing prompt anti-crisis actions. In addition, a firm needs a mechanism for determining the individual responsibility for announcing a state of emergency. It should be clear how to make a decision about shifting to the emergency regime and what actions this decision should trigger. The importance of triggering the 'red alert' mechanism is often underestimated or even fully ignored. In reality, the role of this mechanism is no less important than the warning signal tool.

I can think of an analogy with the fire alarm system of a building. There are two crucial components in the system:

- an initiating device, which identifies the fire in the premises (e.g. a smoke or heat detector);

- notification devices, which produce the signals (audio or visual) to alert residents and emergency services.

If the initiating device does not properly connect to the notification device or, even worse, if the notification device is out of order or not installed at all, this fire alarm system is useless. The same process should be applied for the crisis identification system in the organisation. The warning signal tool ('the initiating device') should be complemented with the triggering mechanism ('notification device'), which declares the state of emergency in the organisation.

I do not propose any automated triggering just because our crisis warning tools are not as reliable yet as smoke detectors. We need to analyse signals coming from the warning tool, interpret them correctly and exercise our own judgement before making any conclusion regarding the crisis alert. I rather suggest that a firm should clearly assign personal responsibility and granted authority to people who make a decision to declare a state of emergency in the organisation and shift the management to the crisis mode. Without proper defined responsibilities for triggering the alert state, a firm runs the risk that this responsibility will fall through the governance cracks. If no one can take responsibility and make the crucial alert decision, then the precious time preceding the crisis could be wasted.

## Contingency Plan Deployment

The second line of defence helps a firm identify the potential threats and prepare the WWWH contingency plans. I have already explained why the detailed contingency plans are of paramount importance for an organisation.

When a crisis starts to unfold and a state of emergency has been declared, the WWWH plan gets deployed. I have no illusions that prior stress tests can accurately predict what would happen in real life and how exactly the particular crisis unfolds. Therefore, I don't expect that all action points set out in a WWWH plan during the stress test can be feasible or achievable. Yet the WWWH plan is the best starting point for crisis mitigation. When a tail risk event strikes, the firm should review its WWWH plans, select the appropriate one and update its action points, taking the current circumstances into account. Without a WWWH plan prepared in advance, the firm is likely to be caught in the crisis behaviour trap.

How can we can ensure that the appropriate WWWH plan exists in a firm's depository? Indeed, the world of extreme and unpredictable events is massive. Life is the best and the most creative writer of stress scenarios. It is true: there is no guarantee that the new extreme risk challenge has been already addressed via prior stress testing and that a WWWH contingency plan is waiting for the implementation. However, even if the crisis has new and previously unknown risk drivers and has never been analysed via the scenario testing, WWWH contingency plans can be very useful. The firm can borrow mitigating actions from different contingency plans and, like Lego blocks, assemble them in the new contingency plan to address the previously unknown challenge.

Recently I have had an interesting chat with the CEO of a company which provides safety and security solutions. I asked how they provided solutions for tail risk events which are largely unpredictable and often stem from 'unknown unknowns'. He gave me an interesting answer. He said that they develop and keep several contingency plans and these plans can cover a large number of tail risk events. He mentioned one example: they developed a contingency plan for evacuation of their clients' employees from Cairo within 24 hours. They did not know what might trigger the need for such an evacuation (presumably a natural disaster). When the Arab spring covered the region in 2011 and riots started on Tahrir squire and spread across the Egyptian capital, clients called and asked for the emergency evacuation of their foreign personnel from Cairo. While the security solutions firm did not anticipated the Arab spring (which was an entirely unpredictable extreme event) and did not have a contingency plan addressing specifically the Arab spring risks, they had the evacuation plan ready. It appeared that this plan was exactly what the firm needed at that time for their emergency response. The firm implemented the contingency plan and the 24-hour evacuation was successfully done in spite of the high complexity of the task and cumbersome logistics as a result of the burnings and shootings in Cairo.

## Extreme Risk Crisis Communication

The role of communication for a firm during the period when the extreme risk event strikes increases exponentially. There was an astonishing number of cases when awkward and incompetent corporate communication during a crisis resulted in the irreversible damage and downfall of the firm's business. On the other hand, there was also a handful of examples when a company survived and emerged as a winner thanks to its efficient internal and external communication during difficult times.

There is no doubt about the importance of external communication during the crisis period. For a firm undergoing a phase of rainy days, it is crucial to obtain the full support of the external stakeholders (regulators, government bodies, clients, rating agencies, equity analysts, mass media, investors' community, etc.). However, it is equally important how the firm communicates the crisis challenges internally because employees are often decisive factors in a firm's survival. While it is difficult or even impossible to prepare the texts and company's press releases that the firm would circulate in the crisis situation in advance, the key tail risk communication principles should be ready before the turmoil begins. The WWWH contingency communication plan should set out details of the tail risk communication approach:

- who should speak to the employees and external stakeholders;

- when and how often the firm should communicate externally and internally;

- what should be the tone of the messages;

- in what form should the communication be and what communication channels should be used.

## Crisis Governance

When a crisis strikes, one of the most serious stumbling blocks to crisis mitigation appears to be the organisation's governance. Who needs to be involved in decision-making processes in the crucial moments? How fast can decisions be made? How quickly can decisions be cascaded down to people involved in mitigating actions? And how can the decision-makers ensure tight control over the crisis situation and the proper implementation of their decisions? Organisational governance should demonstrate a high degree of efficacy to steer the organisation through the turbulence of a crisis.

Traditional corporate governance establishes an administration and control under normal circumstances. The governance structure ensures the necessary balance of power and several layers for decision-making processes and internal controls. This 'well-balanced' governance structure comes at some costs. These costs are not only direct financial costs, but also the slowness of taking strategic decisions. While perfectly reasonable for normal situations, this governance does not sound great for the crisis. Numerous and large committees appointed as decision-making, controlling or consultation bodies are not an ideal option for crisis-plagued times.

The management requires a different sort of governance during the crisis period. A crisis situation with a shortage of time and scarce information requires a very different, simple, dynamic and a more military-style type of governance. I know that for some people the proposal of having a military style governance cannot sound like a great idea. But, firstly, I am talking only about extreme crisis situations. Secondly, experience suggests that in order to survive in extreme situations (e.g. a war, a natural disaster or severe social turmoil) society naturally shifts to a more military-style type of governance. During the crisis, life-or-death decisions should be made very quickly. It leaves no room for discussions in various governance bodies and consultations with various stakeholders. The key decisions should be taken by a small group of people who have power, expertise and influence to do this quickly. The crisis governance needs also to include an effective mechanism of decisions cascading from the top to the bottom of the firm's hierarchy and a simple but effective decision-implementation control and feedback.

Crisis governance should be designed, approved and set up well before the moment when the extreme risk event crystallises. It is a very bad idea to design crisis governance during the turmoil. Previously I analysed the Eurozone crisis reaction trap. One of the reasons for such a terrible inefficiency of the Euro crisis management was the absence of clear crisis governance, while the traditional Eurozone governance structures were struggling to provide an adequate response to the multi-country financial disaster.

Crisis governance (including the mechanism of decision cascading across the organisation) needs to be included in a firm's policy documents and receive full approval in order to be legitimate. It will eliminate the stumbling blocks of traditional governance. When a state of emergency is declared, the firm should swiftly switch to the new governance type.

## IT Infrastructure and Management Information

During the crisis, information goes from being a highly valuable resource for decision-making to a 'life-or-death' resource. When an extreme event unfolds, the IT infrastructure and management information should be able to process data and generate information to address the crisis situation. The IT and reporting systems are usually consistent with fully meeting the goals set under normal circumstances, but not necessarily with working successfully during the crisis times.

Two aspects of crisis information flow are paramount for IT and management information systems:

1.  Time 'compression': a crisis compresses time. Not actually, of course, but virtually. People who find themselves in the midst of a crisis feel like time starts to flow much faster than during normal days. One crisis day can bring more information than one month of a benign period. It also means that during the crisis, information becomes outdated much more quickly. This creates a challenge for IT systems. Suppose that an IT system sets to provide a bi-weekly report on a credit portfolio performance. This frequency looks absolutely appropriate for effective decision-making in a normal situation. However, if a credit crunch unfolds, information which is two weeks old is deemed to be outdated and can even be misleading. Two weeks during the crisis can be equal to two or more months of a normal period.

2.  Event-driven situation: the benign business periods are characterised by clear and stable trends. New information or events normally bring little or no change to existing trends. During the crisis, the world is driven by large events. Each event not only can substantially influence the trend but also can be a signal that the world has moved to the new state. The default of a major counterpart, riots on the streets, resignation of a top executive, cancellation of a large credit facility – all these events can drastically change the business environment.

What do these two aspects mean for IT and management information? The first one is pretty straightforward. Effective crisis management can be achieved only if decision-makers and people who are involved in the implementation of mitigating actions are able to receive up-to-date information in the fast-changing crisis situation. This requires the IT and reporting systems to be ready to process the information faster than normal. The IT and management information (MI) systems need to define and set up the crisis mode: a regime which provides a solution to use shortcuts and, where possible, alternative information channels that help to reduce time to distil information and produce reports. It is likely that in order to speed up the information flow the volume of information needs to be compromised. During the crisis, key information should be delivered faster, while non-essential information can be excluded. Therefore, key information should be properly defined and ways of obtaining this information should be established.

The second aspect of the crisis information flow reflects the event-driven nature of information. That's a big thing. This means that the whole traditional ideology of management information and reporting should be reconsidered. The traditional reporting is driven by a calendar. There are normally various reports flying around an organisation and all these reports (or at least the vast majority) are linked to a calendar: people receive daily, weekly, monthly and quarterly reports. In the crisis mode, the MI and reporting system should be driven not by a calendar, but by events. The event-driven approach (contrary to the traditional 'calendar'-driven one) means that the MI system moves towards the ad-hoc nature of MI and reporting. Therefore, the system should:

- be able to generate non-scheduled reports as often as necessary, reflecting key internal and external events;

- allow a much higher degree of flexibility in data extraction, filtering and aggregating that traditional rigid MI systems. IT infrastructure should be flexible enough to be able to generate not only pre-defined reports, but also to slice and dice information to address non-standard requests.

## Connecting All the Dots: Three Lines of Defence

The development and implementation of the bespoke risk management framework focusing on large and catastrophic loss prevention is paramount to the successful survival of a firm and makes a positive difference in the way that the firm copes with future crises. I have previously described what this framework can look like. The beauty of the approach is that this framework does not require huge investments and many years of hard work to implement it. Basel II implementation takes years: a firm needs to build dozens of risk models (for global banks – hundreds), design the data infrastructure and the risk engine to aggregate risk data and calculate risk-weighted assets (RWAs). It requires creating teams of model developers, valuators, Basel reporting, etc and etc. The extreme risk management approach described above aims to utilise what already largely exists in most financial institutions: no more complex models, databases, additional teams of risk managers or quants. What we need is to use existing resources in a more intelligent way. We need to change the scope to think more about things that can kill the financial institution. We need to modify the existing risk frameworks and infrastructure to address challenges of extreme risk.

For example, today each and every large bank has its risk appetite framework. What we need is to stop replicating the financial and performance metrics from annual plans, proudly calling them risk appetite statements. We need to analyse the business model and businesses, which we run outside the comfort zone, and make a decision about the strategic appetite to run business inside and outside our comfort zone and then convert this message into metrics and cascade them.

Today, all financial institutions have their stress-testing programmes, stress-testing infrastructure and dedicated specialists who run stress tests. What we need is to focus on extreme risks: to develop really useful tail risk scenarios to uncover the Achilles' heel of the firm, to shift focus from number-crunching to contingency-planning, to make processes free from the conflict of interest. This is not about extra investments, headcounts and costs. This is all about doing things right.

The described approach was designed to address different strategic and tactical aspects of tail risk management and includes three lines of defence. Within each line, there are a number of different solutions. While implementation of each solution can add significant value, an implementation of the entire architecture (Figure 9.3) across a firm will provide a holistic defence from extreme events and will drastically enhance a risk culture within the organisation.

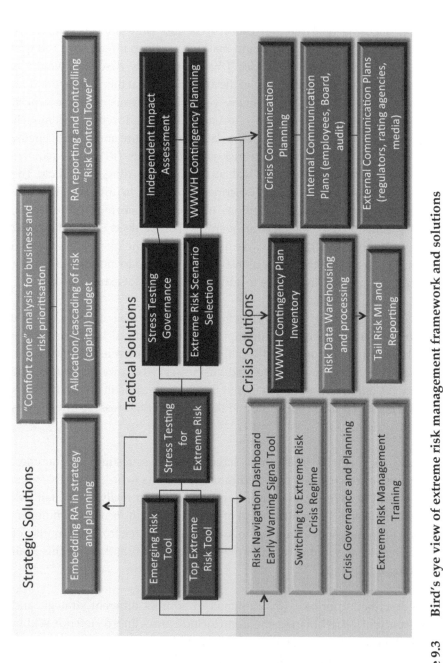

**Strategic Solutions**

"Comfort zone" analysis for business and risk prioritisation

RA reporting and controlling "Risk Control Tower"

Allocation/cascading of risk (capital) budget

Embedding RA in strategy and planning

**Tactical Solutions**

Independent Impact Assessment

WWWH Contingency Planning

Stress Testing Governance

Extreme Risk Scenario Selection

Stress Testing for Extreme Risk

Emerging Risk Tool

Top Extreme Risk Tool

**Crisis Solutions**

Crisis Communication Planning

Internal Communication Plans (employees, Board, audit)

External Communication Plans (regulators, rating agencies, media)

WWWH Contingency Plan Inventory

Risk Data Warehousing and processing

Tail Risk MI and Reporting

Risk Navigation Dashboard Early Warning Signal Tool

Switching to Extreme Risk Crisis Regime

Crisis Governance and Planning

Extreme Risk Management Training

**Figure 9.3    Bird's eye view of extreme risk management framework and solutions**

# 10

# If the Blind Lead the Blind:
# Dear Regulator ...

*They are blind leaders of the blind. And if the blind lead the blind, both will fall into a ditch.*

(Holy Bible, Luke 6: 39)

## Too Big to Fail

Dear Regulator,

I am writing to share my concern about the new regulatory rules. I waited anxiously for the regulatory response to the global financial crisis. It was clear that the Basel II approach failed to weather the financial disaster. The financial sector needed measures that would focus on the effectiveness of extreme risk management. Basel III came as a big disappointment to me and early in this book I explained why I believe the regulatory reform will not achieve the goal. I understand that regulators experienced huge political pressure to deliver proposals quickly, but the three 'silver bullets' of new Basel – higher capital ratios, more liquidity and capped financial leverage – will not kill the beast of large systemic and catastrophic losses. I do not want to repeat myself on how regulators missed the point ...

... Basel III capital rules do not provide solutions for improvements of extreme risk quantification, so the fundamental problem persists. The idea to increase risk-based capitalisation, while the entire concept of the risk quantification fails, sounds strange to me. But I fully understand the position of regulators. They implicitly say: 'OK, we don't know how to calculate risk and risk-weighted assets correctly. Therefore, as a mitigation we propose to increase the percentage of capital for each unit of risk (even if this risk has been miscalculated).

As a result, if before Basel III the estimated risk-weighted capitalisation was wrong, now it is conservatively wrong.' I already explained in detail why I believe that it is unlikely that the new liquidity framework will be able to prevent the systemic liquidity crisis in case of the market panic.

One innovation of the new regulation that I have not mentioned before and would like to touch on here is the approach to systemically important financial institutions (SIFIs). The global financial crisis for the first time highlighted so starkly the problem of interconnectivity of financial institutions and the 'too big to fail' problem. If SIFIs crashed, the whole financial system could experience a domino effect with disastrous consequences. During the crisis, to avoid the worst, governments had to bail out failed SIFIs at the taxpayers' expense (e.g. RBS, Lloyds Banking Group, UBS, ING Bank, Citigroup, Bank of America). What was the response of the regulators to address the 'too big to fail' problem?

'You do not need to be Sherlock Holmes with his superb deductive reasoning to guess what regulators proposed.'

'Damn, was it again more capital?'

'Yes, indeed!'

'Was it as a percentage of risk-weighted assets?'

'Yes, of course.'

'Oh dear! Do regulators understand that the calculation of risk-weighted assets suffers a conceptual problem and estimated RWAs never correctly reflect the actual extreme risk that a financial firm is exposed to?'

'They don't care.'

The BIS paper 'Global systemically important banks: assessment methodology and the additional loss absorbency requirement' (BIS, 2011) explains that the introduction of the add-on capital requirement needs to reduce the probability of failure by increasing their going-concern loss absorbency.

Once again, normally financial institutions fail not because they have insufficient capital, but because they suffer unbearable losses. They face losses because they cannot manage extreme risk properly by opting for reckless business strategies, flawed business models or by making unforgivable mistakes. I don't dispute the idea of sufficiency of capital, but loss absorbency is no more than an 'airbag'. Yet regulators keep on referring to the same mantra: 'More capital, more capital, more capital ...'

## UBS CASE STUDY

Take UBS AG. Did the bank fail during the global financial crisis due to insufficiency of capital? UBS started the year 2007 as one of the best capitalised banks in the world with almost CHF40.5 billion of equity capital and BIS Tier 1 capital ratio of 11.9 per cent! But when the sub-prime crisis started, UBS has been exposed to catastrophic losses, mainly from their sub-prime mortgage investments. By April 2008, the bank had to write down an astonishing circa CHF38 billion (about US$37.3 billion). This eroded the bank's capital and pushed the bank into massive recapitalisation. In October 2008, the Swiss Confederation had to step in, and bailed out UBS. This bailout pushed the federal budget into a deficit of 5.3 per cent of spending. Overall during the financial crisis, UBS experienced catastrophic write-downs of more than $50 billion.

I have a question to regulators: If the proposed approach for SIFIs was in place at the beginning of 2007 and UBS was to increase its common equity by an extra 2 percentage points, would it have saved the bank from the financial fiasco?

Firstly, by 2007 UBS already had its capital ratio sufficiently higher than the minimum requirement, so the bank would not need to add 2 percentage points more. But even with the additional 2 percentage points, the disaster would be inevitable. Why was UBS doomed for disaster? Not because of insufficiency of capital, but because of its Investment Bank's reckless growth strategy and the failure to properly assess and manage extreme risks.

We can use the UBS case to demonstrate to the regulators how the 'too big to fail' problem should be addressed. UBS is not only a typical SIFI but its failure also represents a classic example of how a SIFI can collapse. UBS has been a brilliant wealth management firm, possibly the best in the world. At the beginning of the 2000s, Marcel Ospel, UBS CEO and then the Chairman, together with John Costas, the CEO of UBS Investment Bank (former UBS Warburg), started to implement an ambitious plan to turn UBS into the leading investment bank with a leading market share in the USA. As a result, UBS dramatically built up its exposure to investment banking areas (mostly in the USA), stepping far outside their traditional comfort zone.

As so often happens, at the beginning UBS' leap outside the comfort zone looked like the right step. Extreme risks remained invisible, but profit grew massively. From 2002 to 2006, the Investment Bank's profit before tax grew from CHF1.3 billion to CHF5.9 billion or by 4.4 times! These results should immediately raise the question: Did UBS invent the money machine or just get free cheese in a mousetrap? Ospel and Costas believed that it was the former, but the year 2007 proved that it was the latter.

## HOW TO SOLVE IT

The UBS case shows how regulators need to approach the 'too big to fail' problem. Instead of applying capital add-on, they need to closely oversee the business and risk strategy of SIFIs using the approach described in Chapter 7 of this book. Regulators need to take the following steps:

1.  Build 'genomes' of all SIFIs to understand their comfort zones and high risk zones.

2.  Analyse SIFIs' current exposures outside comfort zones and establish the tolerances for each SIFI to run business outside comfort zones.

3.  For each SIFI, the approval of the business and risk strategy to outline the maximum accepted growth in key business areas inside and outside comfort zones.

4.  Control the agreed strategy implementation and, where necessary, exercise the veto right to prevent SIFIs taking excessive risks.

This approach allows regulators to spot and stop the warehousing of extreme risk at its early stages. If this approach had been used for UBS and other failed SIFIs, the industry would avoid the massive bail-outs of 'too big to fail' firms in 2008–9.

Of course, this approach requires very different skills from regulators: the ability to analyse instead of number crunching, the deep understanding of financial businesses instead of regulatory reporting data checking, judgemental decision-making instead of a formal technical approach. And additional responsibility: once regulators approve business strategies for SIFIs, they become responsible for the consequences. It is a big step for the regulators and a steep learning curve. But without clearing this big hurdle, we cannot fix the 'too big to fail' problem.

Do regulators need to approve and tightly control business strategy for other financial institutions outside the SIFI list? I believe that small banks should not be subject to regulatory strategy control. Small banks need to be able to search for their business niche and can afford to take risky steps outside their comfort zones. At the end of the day, this is how small firms can find their place in the sun and grow to be large players. But as soon as financial firms become large enough such that their collapse would be significant enough to threaten the system, the regulators need to step in and impose strategy control. I am absolutely convinced that the freedom of choosing business strategy ends when the stability of the financial system is at stake.

The idea of regulatory control for SIFIs' strategy is hardly very original. We need to look at other areas of life. Why do you think the traffic rules impose much lower speed limits for heavy vehicles compared to light ones? The answer is: because heavy vehicles are 'systemically important'. The error of the truck driver could be costly. That is why we find the extra speed limit of heavy vehicles logical and appropriate. The regulatory control for strategy will be a 'speed limit' for SIFIs. Those who prefer to drive faster should swap trucks for cars.

For banks such as UBS, it was not morally admissible to exercise a strategy that put not only millions of customers at risk but also the entire nation's wealth. In 2009, the newspaper *Le Quotidien Jurassien* rightly said: 'Ospel and his like have truly failed the country' and Suedostschweiz wrote that Ospel's efforts to grab market share for UBS in the USA had 'left its home country in a shambles' (Ligi and Holland 2009).

What regulators need to push for is for all financial institutions to implement an extreme risk management framework. Regulators need to oversee the level of robustness of this framework in place. Moreover, regulators need to lead and be a part of this process. A systemic crisis cannot be resolved by one isolated financial firm. The individual firm can create an effective three-line defence from systemic and catastrophic losses and successfully withstand the extreme risk shock. But working together with regulators, the firms can make their defence much stronger. Regulators need to not only encourage firms to build an effective framework for managing extreme risk events, but lead and coordinate this work.

Let me give you an example. I explained earlier that contingency planning is an essential part of the defence approach. But when a firm is preparing its contingency plan and response actions for the systemic crisis, it needs to take into account the actions of the key players of the financial system. These key players are the Central Bank and systemically important financial institutions. The risk-mitigating actions of the firm will depend on, for example, how the Central Bank will react to the crisis. Therefore, the WWWH contingency plan needs to include coordinated mitigating actions of the central bank and the major player of the financial system. The role of regulators should be to build their own contingency plan and coordinate it with all systemically important banks and other market players.

## Culture of Collective Blindness

> *But as long as the music is playing, you've got to get up and dance. We're still dancing.*
>
> (*Charles 'Chuck' Prince, CEO and Chairman of Citigroup*)

---

Dear Regulator,

Another worry that I would like to share with you relates to business culture. In the last several years, I have studied many cases of financial institutions' failures. I tried to understand why some banks running profitable 'sexy' businesses and having advanced risk management collapsed while others, being less advanced, survived and succeeded. For example, Lehman Bothers' risk management department had more PhDs than some UK universities! And Lehman's top managers were not stupid and were highly educated. I was struggling to explain this phenomenon until I found and read a book that has nothing to do with the finance world ...

---

... The book was called *Collapse* and was written by the American scientist Jared Diamond (2005). In the book, he analysed past civilisations and revised the conventional explanation as to why societies collapsed. Usually, a civilisation collapse is explained by some catastrophic events outside the society's control (e.g. disease outbreak, a war, acts of God). Diamond provided the analysis of collapses of several civilisations, one of which was the Norse Vikings. Here, I need to repeat this story in brief.

## LESSONS OF PAST CIVILISATIONS

Thousands of Norse Vikings settled in Greenland in the eleventh century and made this island their home for almost 500 years, from 1000 to 1450 AD. The disappearance of the Norse Viking civilisation in Greenland was commonly attributed to the Little Ice Age. Diamond argued that while the Little Ice Age played some role, it was not the main factor leading to the Viking civilisation's collapse. It did get cold, but the change of climate came gradually, leaving the Vikings with about 200 years to adapt. Two hundred years is a long time (consider, for comparison, a time period from Napoleonic wars until our days). It didn't get so cold that Greenland became uninhabitable: a more primitive civilisation of the Greenland Inuit (Eskimos) survived long after the Vikings died out. Compared to the Eskimos, Vikings had all the competitive advantages needed to survive and thrive:

- more advanced knowledge and ways to organise their lives: Norse Vikings wrote in Latin and Old Norse and they followed the latest European fashions in clothing;

- more diverse food supply (they even herded farm animals);

- better equipment for survival: they made and used iron tools;

- ready access to Europe: they regularly traded with Norway.

Yet the Inuit survived, while the Norse Vikings vanished. 'The lesson of *Collapse* is that societies, as often as not, aren't murdered. They commit suicide: they slit their wrists and then, in the course of many decades, stand by passively and watch themselves bleed to death' (Gladwell 2005). Diamond concluded: Norse Vikings' culture predetermined their collapse. The culture dictated three behavioural priorities for their elite:

- to maintain their own status in society;

- to please the clergy, who regulated the life of Viking society;

- to stubbornly stick to their traditional cultural heritage and values, which became inappropriate and even suicidal when the environment adversely changed.

For example, to survive, the Vikings needed to stop damaging the fragile Greenland environment. By chopping down trees and maintaining a large livestock, the Vikings damaged the soil, which started to erode progressively due to strong winds. To survive, they needed to reduce their reliance on livestock ... But cows were a sign of high status and the local elite continued to herd cows.

To survive, Vikings needed iron to make iron tools and wood for building purposes (scarce local lumber resources almost disappeared due to their overuse). The local elite traded walrus tusks and polar bear skin with Europe, but not for iron and wood as you might expect. Diamond wrote: 'much of that arriving cargo capacity was devoted to materials for churches and luxuries for the elite' (Diamond 2005: 238). Instead, from Norway they brought church bells, priests' robes, communion wine, stained-glass windows and bronze candlesticks to adorn their churches as well as silk, silver and jewellery.

Why were the elite so short-sighted? Even while the Vikings depleted their resources, their elite were still being fed well, continued living in their 'ivory towers' and protecting their own interests. As Diamond wrote:

> There were many innovations that might have improved the material conditions of the Norse, such as importing more iron and fewer luxuries ... and copying (from the Inuit) or inventing different boats and different hunting techniques. But those innovations could have threatened the power, prestige, and narrow interests of the chiefs. In the lightly controlled, interdependent society of Norse Greenland, the chiefs were in a position to prevent others from trying out such innovations.
> (Diamond 2005: 276)

And the chiefs didn't recognise that they were making a big mistake until it was too late. I asked myself what a Viking chief was thinking when he ordered what to buy from Norway. He knew that another cold winter and harsh times were coming soon. Yet he exchanged walrus tusks for jewellery and silk for his wife and silver plates, church bells and communion wine for the church to please the bishop. Why? Because the Viking's culture dictated the priorities: to maintain status in the Viking society and 'maintain relationship' with bishops, who ruled the Norse society and influenced the social hierarchy. 'Thus, Norse society's structure created a conflict between the short-term interests of those in power, and the long-term interests of the society as a whole. Much of what the chiefs and clergy valued proved eventually harmful to the society' (Diamond 2005: 276).

Surprisingly, when I studied failed firms, I found that this Viking culture of collective blindness was quite typical for those firms. We can see any large firm as an example of a 'society' with its own elite, social structure and traditions. A firm's strategy, business agenda and resource allocation are determined by the firm's chiefs and driven by the firm's internal culture. In failed firms, the chiefs made decisions that were good for them in the short run and ruined the 'society' in the long run. In particular:

- The elite were well fed and well paid and their internal culture focused on short-term priorities. Actions that can ensure a firm's long-term survival (focus on extreme risks) were not a part of their agenda.

- The chiefs' priorities were to maintain their own status in society and to please the 'modern clergy' (i.e. regulators, politicians) who regulated life in the financial community. These firms all had chances to survive, but their elite ignored the obvious threats because they focused on different priorities (a phenomenon of collective blindness). That is why they were not able to recognise what a mess they made until it was too late.

I would like to stress one more element of commonality between the Norse Vikings and modern financial firms. Diamond wrote: 'The Greenland Norse also carried over from Iceland and Norway a sharply stratified, hierarchically organized social organization, such that a small number of chiefs dominated owners of small farms, tenants who didn't even own their own farms, and (initially) slaves' (Diamond 2005: 248). The centralised social structure per se increases extreme risks for a society. The concentrated power at the top can bring the society to its glory (if the chiefs implement the right strategy) or to its disaster (if the strategy is flawed). When a very few people dominate the whole society and if these chiefs make a major strategic mistake, there is nobody who can correct the mistake and the whole society will suffer the consequences. Most of the failed firms that I studied had a 'sharply stratified, hierarchically organised' Viking type structure with the domination of a small number of charismatic leaders. Even when these chiefs were terribly wrong, 'society' accepted their decisions.

Therefore, once again I arrive at the conclusion that:

- The majority of failed financial institutions were not innocent victims of external systemic extreme events but rather committed collective suicide.

- Top management of failed firms created the culture of collective blindness and did not recognise extreme risks until it was too late.

- The key factors of success or failure were not risk tools, risk infrastructure or the level of capitalisation but 'soft' elements – the business and risk culture and people. Firms with a 'Viking culture' and a lack of survival instinct choose to fail. Inuit-type culture leads to survival.

## TO SURVIVE THE FINANCIAL ICE AGE

In the modern financial world, we cannot see the 'Inuit culture' very often. I studied many financial institutions to find banks with the 'Inuit culture' where the local elite give priority to a long-term survival of the 'society' rather than their own high social status. One of the banks which I admire for their strong 'Inuit culture', is Rabobank, a Dutch cooperative bank. The bank was included in the Top 10 world's safest banks in 2012 by Global Finance. Key elements of Rabobank's uniqueness are their internal culture with their focus on long-term tasks and a decentralised structure, which includes checks and balances, making reckless risk-taking by any of Rabo's entities impossible.

Unfortunately, the majority of financial institutions have more 'Viking culture' and this is not good news at all. In a world dominated by 'Vikings', we are destined to fail. How can we change the culture of collective blindness? I do not believe that the culture can be changed overnight. It requires transforming not only decision-making processes and governance but more fundamental things – basic values of the firm's elite. It is likely that we need a new generation of people to take the top position in the financial firms.

However, while the cultural transformation takes a long time, we can try to exploit some traits of 'Viking culture' to enhance the survival ability. One strong trait of 'Viking culture' is the aspiration of the local elite to please the 'bishops' who regulate life in the financial community. Using the Vikings analogy, if the clergy were to ask the Viking elite to send ships for wood and iron instead of church bells and bronze candlesticks and encourage Vikings to learn from the Inuit their strategy of survival in the cold winter, the Norse Viking society would have had a chance to withstand the Little Ice Age.

Who are the modern 'clergy' in the financial industry? First of all, regulators and policy-makers. Currently, these 'bishops' stay as blind as the financial elite to the long-term survival challenges. After the introduction of Basel II, the modern 'bishops' told the financial elite that they would like the financial elite to build risk models and deliver high capital ratios for the newly built 'Basel II Cathedral'. The modern 'Vikings' delivered exactly what the 'bishops' asked. But it did not help much during the first cold winter of the 'Little Ice Age' (the global financial crisis). Many 'Vikings' died or narrowly escaped the worst.

To those who survived the first extreme winter, 'bishops' said that they knew what was needed to be done to withstand the next winter. The modern 'clergy' decided to build an even larger 'cathedral' called Basel III. They ordered financial chiefs to deliver even higher capital ratios and things like ample liquidity to decorate the new 'giant regulatory cathedral'. I am sure that to please the 'bishops', the financial elite will bring these 'bronze candlesticks and church bells', but they are not crucial for the survival in the next extreme winter. If the modern 'bishops' are not able to recognise what the financial society needs to successfully withstand the 'Little Ice Age', the financial society will continue the grim trajectory that started in 2008–9.

We know what happened with Norse Vikings when the local chiefs and clergy developed a culture of collective blindness. The Vikings needed to learn from the Inuit tribes how to survive and the bishops must have initiated the cultural transformations to adopt the right survival habits. Yet they failed to change their culture. They did things that resulted in their own decline and failed to see the mess that they were getting into. As a result, the Vikings' society together with their 'blind' clergy vanished.

The modern 'bishops' have a chance not to repeat the grim experience of Norse Vikings. What they need to do now is to answer the question: what were the solutions that helped modern 'Inuit' to survive cold winters? Instead of 'bronze candlesticks and church bells' for the 'giant regulatory cathedral', they must tell the financial elite to start building three lines of defence against extreme risk events. The Viking culture can help to make this happen: the financial elite will be eager to please 'bishops'. It's important that 'bishops' ask for the right things to be done. The cultural transformation – the long-term task – will follow.

We all need to clearly realise the fact that in 2008–9 the financial industry entered its 'Little Ice Age'. The global financial crisis has been a 'first extreme winter'. Many financial firms died but those who survived need to understand that another cold winter is coming. For regulators and for the financial elite, it's the right time to decide whether to fail or survive. It's the right time to start transforming a society to make it resilient to extreme risk shocks.

## Selecting the Financial Elite

---

Dear Regulator,

One more issue that I feel necessary to bring to your attention is the problem of leadership in the financial sector. The key elements that predetermine the resilience of a financial firm to extreme risk shocks remain the business and risk culture and people. First of all, I am talking about top executives who manage the firm and make strategic decisions. This is a sort of chicken-and-egg problem. A firm's culture to a large extent drives the process of career movements within the organisation – who can get on the very top and who cannot go through the invisible career filters. The people who receive the top jobs in the organisation are usually well-matched with firm's culture and share the similar cultural values. In this sense, top executives are products of a firm's culture. On the other hand, top executives (e.g. CEOs) shape a firm's culture and their personalities reflect the corporate culture. Some CEOs with a very strong personality can not only change the organisational culture but can fully dominate it. Hank Greenberg, who was AIG's CEO for 18 years, is a good example of how a top executive can shape a firm's culture. He had such a dominant personality in the firm that employees joked that AIG actually stood for 'All Is Greenberg' …

---

… The role of the top executives in a business's success or failure is very substantial, and often crucial. That is one of the most important tasks for shareholders: to choose the right captain for their business. But this task becomes not only the shareholders' headache when it comes to the financial firm which manages the money of thousands or millions of clients, and especially if this firm is systemically important for the national financial system. That is why regulations in many countries require key people in financial institutions to be approved by government bodies like the central bank or financial regulators. The main management roles like Chairman, CEO, Chief Risk Officer and Chief Financial Officer are included in the list of approved functions.

## WHY HAVE THEY BEEN APPROVED?

The global financial crisis highlighted a serious problem in the selection and approval of top executives in financial institutions. In spite of the dual approval process, the appointments of financial captains resulted in massive errors: so many bank CEOs and Chairmen appeared to be incapable of managing their financial institutions effectively and responsibly. Was it the shareholders' mistake to appoint Martin Sullivan as the CEO of AIG, who crashed this iconic American company? If yes, why did the US taxpayers have to pay $182 billion for this terrible error? It became a problem for all US taxpayers. The appointment of Fred Goodwin, who played a key role in RBS's failure, became a problem for all UK taxpayers.

The names of some former financial captains have already become synonymous with greed, unethical behaviour and irresponsibility. Nicknames such as 'Fred the Shred' (Fred Goodwin, the former RBS CEO) and the 'Gorilla of Wall Street' (Dick Fuld, Lehman's CEO) tell a lot about the reputation of these captains of financial business. But people like Fred Goodwin and Dick Fuld successfully passed all regulatory filters and received their approval. How can taxpayers ensure that in the future we will not suffer the consequences of the wrong selection of bank executives? What do regulators need to do to enhance the effectiveness of their approval process? This is not an easy question to answer.

If we look at the list of top executives who received the approval of their shareholders and regulators and later crashed their firms, we can find that on paper all of them look very capable. In their CVs, we can find diplomas from the best universities, impressive career track records, facts supporting their management skills and experience in business and finance. It is not part of their CVs, but I have no doubt that all of them had very high IQs. In most cases, their failures were down to their personalities. Unfortunately, personal traits cannot be scanned during the CV assessment. Hubris, greed, arrogance, aggression, blind optimism and also the ability for deep analysis and making crucial decisions about the situation of uncertainty are not what one can find in professional CVs. I understand that it is not realistic to expect that regulators can thoroughly scan the personality and moral qualities of a candidate during the approval process. They have to stick to the formal requirements like education, skills, experience, absence of misconduct, and criminal records, etc. However, I am convinced that the formal approval framework needs a substantial enhancement. I would like to stress at least one point: the formal requirements should include relevant education in economics, finance, banking or related disciplines.

## LET'S START FROM EDUCATION

I strongly believe that people who take top banking roles should have a formal education in disciplines such as economics, finance, banking, etc. A person who will manage billions of dollars belonging to millions of customers must have a fundamental education in one of those disciplines. The financial crisis became a reminder of how important the role of a banker is for the society and how high the price can be for creditors, investors and taxpayers if the banker makes a mistake. Top banking jobs should follow the rule applicable for some 'high stake and high risk' professions where relevant education is compulsory.

Let's quickly turn our attention outside the financial sector. I have not heard of cardiac or neurological surgeons without medical education. Do you like the idea of going to a hospital for a medical appointment with, let's say, a urologist who was educated in law or international business? This is nonsense for medicine in the twenty-first century. Have you ever met a lawyer or a barrister without a degree in law but with a diploma, for example, in archaeology or astronomy? That's impossible. Why should it still be possible that a person educated in literature, geography, law, languages or history can run a systemically important financial institution which accumulates and manages money of millions of clients?

In the past, doctors and lawyers did not necessarily have a relevant core education. But then society made a decision that allowing people without a relevant education in the core subject to practise medicine or law was an unacceptable risk. That was the right decision. By setting the requirements for core education/qualification, the society defends itself from running the risk in the areas that are socially important (like healthcare or law). Yet finance and banking are not part of this list. Even for plumbers who install electrical appliances, the state requires a professional certificate to be obtained. That is how the state ensures safety for the plumbers' customers.

In banking, however, core education in economics or finance or related disciplines for top executives is still considered unnecessary. Why do I care so much about the core education? Does the 'right education' provide a guarantee that the top executive will not crash the bank? Of course not. We know from the grim LTCM experience that even two winners of the Nobel Prize in Economics (Miron Scholes and Robert Merton) could ruin a financial business.

There are two reasons why I consider that relevant education of top bankers should be made compulsory. Firstly, in my view, an education is not only (and not at all) textbook knowledge. Education to a large extent shapes the way of thinking, analysis and decision-making. A person who received a Bachelors or a Masters degree in modern art has substantially different ways of absorbing and analysing information than a person with a degree in mathematics. They look at the world around us from different angles and often see things differently.

I have my own experience. Once I recruited a quantitative risk analyst to my team. I got an application from a person with a PhD in astrophysics. I was very curious to talk to this person who had worked in a nuclear research centre for many years but had decided to move to finance. We met and had a long chat but I refrained from hiring him. This highly intelligent person had a superb quantitative mind. Yet his main drawback was that he saw the financial world as another deterministic model which, like elementary particles, can be described well via formulae. Of course, he was smart enough to learn the financial jargon, understand the banking products and obtain knowledge on banking risk regulation. But to develop a deep and comprehensive understanding of banking risk he needed to adjust his way of analysis, reasoning and decision-making.

## WHEN A BANK IS RUN BY AN ENGLISH LITERATURE SPECIALIST

The second reason is the alarming factual database of this book's 'heroes'. When preparing this book, I studied not only cases of failures of banks and other firms but collected and analysed information about their top executives, their professional career and personalities. What struck me was that too often, these people have been extremely bright and charismatic (often labelled as 'superstars') but have been educated in disciplines far outside the scope of economics/finance and often had insufficient practical banking experience – insufficient for the top roles in systemically important financial institutions. This led to what I can call a lack of financial wisdom.

Consider HBOS. This bank was formed from two old-fashioned British banks – Halifax, the rock solid world's largest old building society with a 90-year history, and Bank of Scotland, founded by an Act of the Scottish Parliament in 1695. You could expect that HBOS would be led by a mature conservative banking mastermind. Not at all. Andy Hornby was appointed as HBOS Group Chief Executive when he was only 38! He was extremely bright, energetic and full of ideas. In other words, a real superstar. He holds a degree in English Literature from Oxford University and did his MBA at Harvard University, where he came out top from the class of 800 MBA students. Hornby came to Halifax in 1999 after a career in a cement-making company, Blue Circle, and a retailer, Asda. By the time of his appointment, his banking experience amounted to only six years! Gordon Rayner wrote about him:

> *Little matter, it seemed, that he knew so little about the nitty-gritty of*
> *high finance. 'I don't pretend to know about pricing banking products,'*
> *he cheerfully admitted when he took on the job'* ... *He was very*
> *charismatic, had a vibrant young board behind him and brought a real*
> *rah-rah effect to the staff.*
>
> (Rayner 2008)

Nobody questioned Hornby's IQ level, which was exceptional. But this was a question of how Hornby used his IQ. As Warren Buffet once said, 'Smart people can do dumb things'. We need to question his ability to make wise, strategic decisions for a systemically important financial firm. The absence of financial wisdom became the factor that predetermined his fiasco as the HBOS CEO. Being the CEO of the systemically important bank, he remained a marketing person and he did not recognise how different financial products were compared to dairy products that he sold in the Asda stores. It is not surprising that after his resignation from HBOS, he went back to retail business.

The other hero of my HBOS story was Peter Cummings, chief executive of HBOS Corporate banking (the division which sunk HBOS). Cummings had no University degree and started his career in Bank of Scotland straight from high school in 1973.

## EDUCATIONAL MISMATCH

Take the RBS top management, which drove the bank off the cliff. The person who started RBS's expansion fever was Sir George Mathewson. He was educated at Perth Academy and the University of St Andrews' Queen's College in Dundee with a degree in mathematics and applied physics. Before joining RBS, he spent 25 years of his career as an engineer in aerospace and the oil industry, as well as the manager of the state-funded agency. Sir Tom McKillop, who replaced Mathewson as the RBS Chairman in 2006, was educated at Irvine Royal Academy and then Glasgow University, where he obtained BSc and PhD degrees in chemistry. He spent 37 years of his career in the pharmaceutical industry before chairing the RBS Board. His last job was as CEO of AstraZeneca, a multinational pharmaceuticals company.

Fred Goodwin, CEO of RBS from 2001 to 2008, was another executive without relevant education. He studied law at Glasgow University. In the first 11 years of his career before he moved to banking, he was a consultant dealing with nationalisation, liquidation and due diligence. Like Andy Hornby from HBOS, he was often referred as a superstar. He was just 42 when he was promoted to RBS Group CEO. His total banking experience by that time amounted to just six years!

The Northern Rock story was different to some extent, but not without a superstar. The Rock's CEO, Adam Applegarth, the actual creator of the recipe for the financial disaster, was a young financial 'genius' who was appointed as the Group CEO at the age of 39. He spent his entire career in Northern Rock and had a degree in economics. He graduated from Durham University, where he read mathematics and economics. This fact just confirms what I already said: even a Harvard economic education and long banking experience do not guarantee that the person will not run for a reckless strategy or make silly mistakes which can destroy a bank.

What is really important is that the firm's culture and governance provides sufficient checks and balances to prevent the CEO from taking dangerous steps. The Chairman should be one of the most important balancing figures. In Northern Rock, Matt Ridley was the Chairman. He was appointed in 2004 at the age of 45. He had a doctorate in zoology from Oxford University, wrote science books and worked as a journalist. He had no banking experience whatsoever. It is not surprising that he could not identify the blunders that the 'star' CEO made.

Steven Crawshaw, the CEO of Bradford and Bingley – a failed UK building society – was promoted to the CEO role at the age of 43. He became the architect of the bank's innovative strategy to move away from the boring traditional mortgages and become the biggest lender to buy-to-let landlords and self-certified borrowers (also known as 'liars loans'). Before coming to banking, Crawshaw was originally a lawyer.

Let's look at my 'heroes' from American financial institutions and start from the anti-record holders. Martin Sullivan, the former President and CEO of AIG, could be regarded as the top anti-record holder. Under his management, AIG reported the largest annual loss in US corporate history. The bail-out costs of $182 billion were another anti-record. Sullivan ended his formal education at the age of 16. He was the only CEO of the Fortune 100 US largest companies list who had no college degree. Joseph Cassano, CFO of AIG Financial Products and the man who was responsible for the downfall of AIG, obtained a political science degree from Brooklyn College.

Dick Fuld, Lehman's CEO, who caused the largest bankruptcy in US history ($613 billion in debt outstanding), was educated in international business. CNBC named him as one of the 'Worst CEOs of All Time'.

Kennedy Thomson, president and CEO of Wachovia Corporation, formerly First Union Corporation, from 2000 through 2008, holds a BA in American Studies, University of North Carolina and an MBA from Wake Forest University.

An individual who made the main contribution to the UBS fiasco was John Costas, former Chairman and CEO of UBS Investment Bank. John Costas graduated from the University of Delaware with a major in political science and a minor in business and did an MBA in the Tuck School of Business. When he became the UBS Investment Bank CEO, Costas declared his ambitions to turn UBS into the largest player among investment banks and orchestrated the reckless growth strategy. He was also Chairman and CEO of UBS's in-house hedge fund Dillon Read Capital Management, responsible for massive losses during the sub-prime mortgage crisis. Overall, UBS wrote down more than $50 billion from sub-prime mortgage investments.

## FORMAL APPROVAL REQUIREMENTS

Unfortunately, the list of top executives without relevant economic educational background is suspiciously long. The more I analyse the failed financial institutions, the more I am convinced that the absence of an economics or finance-related education of the top bank executives is a 'red flag', one of the warning signals that we need to watch out for.

For top central banker roles, relevant economic education is already a must, with almost no exceptions.

Interestingly, while the relevant economic or finance education is not yet compulsory for the role of a bank's CEO, the new generation of CEOs of the largest UK banks predominantly have an economic educational background. Consider the big five systemically important UK banks. With exception of HSBC, current CEOs of Barclays, Lloyds Banking Group, RBS and Santander have been educated in economics.

I am convinced that compulsory economics/finance education is a logical step. If somebody has ambitions for a high-flying career in finance and to become the top executive of a large financial firm, he or she must go to university and learn the fundamentals of economics and finance. To me it doesn't sound like an excessive requirement for a top banker. I also found it surprising that so far in their approval practice, regulators did not apply this filter to candidates at the top roles in large and systemically important banks.

The regulatory approval process needs an urgent reform. The current top executive approval practice is flawed. Too many wrong people managed to get the green light for top executive roles from the regulators. Andy Hornby's case demonstrates it. If a 32-year old person, educated in English Literature, with no banking experience, becomes the Chief Executive of Halifax Retail – the world's largest building society – something went wrong with his regulatory oversight! And then at the age of 38 with only six years of banking experience he gets the top job of a systemically important and fourth largest UK bank, which manages the money of 23 million UK customers! Something went terribly wrong in the regulatory approval process.

Regulators need to enhance the formal criteria for top executive approval. With possible exceptions for small financial institutions, the approval requirements among others should clearly define:

- the minimum age of a candidate;

- the minimum practical banking experience;

- the minimum educational level, including requirements to have an economics or finance-related university degree.

People have always been and remain one of the key risk factors for financial institutions, too important to warrant the use of various loose and open-for-debate interpretations in the approval processes.

## Optimist's Closing Remark

In one of his interviews, Nassim Taleb told about the disappointing results of his efforts to warn regulators, policy-makers and captains of financial business about the upcoming disaster well before the global financial crisis:

> I no longer care about the financial system. I gave them my roadmap. OK? Thanks, bye. I've no idea what's going on. I'm disconnected. I'm totally disengaged. People read 3 m copies of The Black Swan. The bulk of them before the crisis. And people love it. They agree with it. They invite me to dinner. And they don't do anything about it.
>
> (Cadwalladr 2012)

I asked myself the same question many times: after the crisis hit the industry, why did the regulators remain ignorant regarding the problem of extreme risk? How was it possible that they kept repeating the same 'more capital' mantra over and over again and overlooked the obvious, such as the importance of a robust tail risk management framework? This problem lies on the surface. Yet they remain blind. After reading Diamond's *The Collapse*, I found the answer – the 'Viking' culture of the collective blindness. In Greenland, not only the Viking elite remained blind to the survival problem but also the bishops who 'regulated' the life of the society. Even when the Viking population started to decline, bishops continued to insist that spending Vikings' scarce resources on churches and decorations was important for the Vikings' survival.

Recently, I had several conversations with people from leading consultancies that run risk management practices. I wanted to find out what the risk areas were for which their clients asked consultancies to provide solutions. Almost all of them answered that more often, banks requested help with the implementation of the new regulation (Basel III) or solutions that addressed the regulators' requests or solutions that helped boost profitability or speed up processes on data processing (also often for regulatory reporting). It reminds me of a Greenland Norse Viking who was sailing from Europe back home in the boat full of bronze candlesticks, silver and church bells to please clergy. The blind still leads the blind.

Nevertheless, I remain hopeful. The human history gives us examples of successful adaptation to the changing environment. The Norse Vikings' elite and their bishops vanished because they were not willing to learn the survival strategy. The Inuit who were sharing the same island with the Norse Vikings, but had very different culture, survived the Little Ice Age. Lehman Brothers, Northern Rock, Wachovia, Merrill Lynch, Fortis NV and many others vanished because their bosses believed in the superiority of their business strategies and did not pay attention to extreme risk threats.

> Ultimately, though, the chiefs found themselves without followers. The last right that they obtained for themselves was the privilege of being the last to starve.
>
> (Diamond 2005: 276)

This quote is not about Lehman's CEO Dick Fuld or Adam Applegarth, Northern Rock's CEO after they crashed their companies, as you might expect. This was written was by Jared Diamond in 2005 about the chiefs of Norse Vikings, a society that vanished in the fifteenth century. You don't even need to change a single word in Diamond's conclusion.

This lesson still needs to be learned not only by remaining financial institutions but also by regulators. Experience from other industries exposed to extreme risk (like aviation, energy, sea transport) suggests that regulators can learn from painful past experience. Often an extreme risk event helped regulators look at the industry risk from a new angle and make vital regulatory changes. I don't see any reason why the same cannot happen in the financial sector. This optimism inspired me to write this book.

# Appendix 1:
# Who Predicted the Crisis?

One of my favourite surveys is the one that the American newspaper *USA Today* did just before the 2008 crisis began. On 2 January 2008, *USA Today* published the article '2008 predictions for the S&P 500' (*USA Today* 2008). The newspaper approached eight stock market experts and asked them to make a forecast of the level of S&P 500 at the end of 2008. The gurus failed to predict not only the market crash but also any form of decline or stagnation! The most conservative prediction came from Abhijit Chakrabortti, Chief Global and US Equity Strategist at Morgan Stanley. He predicted that by the end of 2008 the S&P 500 would reach 1,520. As at the beginning of the year, S&P stood at 1,447. As such, this meant a 5 per cent increase. Richard Bernstein, Chief Investment Strategist and Head of Merrill Lynch's Investment Strategy Group, was also pretty conservative, predicting 1,525 points.

The most optimistic forecast came from Jason Trennert of Strategas Research Partners. He expected that the economic growth would continue in the USA and that S&P would reach 1,680 (16 per cent return for the year). The other six gurus predicted that S&P would stay between 1,580 and 1,675 points at the end of 2008 (Figure A1.1). The reality, however, was very different: the market crashed and S&P 500 traded at 903 points on the last day of 2008. The annual return was negative 37 per cent!

I am not surprised that the Wall Street gurus' predictions turned out to be completely wrong, even directionally. There were two things that struck me about this expert judgement. The first one relates to the way in which the gurus made their forecasts. All gurus predicted the S&P index to grow within the range of 5–16 per cent. Interestingly (and I suspect that it was not just a coincidence), in all three years preceding the 2008 crash, the S&P annual return was positive, with its total return being between 5 and 16 per cent. I strongly suspect that the gurus made their forecasts for 2008 looking in the

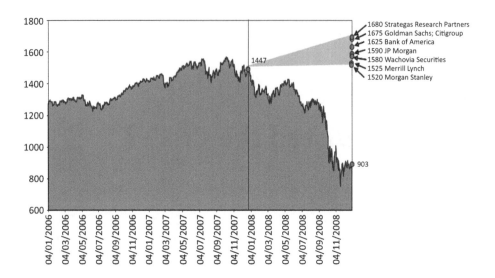

**Figure A1.1   S&P 500 Index: forecast vs. actual**

*Source*: Author's own figure using data from *USA Today*, Bloomberg.

rear view mirror. If I am right, the potential advantage of the expert judgement compared to backward-looking statistical models is no more than an illusion or a theoretical concept.

The second thing that I found interesting was what happened to the gurus after they made completely wrong predictions for 2008. Since all of the gurus were in the driving seats of their firms' investment vehicles (e.g. Chief Investment or Equity Strategists), it is likely that their wrong predictions also resulted in wrong investment decisions and, presumably, large losses for their companies. I tried to find out what happened to the stock market gurus after 2008.

Abhijit Chakrabortti from Morgan Stanley, who gave the most conservative forecast for 2008 (yet incorrect), resigned from his role of Chief Global and US Equity Strategist in January 2009, according to Reuters (Wilchins 2009). I could not find where he ended up after he left Morgan Stanley.

I discovered that Jason Trennert from Strategas, who made the most bullish and incorrect prediction among the gurus, was still in the driving seat of Strategas. Strategas' website provides the following information:

*Mr. Trennert is the Managing Partner of Strategas and the Chairman and Chief Executive Officer of the Firm's broker–dealer subsidiary, Strategas Securities, LLC. Also the Firm's Chief Investment Strategist, Mr. Trennert has been ranked consistently by Institutional Investor magazine as one of the top Strategists on Wall Street and has been named to SmartMoney magazine's Power 30 list of the most influential people in the world of investing.*

*(Strategas)*

Tobias Levkovich, from Citigroup, whose forecast was almost as bullish as Trennert's (Levkovich predicted S&P 500 of 1,675), continued in his role of Chief US Equity Strategist in Citigroup. The National Investor Relations Institute's website gives the following information:

*Tobias M. Levkovich is a Managing Director, Chief U.S. Equity Strategist for Citi Investment Research and Analysis and is a member of the firm's Investment Strategy Committee. In this role he is responsible for assessing the direction of the market, setting the firm's investment sector allocations, and compiling its Recommended List, a list of specific investment that he expects to appreciate in value. Tobias assumed his current role in 2001. He is a member of Institutional Investor's (2009) All-America Research Team, a recognition that he has received previously. SmartMoney magazine has also recognized Tobias as one of its 'Power 30 Thinkers' (November 2004), its 'Best Market Seer' (December 2003) and its '30 Smartest People in Investing' (December 2002).*

*(NIRI)*

Overall, the successful careers of the gurus before and after 2008 suggest that *USA Today* collected opinions of the top-notch industry specialists who were and remain, presumably, the most skilful people in their area. They were in a better position than anyone else to make a correct forecast of the upcoming tail risk event of 2008. If they were not able to give the right projection, then who could?

Wall Street's gurus, as well as economists, academics, regulators and central bankers, failed to predict the 2008 crisis. Speaking at the Financial Crisis Inquiry Commission, Ben Bernanke, US Federal Reserve Chairman, was very honest about it:

*We knew all those numbers, of course. But a lot of smart people – and you asked the question about anticipation, people like Paul Volcker and others thought it was going to cause a crisis. But they got it wrong. They thought it was going to cause a dollar crash. It didn't do that. It caused a different kind of crisis. Just another example of how difficult it is to predict.*

(*Financial Crisis Inquiry Commission 2009: 78*)

David Stockton, who used to work for the Federal Reserve, prepared a report on the forecasting capabilities of the Bank of England (Stockton 2012). In particular, he analysed the information on forecasts made by the Monetary Policy Committee (Bank of England) and 25 other bodies (collected by Consensus Economics survey of forecasters) at the beginning of each calendar

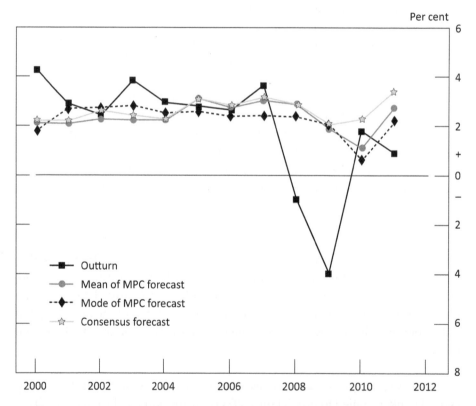

**Figure A1.2   Central forecasts for calendar year average GDP growth made at the beginning of the previous year**

*Source*: Stockton 2012: 16, Consensus Economics and Bank of England.

year on the GDP growth for the following year. The results are presented in Figure A1.2.

The graph clearly shows that the gap between forecasted and actual GDP has been the smallest in the 2004–6 period, when the economy demonstrated steady growth. However, the forecasting error grew materially in 2008–9 as the crisis took the forecasters by surprise. Stockton concludes: 'Neither the MPC nor external forecasters anticipated the deep recession which began in 2008 following the onset of the global financial crisis' (Stockton 2012: 17). He also clarifies:

> It is not surprising that the MPC did not foresee the onset and intensity of the recession over 2008 and 2009 – other forecasters of the UK economy made similar errors during that period, and both the ECB and the Fed also failed to anticipate the depth of the impending recessions in their economies.
>
> (Stockton 2012:18)

# Appendix 2:
# Good Years vs. Bad Years

There is nothing new in the idea that the economic development exhibits a natural cyclicality. The phase of an accelerated growth changes to the contraction phase. The economic contraction often comes together with a systemic crisis. If we look back, we can find that on average once in 10 years the economy suffers from a systemic crisis. This can be clearly seen in Figure A2.1, which depicts corporate defaults in the last 30 years.

There were three peaks of defaults, in 1989–91, 2000–2 and 2008–9, which reflect systemic crises simultaneously occurring in the USA and Europe (Moody's default database is dominated by US and European corporates, which account for about 95 per cent of the defaulted population).

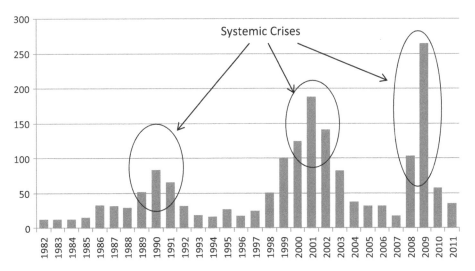

**Figure A2.1  Global corporate defaults (counts)**

*Source*: Author's own figure using data from Moody's default database.

The recent track record of systemic crises demonstrates that the extreme risk events (a systemic crisis obviously belongs to this category) are not as rare as one might believe. The fact that Black Swan events happen much more frequently than expected has already been highlighted by many economists and risk management specialists. That is why when defining extreme risk events I deliberately stressed the low *perceived* probability. If we talk about probability as a statistical property, for most extreme events the real probability of their occurrence is unknown and cannot be calculated with acceptable level of accuracy. Yet people can (often wrongly) perceive that the probability is very low, which makes the extreme event more unexpected and, hence, far more devastating.

How seriously do extreme events affect the business and who suffers most? We can look at the aggregated picture since 1980.

If we aggregate data to get a 'bird's eye view', in the past 32 years the USA and Europe enjoyed a robust economic growth in 24 years. Yet for 8 years the economy suffered contractions or minor growth. For the sake of simplicity, we can call these years 'bad' years. Statistically bad years accounted for exactly 25 per cent of the period in question. Using Moody's default database, we can segregate the data of 1,746 corporate defaults which happened between 1980 and 2011 in two groups – good years and bad years (Figure A2.2).

While bad years and good years are divided in a proportion of 1:3 over the last 32 years, corporate defaults are distributed roughly 1:1 between these two periods. In other words, defaults increased threefold during bad years. Not surprising that during the contraction phase, corporates experienced the high default rates. The similar proportion holds for low rated corporates – companies that had a speculative credit rating. That is because out of 1,746 defaulted companies the vast majority belonged to corporates that had a speculative credit rating. Only 65 companies with the investment credit rating (or 3.7 per cent of the defaulted pool) experienced the default in this period.

If we look at the volume of defaulted debt, however, the picture becomes different. While one bad year is accompanied by three good years, the dollar volumes of defaulted debt in bad and good years have the proportion of 3:1. In other words, in bad years not only the number of defaults tripled but also the dollar volume of defaulted debt almost tripled: in a good year on average each default represents $411 million of debt, while in a bad year it rises to $1,150 million.

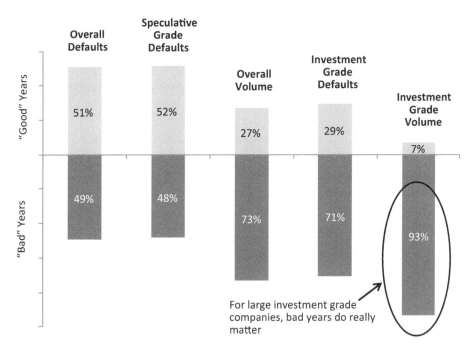

**Figure A2.2   'Good' vs. 'bad' years: distribution of corporate defaults**
*Source*: Author's own figure using data from Moody's default database.

The picture becomes even scarier when we take statistics of investment grade companies in the defaulted pool. 71 per cent of investment grade companies (46 out of 65) defaulted in bad years. This means that in a good year we have statistically less than one default of investment grade companies, while in a bad year – almost six defaults! Moreover, in dollar volume terms bad years accounted for 93 per cent of all defaulted debt of investment grade companies! On average, bond/loan default dollar volume per each default increases from $1.3 billion in a good year to $7.5 billion in a bad year.

Paradoxically, it appears that to manage systemic and extreme risks is more important for solid firms with strong risk management than for firm of mediocre creditworthiness. The firms with strong risk management can normally eliminate and effectively mitigate most of the regular day-to-day risks. They do not lose much money on obvious things, they do not default in good times. The only door that always remains open is 'unknown unknowns', rare and exceptional events (systemic crisis) that they do not anticipate. I would even say that the more robust is the risk management of a firm, the more important the task to create the risk management capability to address extreme risk events. For firms with the weak risk management, the number one task is to learn how to manage obvious risks as they possess the most threats for the firm (the obvious risks are always nearby while the Black Swans are very rare). For firms with the strong risk management, the area of extreme risk becomes a priority.

To conclude, in good times, companies with strong credit ratings fail very rarely and on a small scale. Yet, in bad years when the economy suffers a systemic risk event the number of investment grade companies' defaults jumps almost sixfold and many of these defaults become spectacularly large failures by their scale. Therefore, for a large investment grade firm only extreme risk events (e.g. systemic crisis) represent a realistic threat for their existence. For them only bad years really matter.

# Bibliography

Aldrick P. 2012. The HBOS horror story is a grim read. *Telegraph*, 9 March. Available at: http://www.telegraph.co.uk/finance/newsbysector/banksand finance/9135277/The-HBOS-horror-story-is-a-grim-read.html [accessed: 24 December 2012].

American International Group Inc. 2007. Annual Report and Accounts 2006. New York: AIG.

Appelbaum B. 2009. Wells Fargo Quarterly Loss: $2.55 Billion. *Washington Post*, 29 January 2009. [Online]. Available at: http://www.washingtonpost.com/wp-dyn/content/article/2009/01/28/AR2009012803630.html [accessed: 15 November 2012].

Awoga T. 2012. Successes and failures in mergers and acquisitions. *Risk Journal* 2012, PRMIA [Online]. Available at: http://www.prmia.org/Chapter_Pages/WashingtonDC/Summer_2012_ful_issue_6.pdf [accessed: 29 July 2012].

Bank of England 2007. The Inflation Report, May. London: Park Communications Limited.

Bank of England 2009. The Inflation Report, February. London: Park Communications Limited.

BBC 2010. Flight disruptions cost airlines $1.7bn, says IATA. BBC, 21 April 2010. Available at: http://news.bbc.co.uk/1/hi/business/8634147.stm [accessed: 27 November 2012].

BBC News 2000. Y2K: Overhyped and oversold? Report BBC News, 6 January 2000. [Online]. Available at: http://news.bbc.co.uk/1/hi/talking_point/586938.stm) [accessed: 23 December 2012].

BBC News 2011. Notting Hill Carnival: Police hail 'peaceful' event. 30 August 2011 [Online]. Available at: http://www.bbc.co.uk/news/uk-england-london-14706924 [accessed: 23 December 2012].

Berkshire Hathaway 1999. Annual report 1999. Omaha: Berkshire Hathaway.

BIS 1988. *International Convergence of Capital Standards*. Basel: Basel Committee on Banking Supervision.

BIS 2006. *International Convergence of Capital Measurement and Capital Standards. A Revised Framework Comprehensive Version*. Basel: Basel Committee on Banking Supervision.

BIS 2008. Range of practices and issues in economic capital modelling. Consultative Document. Issued for comment by 28 November 2008. Basel: Bank for International Settlements.

BIS 2010a. *Basel III: A Global Regulatory Framework for More Resilient Banks and Banking Systems*. Basel: Basel Committee on Banking Supervision.

BIS 2010b. *Basel III: International Framework for Liquidity Risk Measurement, Standards and Monitoring*. Basel: Basel Committee on Banking Supervision.

BIS 2011. Global systemically important banks: assessment methodology and the additional loss absorbency requirement. Rules text. November 2011. Basel: Bank for International Settlements.

Blundell-Wignall A., Wehinger G., Slovik P. 2009. The Elephant in the Room: The Need to Deal with What Banks Do. *OECD Journal: Financial Market Trends*, 2009 (2), ISSN 1995-2864, OECD 2009. Available at: http://www.oecd.org/finance/financialmarkets/44357464.pdf [accessed: 24 November 2012].

Brisson M., Campbell B., Galbraith J.W. 2003. Forecasting some Low-Predictability Time Series Using Diffusion Indices. *Journal of Forecasting* 22, 515–31.

Buehler K., D'Silva V., Pritsch G. 2004. The business case for Basel II. *Risk Magazine*, McKinsey Quarterly 2004 [Online]. Available at: http://www.mckinseyquarterly.com/Public_Sector/Government_Regulation/The_business_case_for_Basel_II_1396 [accessed: 2 November 2012].

Buffett W. 1990. To the Shareholders of Berkshire Hathaway. Available at: http://www.berkshirehathaway.com/letters/1990.html [accessed: 23 December 2012].

Cadwalladr C. 2012. Nassim Taleb: my rules for life. *Guardian*, 24 November. Available at: http://www.guardian.co.uk/books/2012/nov/24/nassim-taleb-antifragile-finance-interview [accessed: 20 December 2012].

Campbell A. 2005. Basel II costs rising, says survey. *Risk Magazine*, August 2005. [Online]. Available at: http://www.risk.net/risk-magazine/news/1506561/basel-ii-costs-rising-survey [accessed: 2 November 2012].

Carney M. 2010. Living with Low for Long. Speech at Economic Club of Canada, 13 December 2010, Toronto. [Online]. Available at: http://www.bankofcanada.ca/wp-content/uploads/2010/12/sp131210.pdf [accessed: 18 December 2012].

CEBS 2010. CEBS Guidelines on Stress Testing (GL32). August 2010. [Online]. Available at: http://www.eba.europa.eu/documents/Publications/Standards – Guidelines/2010/Stress-testing-guidelines/ST_Guidelines.aspx [accessed: 2 January 2013].

CNBC 2011. Jon Corzine, MF Global Chairman and CEO. CNBC Video. 21 January 2011 [Online]. Available at: http://video.cnbc.com/gallery/ ?video=3000002448&play=1#eyJ2aWQiOiIzMDAwMDAyNDQ4IiwiZW 5jVmlkIjoiQUhyWTNueWowU0pvVlRQd3BsNWRjUT09IiwidlRhYiI6ImluZm 8iLCJ2UGFnZSI6MSwiZ05hdiI6WyLCoExhdGVzdCBWaWRlbyJdLCJn U2VjdCI6IkFMTCIsImdQYWdlIjoiMSIsInN5bSI6IiIsInNlYXJjaCI6IiJ9 [accessed: 25 December 2012].

CNN Money 2009. The 10 largest U.S. bankruptcies [Online]. Available at: http:// money.cnn.com/galleries/2009/fortune/0905/gallery.largest_bankruptcies. fortune/index.html [accessed: 28 February 2013].

Conway E. 2009. IMF puts total cost of crisis at £7.1 trillion. *Telegraph*, 9 August. [Online]. Available at: http://www.telegraph.co.uk/finance/newsbysector/ banksandfinance/5995810/IMF-puts-total-cost-of-crisis-at-7.1-trillion.html [accessed: 20 December 2012].

Coote S. 2011. The truths behind the M&A myths. Available at: http:// www.vscgrowth.com.au/index.php?option=com_content&view=article &id=111:the-truths-behind-the-myths-2&catid=3:newsflash&Itemid=158 [accessed: 26 July 2012].

Croft J. 2009. Risky US purchase rued in hindsight. *Financial Times*, 2 March 2009. Available at: http://www.ft.com/cms/s/0/a0db8604-0767-11de-9294-000077b07658.html#axzz2FFiqXXAB [accessed: 16 December 2012].

Dash E. 2008. Wachovia Reports $23.9 Billion Loss for Third Quarter. *New York Times*, 22 October. Available at: http://www.nytimes.com/2008/10/23/business/ 23wachovia.html?_r=0&adxnnl=1&adxnnlx=1353798112-BUCb69aRukNzpx R7Chl8mA [accessed: 15 November 2012].

Davenport J. 2012. Feel-good factor cuts crime. *Evening Standard*, 13 August 2012.

Davies B. 2012. Tools of the trade. *Quantum Finance Magazine*, Issue 20, October 2012, 18–23. [Online]. Available at: http://www.quantummagazine.com/ Q20_Final_68pp-low.pdf [accessed: 21 November 2012].

Denrell J., Fang C. 2010. Predicting the Next Big Thing: success as a signal of poor judgement. *Management Science* [Online], 56 (10), 1653–67. Available at: http://papers.ssrn.com/sol3/papers.cfm?abstract_id=1621800 [accessed: 28 October 2012].

Derbyshire, D. 2011. The moment nuclear plant chief WEPT as Japanese finally admit that radiation leak is serious enough to kill people. *Daily Mail*, 19 March 2011. [Online]. Available at: www.dailymail.co.uk/news/article-1367684/Japan-earthquake-tsunami-Fukushima-nulear-plant-radiation-leak-kill-people.html [accessed: 22 December 2012].

Diamond, J. 2005. *Collapse: How Societies Choose to Fail or Survive: How Societies Choose to Fail or Succeed*. New York: Penguin Group.

Elias C. 2011. MF Global and the great Wall St re-hypothecation scandal. Available at: http://newsandinsight.thomsonreuters.com/Securities/Insight/2011/12_-_December/MF_Global_and_the_great_Wall_St_re-hypothecation_scandal/ [accessed: 07 August 2012].

Elliott L. 2010. No EU bailout for Greece as PM promises to 'put house in order'. *Guardian*, 28 January 2010. Available at: http://www.guardian.co.uk/business/2010/jan/28/greece-papandreou-eurozone [accessed: 10 December 2012].

Energy Information Administration, 2001, *International Energy Outlook* 2001. Washington: EIA.

European Commission 2009. Greece: Commission assessment in relation to the Commission recommendation for a Council decision under Article 104(8) of the Treaty, November 2009. Brussels: European Commission.

Everitt V. 2012. Letter to TfL Customers. TfL Managing Director. 13 August 2012. [Online]. Available at: http://info.tfl.gov.uk/public/read_message.jsp;jsessionid=0;apw18?sigreq=1413658821[accessed: 1 September 2012].

Financial Crisis Inquiry Commission, 17 November 2009, p. 78 [Online]. Available at: http://www.scribd.com/doc/48878840/FCIC-Interview-with-Ben-Bernanke-Federal-Reserve) [accessed: 1 November 2012].

Fortis 2007a. Fortis Financial Statements 2007. Brussels: Fortis.

Fortis 2007b. Solid foundation, exciting perspectives. Annual Report 2007. Brussels: Fortis.

FSA 2005. Expert Group Paper on Low Default Portfolios. [Online]. Available at: http://www.fsa.gov.uk/pubs/international/default.pdf [accessed: 12 December 2012].

FSA 2008. Stress and scenario testing. Consultation paper 08/24. December 2008, London: FSA.

FSA 2011. The failure of the Royal Bank of Scotland. Financial Services Authority Board Report, December 2011. London: FSA.

FSA 2012. Results of 2011 Hypothetical Portfolio Exercise for Sovereigns, Banks and Large Corporate. London: FSA. [Online]. Available at: http://www.fsa.gov.uk/static/pubs/international/2011hpe.pdf [accessed: 13 November 2012].

Galbraith J., Tkacz G. 2007, How far can we forecast? forecast content horizons for some important macroeconomic time series. *Canadian Journal of Economics*, 40 (3), 935–53, August 2007.

Gladwell M. 2005. The vanishing. *New Yorker*. January 3, 2005. Available at: http://www.newyorker.com/archive/2005/01/03/050103crbo_books#ixzz1vcEYkPzn [accessed: 28 December 2012].

Granger C.W.J. 2001. Can we improve the perceived quality of economic forecasts? *Essays in Econometrics. Collected Papers of Clive Granger*, Vol. 1. Cambridge: Cambridge University Press.

Gupton G., Finger C., Bhatia M. 2007. CreditMetrics™ – Technical Document. RiskMetrics Group.

Haldane A., Madouros V. 2012. The dog and the Frisbee. Speech at Federal Reserve Bank of Kansas City's 36th economic policy symposium. Available at: http://www.bankofengland.co.uk/publications/Pages/speeches/2012/596. aspx [accessed: 24 November 2012].

Härle P., Lüders E., Pepanides T., Pfetsch S., Poppensieker T., Stegemann U. 2010. *Basel III and European Banking: Its Impact, How Banks Might Respond, And The Challenges Of Implementation.* November 2010. EMEA Banking, McKinsey & Company.

HBOS 2007. HBOS Annual Report and Accounts 2007. Edinburgh: HBOS plc.

HBOS 2008, Annual Report and Accounts 2008. London: HBOS.

House of Commons Treasury Committee, 2010. Too important to fail – too important to ignore. Ninth Report of Session 2009–10, Volume I. London: The Stationery Office Limited.

HSBC 2002. A Transforming Transaction Combining Two Successful Business Models – HSBC and Household [Online: HSBC]. Available at: www.hsbc. com/1/PA_esf-ca.../hsbc11142002_presentation.pdf).

HSBC 2003. HSBC Holding plc Annual Reports and Accounts. London: HSBC.

Hypo Real Estate, 2007. Annual Report 2007. Munich: Hypo Real Estate.

IMF 2008a, World Economic Outlook: April 2008. Washington: IMF

IMF 2008b, Iceland: Financial Stability Assessment update [Online: International Monetary Fund]. Available at: http://www.imf.org/external/pubs/ft/scr/2008/ cr08368.pdf [accessed: 15 July 2012].

IMF 2010a. Global Financial Stability Report: Sovereigns, Funding, and Systemic Liquidity, October 2010. Washington: IMF [Online]. Available at: http://www.imf.org/External/Pubs/FT/GFSR/2010/02/pdf/text.pdf [accessed: 20 December 2012].

IMF 2010b. *Global Financial Stability Report: Meeting New Challenges to Stability and Building a Safer System.* April 2010. Washington: IMF. Available at: http://www.imf.org/external/pubs/ft/gfsr/2010/01/pdf/text.pdf [accessed: 23 November 2012].

Jones S. 2009. The formula that felled Wall St. *Financial Times*, 24 April. [Online]. Available at: http://www.ft.com/cms/s/0/912d85e8-2d75-11de-9eba-00144fe abdc0.html#axzz2Fd1jDiEX [accessed: 20 December 2012].

Kealhofer S., Bohn J. 2001. Portfolio Management of Default Risk. San Francisco: KMV.

Landsbanki 2007. Annual Report 2007. Reykjavík: Landsbanki.

Lehrer J. 2011. Do Political Experts Know What They're Talking About? Wired. com [Online] Available at: http://www.wired.com/wiredscience/2011/08/

do-political-experts-know-what-theyre-talking-about [accessed: 27 October 2012].

Ligi A., Holland B. 2009. Why Bernie Madoff Is No Marcel Ospel as Man Swiss Love to Hate. February 23, 2009. Bloomberg. Available at: http://www.bloomberg.com/apps/news?pid=newsarchive&sid=aApnFtmhFswQ [accessed: 28 December 2012].

Linklaters 2011. *Basel III: Liquidity Rules*. London: Linklaters.

Macroeconomic Assessment Group 2010. Assessing the macroeconomic impact of the transition to stronger capital and liquidity requirements. Final Report. Basel: BIS.

McNeil A. 2008. Economic Capital Models for Basel/Solvency II, Pillar II. Paper to the FIRM Conference, Manchester, 15–17 June 2008. Available at: www.actuaries.org.uk/system/files/documents/pdf/McNeil.pdf [accessed: 25 December 2012].

Menand L. 2005. Everybody's An Expert: Putting predictions to the test. *New Yorker* [Online] Available at: http://www.newyorker.com/archive/2005/12/05/051205crbo_books1 [accessed: 28 October 2012].

Moody's Investors Service. 2003. *Default & Recovery Rates of Corporate Bond Issuers: A Statistical Review of Moody's Ratings Performance, 1920–2002*, New York: Moody's Investors Service.

Morgenson G. 2008. Behind insurer's crisis, blind eye to a web of risk. *New York Times*, 27 September 2008. Available at: http://www.nytimes.com/2008/09/28/business/28melt.html?_r=0 [accessed: 2 December 2012].

Neather A. 2012. The best 2012 legacy? Spend to fix the Tube. *Evening Standard*, 17 August 2012, 2.

NIRI [Online]. Available at: http://www.niri.org/Main-Menu-Category/learn/annualconference/AC2012/sp.aspx?param1=1358 [accessed: 28 October 2012].

Northern Rock 2006. Annual Report and Accounts 2006. Newcastle upon Tyne: Northern Rock.

Northern Rock 2007. Northern Rock plc Interim Results 6 Months Ended 30 June 2007. Newcastle upon Tyne: Northern Rock.

Ohmae K. 2008. America must seek aid for a global credit line. *Financial Times*, 30 September 2008. Available at: http://www.ft.com/intl/cms/s/0/d44a3c0a-8ef0-11dd-946c-0000779fd18c.html [accessed: 23 November 2012].

Oller L.-E. 1985. How far can changes in business activity be forecast? *International Journal of Forecasting* 1, 135–41.

Pierce A. 2008. Financial crisis: Our masters' summer of denial. *Telegraph*, 24 October 2008. Available at: http://www.telegraph.co.uk/finance/recession/3255908/Financial-crisis-Our-masters-summer-of-denial.html [accessed: 15 July 2012].

Rayner G. 2008. HBOS's Andy Hornby must now dance to Lloyds' quiet tune. *Telegraph*, 18 September. [Online]. Available at: http://www.telegraph.co.uk/finance/newsbysector/banksandfinance/2982326/HBOSs-Andy-Hornby-must-now-dance-to-Lloyds-quiet-tune.html [accessed: 24 December 2012].

RBS Group 2006. Annual Report and Accounts 2006, Edinburgh: RBS plc.

RBS Group 2007. RBS Annual Report and Accounts 2007. Edinburgh: RBS plc.

Reinhart C., Rogoff K. 2009. *This Time Is Different: Eight Centuries of Financial Folly*. Princeton, NJ: Princeton University Press.

RiskMetrics Group. 2007. CreditMetrics – Technical Document. RiskMetrics Group.

Roth A. 2010. Gary Schilling's 2009 Predictions – What Went Wrong? CBS Money Watch [Online]. Available at: http://www.cbsnews.com/8301-505123_162-37740934/gary-schillings-2009-predictions---what-went-wrong/?tag=mncol;lst;1 [accessed: 27 October 2012].

Rothacker R. 2008. $5 billion withdrawn in one day in silent run. *Charlotte Observer*, 2008-10-11. Available at: http://www.charlotteobserver.com/2008/10/11/246983/5-billion-withdrawn-in-one-day.html [accessed: 23 November 2012].

Sender H. 2011. Breakfast with the FT: Stuart Gulliver. *Financial Times*, 25 February 2011. [Online]. Available at: http://www.ft.com/cms/s/9f34a2bc-4064-11e0-9140-00144feabdc0,Authorised=false.html?_i_location=http%3A%2F%2Fwww.ft.com%2Fcms%2Fs%2F0%2F9f34a2bc-4064-11e0-9140-00144feabdc0.html&_i_referer=http%3A%2F%2Fen.wikipedia.org%2Fwiki%2FStuart_Gulliver#axzz1rofKo8IH [accessed: 24 December 2012].

Solman P. 2008. Top Theorists Examine Rippling Economic Turbulence, PBS Newshour, [Online]. Available at: http://www.pbs.org/newshour/bb/business/july-dec08/psolman_10-21.html [accessed: 27 October 2012].

Stockton D. 2012, Review of the Monetary Policy Committee's Forecasting Capability. [Online]. Available at: http://www.bankofengland.co.uk/publications/Documents/news/2012/cr3stockton.pdf [accessed: 2 November 2012].

Strategas [Online]. Available at: http://www.strategasrp.com/ourteam_analysts.aspx [accessed: 28 October 2012].

Suttle P. 2011. Measuring The Cumulative Economic Impact of Basel III. The 9th Annual Ri$k Capital Conference, Frankfurt, 19 September 2011. Available at: iif.com/download.php?id=wT7xSI3009Q= [accessed: 25 October 2006].

Taleb N. 2007. *The Black Swan: The Impact of the Highly Improbable*. New York: Random House.

Tetlock P. 2005. *Expert Political Judgement. How Good Is It? How Can We Know?* Princeton, NJ: Princeton University Press.

Thesing G. 2010. Greece Should Be Prepared to Abandon Euro, German Lawmaker Schaeffler Says. *Bloomberg*, 22 April 2010. Available at: http://www.

bloomberg.com/news/2010-04-22/greece-should-be-prepared-to-abandon-euro-german-lawmaker-schaeffler-says.html [accessed: 22 December 2012].

Treanor J. 2012. Banned former HBOS banker attacks City regulators. *Guardian*, 14 December. Available at: http://www.guardian.co.uk/business/2012/dec/14/hbos-banker-attacks-city-regulators [accessed: 24 December 2012].

Tucker P. 2009. Speech at SUERF, CEPS and Belgian Financial Forum Conference: Crisis Management at the Cross-Road, 16 November 2009, Brussels. Available at: http://www.bankofengland.co.uk/publications/Documents/speeches/2009/speech410.pdf [accessed: 22 November 2012].

UBS 2008. Shareholder Report on UBS's Write-Downs. 18 April 2008, Zürich: UBS AG.

*USA Today* 2008. 2008 predictions for the S&P 500, *USA Today*, 2 January 2008 [Online]. Available at: http://usatoday30.usatoday.com/money/markets/2008-01-02-predictions-numbers_N.htm [accessed: 28 October 2012].

Wachovia 2007. Annual report 2007. Charlotte: Wachovia Corporation. Washington Post Editorials 2010.

*Washington Post* 2010. Angela Merkel's mistake: Battling the financial markets. *Washington Post*, 22 May 2010 [Online]. Available at: http://www.washingtonpost.com/wp-dyn/content/article/2010/05/21/AR2010052104489.html [accessed: 10 January 2013].

Wente M. 2009. Nassim Taleb on the economy 'We still have the same disease'. *The Globe and Mail*, September 13 [Online]. Available at: http://www.theglobeandmail.com/report-on-business/economy/we-still-have-the-same-disease/article1202455/ [accessed: 20 December 2012].

Wilchins D. 2009. Morgan Stanley strategist Chakrabortti leaves. *Reuters*, 27 January 2009. [Online]. Available at: http://www.reuters.com/article/2009/01/27/morganstanley-chakrabortti-idUSN2748436620090127 [accessed: 28 October 2012].

Wray R. 2010. Angela Merkel: EU summit should not discuss bailout for Greece. *Guardian*, 21 March 2010. Available at: http://www.guardian.co.uk/business/2010/mar/21/eu-greece-angela-merkel [accessed: 10 December 2012].

# Index